The Politics of Wartime Aid

CHOICE   JAN. '79

History, Geography & Travel

DOUGHERTY, James J. **The politics of wartime aid: American economic assistance to France and French Northwest Africa, 1940–1946.** Greenwood, 1978. 264p bibl index 77-84770. 17.50 ISBN 0-8371-9882-8. C.I.P.

Franco-American wartime relations had more than their share of controversial personalities (Jean Darlan, Charles de Gaulle, Henri Giraud, Robert Murphy) and troublesome issues (among them recognition of Vichy France by the U.S., the St. Pierre-Miquelon dispute, French troops under General Eisenhower's command). While Dougherty's study touches on these figures and problems, he is more concerned with yet another matter, American economic assistance and aid through Lend-Lease to Vichyite France and the Free French. This is an exceedingly complex story, and what with statistics, acronyms for more than a dozen agencies and boards concerned with the question, and the many personalities involved, it is not an easy story to follow. Yet it closes a gap in the historiography of World War II diplomacy, and it helps fill out the story of America's relations with the nations of North Africa. Interested readers should also consult John M. Haight's *American aid to France, 1938–1940* (1970). Eight appendixes, bibliography, and index; maps and illustrations would have been helpful. Recommended for graduate and strong undergraduate collections in history.

The Politics of Wartime Aid

American Economic Assistance to France and French Northwest Africa, 1940-1946

James J. Dougherty

Contributions in American History, Number 71

Greenwood Press
WESTPORT, CONNECTICUT ● LONDON, ENGLAND

Library of Congress Cataloging in Publication Data

Dougherty, James J   1939-
    The Politics of wartime aid.

    (Contributions in American history ; no. 71
ISSN 0084-9219)
    Bibliography: p.
    Includes index.
    1. Lend-lease operations (1941-1945) 2. World War,
1939-1945--France. 3. World War, 1939-1945--Africa,
Northweast. I. Title.

D753.2.F8D68   940.53'14   77-84770
ISBN 0-8371-9882-8

Library of Congress Catalog Card Number: 77-84770
ISBN: 0-8371-9882-8
ISSN: 0084-9219

First published in 1978

Greenwood Press, Inc.
51 Riverside Avenue, Westport, Connecticut 06880

Printed in the United States of America

10 9 8 7 6 5 4 3 2 1

To Mary and Michael

Contents

Preface

The history of wartime aid to the civilian populations of French Northwest Africa and Metropolitan France is an involved and somewhat controversial story. Most of the aid was eventually furnished through lend-lease, but lend-lease to North Africa did not commence until after the invasion in November 1942, and it did not flow to France until some time following D day. From the fall of France until the North African invasion, however, the United States, much to the dissatisfaction of the British, furnished limited quantities of civilian supplies to unoccupied France and the Vichy government in Northwest Africa. Only after severing relations with Pétain's government did the United States abandon the assistance programs to France. But these early efforts, despite their limitations, are an important part of the entire picture of wartime assistance. Through these economic contacts the United States hoped to maintain a closeness with the French people, and in North Africa the purpose was to influence the military government and to demonstrate to the Arabs that the United States was interested in their welfare. Once lend-lease began to North Africa, few better examples before the Marshall Plan and foreign-aid programs can be found of American attempts to restore economic health to strategic depressed areas. At the same time, many of the problems faced in North Africa were harbingers of those that the United States encountered in other parts of the third world.

In the early stages of this study it became quite evident that on economic matters, even if internal divisions over policy existed, the French position was clear. The consistency and clarity must be attributed to the wisdom and astuteness of Jean Monnet, who later became the father of the European Common Market. He spoke for the French on virtually every economic matter and negotiated the interim lend-lease arrangements as well as the final Master Agreement, signed in February 1945. The French policies are revealed in his correspondence and in summaries prepared by American officials. Thus no attempt has been made to analyze the complex intra-French political struggles.

The material was gathered solely from the abundant sources within the United States, especially from the huge Foreign Economic Administration collection. Gradually the French operation became less of a mystery, and in the end I was inundated with details. I had a brief correspondence with Jean Monnet, but his work prevented him from returning a questionnaire. Lloyd Cutler and Robert Murphy took time from their busy schedules to discuss at length their impressions of the aid programs, and their insights proved to be extremely useful.

My research was facilitated by the efficient and polite assistance of archivists and librarians. I am indebted to the diplomatic division of the National Archives and especially to William Lewis, who waded through hundreds of boxes of material, many of which were inadequately described and were being examined for the first time. The staffs at the Franklin Delano Roosevelt Library, the manuscript division of the Library of Congress, the Yale University Library, and the University of Virginia Library all provided valuable assistance.

The opportunity to appreciate research and writing was given to me by my parents. As my years in education continued, I am certain that they often wondered what, if anything, would ever come of it all. For their generosity and for not wondering too audibly, I am very grateful. My thanks and appreciation go to Professor Horace S. Merrill for his careful guidance, encouragement, and sustained interest. His attention and concern were far more than any student has a right to expect. I would also like to thank Wayne Cole, Gordon Prange, and Richard Farrell for reading the manuscript and offering suggestions. Jon Wakelyn and Lisle Rose carefully reviewed the work and encouraged me to make the revisions necessary for publication. Marcia Castaneda gave up much of her time to assist with the typing and editing of the final revisions.

Finally, this book would never have been possible without the understanding and sacrifices of my wife, Mary. She shared all the burdens and, in some instances, carried the entire burden, while teaching and raising a son, who is now old enough to appreciate a published work.

Abbreviations

BEW	Board of Economic Warfare
CCAC	Combined Civil Affairs Committee
CLAC	Combined Liberated Areas Committee
DNA	National Archives
FCNL	French Committee of National Liberation
FEA	Foreign Economic Administration
LAC	Liberated Areas Committee
LACs	Subcommittee of Liberated Areas Committee
NAEB	North African Economic Board
NAJEM	North African Joint Economic Mission
OFEC	Office of Foreign Economic Coordination
OFRRO	Office of Foreign Relief and Rehabilitation Operations
OLLA	Office of the Lend-Lease Administration
OWI	Office of War Information
SHAEF	Supreme Headquarters, Allied Expeditionary Force
UNRRA	United Nations Relief and Rehabilitation Administration
WPA	Works Progress Administration
WPB	War Production Board
WSA	War Shipping Administration

The
Politics of
Wartime Aid

Introduction

On March 11, 1941, President Franklin D. Roosevelt signed the Lend-Lease Act. Cited as "An Act to Promote the Defense of the United States," it conferred extraordinary power on the executive branch of the government. Originally intended to aid England with goods and war materials, despite her inability to pay for them, lend-lease eventually expanded to include over forty countries and became an invaluable source of military and civilian supply.

Following the Allied invasion of North Africa the administration employed lend-lease as an instrument for large-scale civilian economic assistance to that area. The civilian-aid programs appeared to distort the original prupose of the act. But the administration justified such aid as essential to the war effort and therefore "vital to the defense of the United States." The civilian programs clearly revealed the magnitude of modern global warfare, in which food, clothing, raw materials, and other civilian supplies played as important a role as guns and munitions. Through these programs the United States became intimately involved with other nations' economic problems and exerted a powerful influence on other countries.

Despite the broad and sweeping provisions of the act, lend-lease remained very susceptible to public opinion. Thus when Congress determined that lend-lease should end with the war, President Harry S. Truman terminated it. The concept of lend-lease, however, survived. When a new force threatened strategic areas, the United States, through the Truman Doctrine and Marshall Plans, revived the principle of economic warfare.

The total cost of lend-lease came to over $40 billion. The French program was the third largest, and from November 1942 until mid-1945 the population of French North and West Africa depended heavily on lend-lease as its major source of economic survival. When the war spread to Metropolitan France, the United States, through lend-lease, attempted to provide civilians with basic economic necessities.

The story of American economic assistance to France and French Northwest Africa, from 1940 through 1945, was one of frustration, controversy, and limited success. From the fall of France until the North African invasion, the United States expressed great concern over the economic deprivations in Vichy France and North Africa. The administration consistently reiterated its intentions of assisting these areas and even agreed to an economic accord with North African officials in order to implement an assistance program. But America's intentions far outdistanced its achievements. The British, who stubbornly adhered to a policy of "no aid for Vichy," opposed the program, and the United States lacked an aggressive attitude. Following the British lead, the administration overreacted to political decisions within Vichy and periodically withheld even token assistance.

While the United States maintained its ties with Vichy, the administration established limited relations with the Free French. Unwilling to jeopardize its Vichy policy, the administration rejected General Charles de Gaulle's appeals for direct economic and military assistance through lend-lease. Rather, the United States instructed the British to retransfer goods to the Free French from their lend-lease program. Despite American assistance relations with de Gaulle deteriorated during 1941 and 1942. The French leader's seizure of St. Pierre and Miquelon infuriated Secretary of State Cordell Hull and Roosevelt. Their distrust of de Gaulle increased, and they excluded him from any knowledge of or participation in the North African invasion. Instead the United States recognized the Vichy commander, Admiral Jean François Darlan, as the military and political authority in North Africa.

The decision of the United States to concentrate on Vichy and then to deal with Darlan and not de Gaulle represented a controversial though extremely wise choice. In 1942, there was no evidence either in France or North Africa of any considerable support for de Gaulle. On the other hand Darlan, as the highest military authority in North Africa, commanded the respect, loyalty, and obedience of the French forces. American overtures to Darlan resulted in the rapid termination of French resistance and eliminated the distasteful possibility of a protracted engagement between French and Allied forces.*

When the Allies landed in North Africa, the lack of assistance combined with two years of German exploitation had reduced the North African economy to a bare subsistence level. The Allies feared that severe economic dislocation would seriously jeopardize the political and military situation. Consequently, through a civilian lend-lease program the United States sought to restore economic health to French North and West Africa. This marked the first attempt at utilizing lend-lease in a liberated area.

The lack of experience in such an operation naturally produced shortcomings that were immediately evident. Yet at the same time the North African operation proved invaluable, as it served as a pilot program for future endeavors. Of utmost importance, the North African experience had demonstrated that the assignment to the civilian agencies of the responsibility for economic assistance created confusion and inefficiency, as well as friction with the military. Thus, although Roosevelt still retained his apprehensions over using the military in civilian affairs, he reluctantly transferred to the army the responsibility for civilian supply during the early stages of liberation.

The French North and West African civilian assistance program differed markedly from those of other lend-lease recipients. From the very beginning of the program the United States insisted that the French pay cash for civilian goods. Since England, China, and Russia received similar assistance on a credit or straight lend-lease basis, the inequity was obvious. But the administration had determined that due to the presence of American troops in North Africa and the large gold and dollar balances held by the French, they possessed sufficient funds to pay for the goods. Naturally the French looked askance at a policy that the United States justified as essential to Allied military operations and then demanded payment for such assistance. On the other hand, the United States was still smarting from the World War I debt debacle and interpreted French reluctance to pay as another example of European evasion of financial responsibility.

In this case, however, the American position was virtually indefensible. The demand for payment was shortsighted and economically unsound because it ignored France's need to retain her funds in order to provide

*For more on the Darlan Controversy, see Chapter 3.

for postwar reconstruction. Furthermore, the United States' demands for payment proved a source of irritation that served to undermine American-French relations.

Another source of friction developed when American private enterprise attempted to exploit France's weakened position in the most lucrative part of her empire. Although lend-lease provided a boon for American manufacturing interests, it stifled overseas commercial activity. The civilian assistance to France flowed on a government-to-government basis, thereby circumventing established import-export houses. With the collapse of the Nazis in Tunisia in May 1943, commercial groups intensified their pressure on the Lend-Lease Administration to restore private trade to North and West Africa. Unfortunately the administration assumed a weak, defensive attitude and continually attempted to appease these groups. Undaunted by their own exhibition of blatant, imperialistic designs, the private traders persisted. They succeeded in gaining support in the administration, which resulted in the application of more pressure on France and further alienated America's ally. The French, wary of American intentions, remained adamant, refused to restore private trade until July 1945, and demonstrated the tenacity of a weakened empire-builder attempting to retain its domination in the face of foreign incursions. The private trade issue rivaled the payment question as the most disruptive feature in American-French lend-lease relations.

The controversial issues of the civilian lend-lease experience in North Africa cast a shadow over the entire operation. The United States expended an enormous amount of time, money, and energy to provide assistance to North Africa. Once the fighting in North Africa terminated, the United States continued its aid, which according to Robert Murphy clearly went beyond its responsibility. But the French exhibited indifference and ingratitude. They aggressively pressed for as much assistance as possible and appeared to American officials as determined to exploit lend-lease to its fullest. With the exception of Jean Monnet, the other French leaders never bothered to grasp the problems involved in wartime supply and shipping. Along with this they demonstrated ineptitude in administering the economic assistance, which constantly dismayed American officials.

The American charges that the primary concern of the French leaders was the maintenance of French domination in North Africa were valid. The French jealously guarded the "treasure" of their empire. They regarded American presence and the power of the United States as a direct threat to their position. At the same time, they insisted upon American assistance but offered few concessions in return. This was particularly true of private trade. Although the American commercial interests had pressured administration officials into an aggressive approach, the French used every devious method to avoid accommodation. The American policy of insistence on cash payment enabled the French to argue that the United States treated them differently than other lend-lease recipients.

At best the civilian assistance to North Africa represented a qualified success. It provided basic subsistence, which pacified the population and thereby prevented any political upheavals. However, the Black Market flourished, the inveterate French discrimination revealed itself in the process of distributing lend-lease goods, and the more grandiose American plans to rehabilitate North Africa and use it as a source of supply for Europe never materialized.

While disagreement over the supply program caused difficulties, the problem that arose with the most pervasive ramifications was the Arab nationalist movement. From the time Murphy and the consuls arrived in North Africa, it was evident that Arab leaders were unsympathetic toward the plight of the French. On the other hand, by supplying aid and driving out the Nazis the United States demonstrated its generosity, wealth, and power; in so doing, however, it unintentionally further undermined France's weakened position in Northwest Africa. Moreover, the Arabs came to view the Americans as their liberators not only from the Nazis but from the French colonial system as well. The dilemma that the United States faced became obvious; American leaders had reassured the French that they had no intention of altering the French North African empire, but, at the same time, they supported the principles of the Atlantic Charter and Four Freedoms. Ultimately the United States could not pursue both pledges, and unfortunately the United States was unprepared to cope with the native movement. Only a handful of Americans recognized its significance, and their advice, namely, that the United States play a major role in postwar North African political settlements, went unheeded. Instead the United States refused to become involved in internal political matters and insisted that only the French should settle them.

The French, still thinking in terms of nineteenth-century colonial relations, initiated reprisals that further alienated the natives. By not intervening, the Americans became identified with the French colonial system, and by the end of the war the United States had lost much of its prestige in North Africa. More importantly, by failing to understand the nationalists, the United States too often accepted French explanations that the communists were responsible for the native turmoil. Thus the United States lost an excellent opportunity to retain and expand its influence, much of which it had acquired through economic aid, in an important area of the third world.

In 1944 the attention of the United States shifted, and the administration began considerations of lend-lease policy in the mother country. Six months after D day France was the only major lend-lease recipient that had not concluded a formal Lend-Lease Master Agreement with the United States.* The responsibility for this situation rested with the United States; the administration had exhibited a reluctance to conclude a formal agreement with the French. It had procrastinated, hoping that the war would end and thereby eliminate the necessity for such an agreement. But the war continued, and with recognition of de Gaulle's government in October 1944, French pressure increased. Thus representatives of the two countries completed negotiations, and on February 28, 1945, the United States and France signed a Master Lend-Lease Agreement. The French accord, which differed considerably from master agreements with other countries, immediately precipitated a controversy. The issue emerged over a list of goods that the United States agreed to supply but that obviously had postwar utility. Such an arrangement aroused a storm of protest in Congress and resulted in an amendment to the original Lend-Lease Act. The reaction influenced Truman's decision to terminate lend-lease abruptly at the conclusion of the war in the Pacific.

Whether the Roosevelt administration attempted to use the French understanding to gauge public reaction to the employment of lend-lease as a postwar measure remains unknown. However, it revealed Roosevelt's continued policy of dealing with the French and other nations on an *ad hoc* basis. Of utmost importance the French understanding demonstrated

---

*In February 1943, Assistant Secretary of State Dean Acheson described the Master Agreements to the House Foreign Affairs Committee: "These Master Agreements are simple, broad documents, designed to establish a framework within which each signatory nation may freely aid the other in such ways as the changing course of the war makes most appropriate."—U.S. Congress, House of Representatives, Committee on Foreign Affairs, *Hearings on H. R. 1501,* 78th Congress, 1st Session, 1943.

that less than three months before VE day Roosevelt had little conception
of any postwar rehabilitation plans and no appropriate instrument to accomplish them. The congressional reaction clearly revealed that Congress
would not sanction the use of lend-lease as a vehicle for postwar assistance.

The Truman administration, cognizant of congressional attitudes, attempted to alleviate postwar economic burdens by writing off most of
the lend-lease debts, but not all of them. In the case of France, the final
settlement, concluded in May 1946, left her with a lend-lease debt of
$720 million—a substantial sum considering France's economic plight.
Moreover, the settlement provided only limited financial assistance and
also revealed that one year after VE day no mechanism capable of restoring the French economy appeared in sight. The subsequent Marshall Plan
and foreign-aid programs attempted to remedy the depressed conditions.
During the postwar period France provided payments on her lend-lease
debt, but in 1957 economic chaos and political turmoil threatened to
cripple her. Consequently in January 1958 the United States agreed to
postpone the payment schedule for 1958 and 1959 to 1981 and 1982.
Thus, an act designed to eliminate the economic hardships that plagued
the post-World War I period had not entirely eliminated the burden of
postwar repayment.

1.

The Setting: French Northwest Africa

The Allied invasion of French North Africa focused world attention on Algeria, Morocco, and Tunisia. It exposed the economic plight of the area and forced the Allies to assume the responsibility for the territories' economic survival. This necessitated the immediate organization of an effective civilian assistance program. The culture, customs, politics, and economy of French North and West Africa, however, were a mystery to officials of the lend-lease administration. The supply agency's introduction to the intricacies of the political and economic life in the French colonies provided a rude awakening. Years of French control had established an economic pattern that not only exploited the territories but subjected them to almost total economic dependence on France. A small minority of self-serving Frenchmen dominated the political and economic life so that the interests of the black natives in West Africa and their Arab counterparts in North Africa remained secondary at best. The economic policies these interest groups pursued and that the government sanctioned prevented other nations from enjoying any extensive trade with French Northwest Africa. Moreover, in addition to the problems inherent in minority control, the area's geography, agricultural structure, industrial complex, and labor organization presented American officials with problems that demanded immediate attention.

Throughout its history North Africa had a European orientation. Its northern boundary, the Mediterranean Sea, and the vast desert that comprised its southern border had determined the area's direction. Not only were communications with Europe more convenient, but the desert provided an effective barrier between Mediterranean Africa and the rest of the continent. Consequently, North Africa developed a civilization more in common with the Mediterranean peoples than with the predominantly Negroid races south of the Sahara. French political and economic control accentuated this tendency. Considered by France as the most prized possession in her empire, North Africa readily complemented France's economic life; it provided a market for all types of manufactured goods and in return exported foodstuffs and raw materials.

In the mid-nineteenth century France began to establish control over North Africa. By 1847 Algeria belonged to France and in most respects functioned as an integral part of Metropolitan France. In 1881 Tunisia became a protectorate, and in 1912 Morocco agreed to accept a similar status. The administration of the protectorates differed somewhat from that of Algeria. The latter functioned without any native administration. The supreme power rested in the hands of the governor-general, who promulgated legislation that emanated directly from the French central government. In Morocco and Tunisia, native governments under the authority of the sultan of Morocco and the bey of Tunis retained control. However, treaty stipulations and French supervision of the resident general insured France of the final decision in all legislative matters.[1]

The geographic features of the territories display a remarkable degree of similarity. The north-south boundaries are arbitrary divisions not determined by physical characteristics. All three countries share the Mediterranean, although Morocco's seacoast belonged to Spain. As a result she employed the Algerian port of Oran as a Mediterranean outlet. However, Morocco is the only country that possesses an Atlantic coastline, and the well-equipped port of Casablanca remained indispensable to its economy and to the Allied war effort. Other North African ports, such as Algiers, Oran, and Bône in Algeria and Bizerte, Tunis-La Goulette, Sfax, and Sousse in Tunisia, furnish each country with adequate harbor facilities. Although no geographical obstructions inhibited inland transportation, not one of the territories ever developed an extensive transportation network. Consequently with the invasion and the subsequent appropriation of railroad cars, autos, trucks, and buses to meet military priorities, large quantities of civilian goods remained stranded in dockside warehouses.

In North Africa the development of the mining industry lagged. Phosphate rock, which was essential to England for the manufacture of fertilizer, was the only mineral that occupied a significant position in the world markets. During the occupation the United States and Great Britain intended to remedy this by stimulating increased production of iron, steel, cobalt, molybdenum, and especially coal. The wartime shortages virtually dictated that North Africa raise its coal production from its prewar level of 250,000 tons per year to at least its consumption level of 1,000,000 tons.[2]

The agricultural products of the area constituted significant contributions to the welfare of France. General agriculture, livestock raising, and fruit growing dominated North Africa's agrarian economy. The cultivation of citrus fruits, dates, garden vegetables, olives, and grapes provided for local consumption as well as exportation. Large-scale sheep raising led to the shipment of millions of pounds of wool to France, which alleviated shortages and sustained the French textile industry. Above all, North Africa's most important contribution to the mother country rested on the regular shipment of huge quantities of wheat and barley. North African grain comprised the major portion of French cereal imports and accounted for more than the total amount from all other countries combined.[3]

The Axis also coveted North African farm products but contributed nothing to maintaining the area's economy. Consequently, when the Allies arrived they found that deteriorated agricultural equipment had considerably reduced North African production and that ruthless Axis exploitation depleted the grain supply to such an extent that the importation of thousands of tons of wheat was essential to keep pace with local consumption.[4]

The population of North Africa exhibited a high degree of uniformity. According to the 1936 census the African population of the three territories numbered 14 million out of a total population of 16 million. In Morocco and Tunisia the French population represented 4 percent of the total, while in Algeria the figure was 10 percent. What the French lacked in numbers they regained in power. Frenchmen dominated virtually every aspect of the area's economic existence. In order to perpetuate their control the French operated in a manner that discriminated against the Arabs as well as the Jews, Spaniards, and Italians. Thus, a small number of import companies controlled the bulk of North African trade. In prewar years these entrenched interests voluntarily organized into groupements or associations of businessmen, industrialists, and workers to promote private interests through group action. The specter of war in Europe and the subsequent Vichy government completed the groupement arrangement.[5]

Prior to the war the French government had approved of the groupements. A French statute of July 11, 1938, provided a legal basis for the previous de facto discrimination by making groupement membership compulsory and requiring government supervision of producers, consumers, and merchants. The reorganization of the groupements along industrial lines produced associations such as the Shoe Groupement, Textile Groupement, and Clothing Groupement. The dependency's administration appointed the heads of each groupement and delegated to each of them so much authority that virtual commercial dictatorships existed. The following year the government further extended the power of the groupements by requiring the consent of both the government and the associations before permitting the expansion of old companies or the establishment of new firms.[6]

Under Vichy the groupements retained their discrimination and power. The associations submitted orders to an organization committee, which in turn distributed the allocations to the groupements. Once received the groupement representative carefully parceled out the goods to its members. By 1942, groupement mergers limited their total number, and memberships became more restricted. Vichy control extended groupement discrimination beyond all previous bounds by excluding not only foreigners but firms and individuals considered politically unsatisfactory.[7]

The groupements posed a dilemma for American officials. They represented the only centralized economic organization in the entire area. At the same time, they failed to serve the needs of the majority of North Africans, in particular those of the huge Arab population. Despite fascist leanings of the groupement leaders, and despite their questionable activities, United States authorities determined that temporary retention of the system offered the only feasible solution for the amelioration of economic hardships. In conjunction with them, lend-lease personnel endeavored to ascertain the basic requirements essential for the pacification of the population and maintenance of the North African economy. They also undertook the more onerous task of supervising the groupements to insure equitable distribution.

From the standpoint of foreign trade North Africa merited her designation as the "brightest jewel" in the French Empire. In 1938 North Africa absorbed more imports from France than the rest of the entire empire and in return exported to the mother country more goods than all the other components of the empire combined. Algeria, the wealthiest and most populated territory, shipped over 80 percent of her foreign trade to France, while the protectorates averaged approximately 50 percent.[8] When France capitulated, the Axis endeavored to exploit this relationship by directing the flow of North African goods to Germany and Italy. Although the intimate details of this procedure remained somewhat obscure, German agents stationed in Marseilles labored to insure the Reich of an ample supply of the fruits and grains that arrived from North Africa. The Kehrl Plans of 1941-42 included textile agreements with provisions for supplying Germany with large quantities of crude and processed wool from North Africa as well as France.[9]

French policies and the low standard of living in North Africa inhibited the expansion of trade with the United States. In 1938 only 3 percent of American exports, with an average value of $2 million per territory, went to North Africa. North Africa furnished a market for American manufactured products such as machinery, agricultural implements, petroleum products, and tobacco. The limited amount of North African exports to the United States included olive oil, animal hides, cork, and a few miscellaneous chemicals.[10]

The absence of extensive trade relations seriously handicapped American efforts to alleviate the North African economic crisis. The secrecy involved in planning military operations excluded the civilian supply agencies from prior knowledge of the invasion. The Board of Economic Warfare had compiled material on the economy of North Africa, but these reports were cursory at best—not extensive proposals for massive economic assistance. Therefore, the immediate problem that confronted the lend-lease administration was to acquire knowledge of the intricacies of the North African economy in order to provide for immediate relief and to develop an effective long-range program. Both of these factors were major influences in the decision to retain the egregious groupements.

France's colonial empire in West Africa consisted of seven provinces and more than 1.8 million square miles of territory. West Africa has a tropical climate and features desert, savanna, and tropical rain forest. Economically and commercially, Senegal was the most important province. Dakar, its capital, served as the political capital of West Africa.

Throughout its history the interests of Metropolitan France dominated territorial considerations while those of the European colonists and natives remained subordinate. Thus a pattern of trade developed that closely paralleled that of North Africa. As an underdeveloped area West Africa imported most of its manufactured products, which the Europeans and assimilated natives absorbed. In 1938 approximately 60 percent of the area's imports came from France while West Africa exported 80 percent of her total to France. As in the case of North Africa the United States received less than 4 percent of West African exports; these included peanuts, cocoa, palm kernels, coffee, bananas, mahogany, and sisal. Although the United States was West Africa's third largest supplier, this accounted for less than 6 percent of her imports.[11]

Large French trading companies dominated West African trade. These organizations had survived and expanded from the early colonial period, so that by 1940 they virtually dictated economic policy. The largest, the United African Company, alone handled approximately 35 percent of all West African imports. The firm controlled all the lighterage on the west coast and owned the chief shipping company between England and West Africa. In addition the company either operated or had interests in the Nigerian railroads, the dock facilities, storage in Port Harcourt, and tin, coal, and magnesium mines. The company recognized no limitations to insure or enhance its position. Other smaller companies, such as the French Company and Charbrier and Fraissent, existed, but none approached the United African Company in power or influence. For American products to enter, orders passed through the main company office in France. French agents purchased the goods in the United States and shipped them directly to West Africa. The system was responsible for the perpetuation of exorbitant prices, abnormal profits, cut-throat trading, company rivalry, and political manipulation.[12]

The central government in France dictated West African policy through the office of the governor-general. With the appointment of the Vichy puppet, Pierre Boisson, the anti-British and anti-Free French policy created a certain amount of unrest. However, the colonists appeared more concerned over the impact of Vichy on the economic structure than over an altered role in the progress of the war.[13]

On March 21, 1941, a French law imposed the groupement system on West Africa. Although the trading companies described government control through the groupements as "colossal influence," there was little overt hostility. In fact the new law did not radically alter the established order; economically, it froze the status quo; politically, it insured the elimination of political undesirables, such as Jews and anti-Fascists. The trading companies exhibited little concern over loyalty to the Axis and readily exported goods destined for Germany.[14]

Unlike North Africa, West Africa did not become a theater of military operations. Nevertheless, American forces occupied it. The United States intended to stimulate the production of West African goods required for the war effort to keep the Allies supplied with essential materials and to promote markets for postwar trade. The occupation halted trade with France, and lend-lease officials assumed the task of the procurement and distribution of civilian supplies. The American army furnished temporary relief in some areas but had to leave many of the colonies without adequate provisions.[15]

With little time to design an intricate distribution network, American authorities sanctioned the established procedure. Despite this decision American incursions promoted suspicions and outright resentment. The trading companies and the colonial administration had spent years developing a working relationship that both pacified and exploited the native population. The French bureaucracy feared that American intervention would disrupt the entire native order by raising wages, improving working conditions, and shortening hours. The trading companies regarded the presence of Americans as a direct threat to their existence.[16]

The attitudes of the natives in North and West Africa about compensation for their labor were identical. Money had no significance beyond its immediate purchasing power. Therefore, the shortage of goods during the war seriously retarded the economy, as the natives simply refused employment when the products they desired were unavailable.[17] As a result, lend-lease personnel faced the awesome task of supplying incentive goods in order to enlist native support. Native labor was indispensable for the successful operation of both the military and civilian programs. Unfortunately the importance of this unique feature of North and West African life, along with many others, remained unappreciated in Washington. Thus, in many respects these area programs revealed the ubiquitous bureaucratic conflicts between field representatives and their colleagues in the States.

NOTES

1. Herbert J. Leibesny, *The African Handbook: The Government of French North Africa* (Philadelphia: University of Pennsylvania, 1943), 9-43.

2. Henry A. Wieschoff et al., eds., *French North Africa: Area Study for the Army Specialized Training Program,* Vol. 1 (Philadelphia: University of Pennsylvania, 1943), 4. This study consists of two extensive volumes of excellent detail concerning all aspects of North African culture, economy, religion, and politics and of French control. The volumes are in the University of Pennsylvania Museum. General information can also be found in secondary works on North Africa; *see* Chapter 7, Notes 2 and 29.

3. Ibid.

4. Ibid.

5. Foreign Economic Administration (hereafter FEA), "The Trade Structure of French North Africa, 1938-1943," January 4, 1943, Box 363, RG 169.

6. Ibid.

7. Ibid.

8. Philip M. Copp, "French North Africa: Economy of a New War Vortex," *Foreign Commerce Weekly* 9 (November 28, 1942), 5-6.

9. Weischoff et al., eds., *French North Africa* 1, 5.

10. FEA, "Trade Structure of French North Africa."

11. FEA, "The Distribution of Imported Goods in French West Africa," November 24, 1943, Box 363, RG 169.

12. Ibid., 2-5.

13. Ibid., 3.

14. Ibid., 6.

15. Ibid., 2.

16. Ibid.

17. Ibid., 7.

2.

Aid to France and French Northwest Africa, 1941-42

From the fall of France until the North African invasion in November 1942, the United States maintained diplomatic relations with Vichy France, despite criticism and controversy. During this period American policymakers engaged in the organization and implementation of economic assistance programs for France and her North African empire. American officials believed that effective economic aid would counter German influence and assist in retaining the goodwill of the French and native populations. However, American efforts encountered stubborn British opposition. Great Britain vehemently objected to any form of economic aid for Vichy, and her attitude clearly revealed the basic differences between the two countries over the treatment of France and her empire. With American officials reluctant to pressure the British into a policy contrary to their wishes, American plans for extensive economic assistance were severely hampered. Consequently, only from a political and strategic standpoint did the program exhibit any success. The economic agreement signed with North Africa permitted the presence of American agents to supervise the distribution of goods. These men provided valuable intelligence data on the most pertinent military, political, and economic developments in that vital area. Along with this, French contacts with the United States, as well as the promise of economic aid, somewhat strengthened the French position in North Africa and tended to offset German incursions.

From an economic perspective, however, the assistance programs were a failure. Only a few relief shipments ever arrived in France, and these were solely for the children of the unoccupied zone. More important and with a much greater long-range impact was the ineffective attempt to sustain the North African economy. Despite a formal agreement and continued promises, North Africa never received sufficient assistance to bolster her sagging economy. Thus, in November 1942, when the lend-lease administration assumed the responsibility for the economic rehabilitation of the area, the shortcomings of the previous inaction were most evident; agency officials encountered a stagnated economy on the verge of total collapse.

On January 4, 1941, Admiral William D. Leahy arrived in France as American Ambassador to the Vichy Government. Leahy's influence, experience in special assignments, and distinguished naval career established him as one of the best available men for the mission. After Leahy had completed his military career as Chief of Naval Operations and had retired from the navy, he served the government in other capacities. To Leahy, comfortably residing in San Juan, Puerto Rico, where he was governor of the island, the call to duty "came as a complete surprise." Although the sixty-five-year-old Leahy professed to know little about European politics and asserted that he was no diplomat, he proved to be an outstanding ambassador. The admiral emphasized his knowledge of military affairs, which he deemed essential during wartime. Through his strong personality he exercised considerable influence at Vichy and served as a deterrent to the extreme collaborationists and as a reminder of America's power and determination. Leahy's sensitivity to the needs of the impoverished and suffering French enhanced his popularity and maintained the impression of America's concern for the people of France. Following his recall in May 1942 Leahy served as President Roosevelt's "personal" Chief of Staff.[1]

Roosevelt regarded the situation in France as extremely critical. Recognizing the possibility that France might actually become involved in the war on the side of the Axis, the president desired an ambassador to France "who can gain the confidence of Marshal Pétain who at the present moment is the one powerful element in the French Government who is standing firm against selling out to Germany."[2]

Roosevelt's chief concern was that the French would employ their fleet against the British. The naval officers in the French high command were intensely anti-British. This resulted from the British attack against part of the French fleet at Mers-el-Kebir on July 3, 1940. The engagement cost the French several vessels and approximately 1,200 casualties. At the time, Robert Murphy, Chargé d'Affaires of the American Embassy at Vichy, reported that American Attachés used all their persuasion in order to prevent the French naval commander, Admiral Jean François Darlan, from turning the fleet over to the Germans.[3]

Roosevelt believed that not only could a man such as Leahy converse with Marshal Henri Pétain in a language they both understood but that his position in the navy would give him "great influence with the high officers of the French Navy who are openly hostile to Great Britain."[4] Shortly after his arrival Leahy justified the president's concern by describing Admiral Darlan as "incurably anti-British."[5]

Since June 25, 1940, the Franco-German Armistice stated the conditions under which France and her empire were to exist. Of utmost importance to the United States was the assurance that French cooperation would not extend beyond the terms of the armistice. Thus, Roosevelt instructed Leahy to convince Vichy officials that excessive collaboration was essentially self-destructive, since "a German victory would inevitably result in the dismemberment of the French Empire and the maintenance, at most, of France as a vassal state."[6] On the crucial issue of the French fleet the ambassador's directives were explicit; if France permitted German acquisition of her fleet or the use of French naval bases, France "would most certainly forfeit the friendship and good will of the United States and result in the destruction of the French fleet to the irreparable injury to France."[7]

By Leahy's arrival the question of economic aid for France in the form of food, medicine, and clothing had already precipitated a controversy between the United States and Great Britain. Moreover, the issue assumed a greater complexity when the French made it clear to Leahy that they considered economic assistance as evidence of American concern and sincerity. The problem defied any immediate solution, and as Leahy described it, "the question of American food supplies for unoccupied France was to be with me during my entire stay at Vichy."[8] The ambiguous nature of Leahy's instructions reflected the dilemma that confronted United States policymakers. The Americans emphasized the necessity of relief in order to maintain the goodwill of the French people; at the same time, they accepted the British premise that such aid had potential value to the Axis.

The relief campaign for France commenced shortly after its capitulation. Former President Herbert Hoover once again demonstrated his administrative skills by effectively organizing various interest groups concerned with the plight of the French people. As a result, within the United States sympathy and sentiment for the French increased substantially.[9]

On December 10, 1940, England clarified her position on the subject in an aide-mémoire. Generally, the foreign office argued that it felt compelled to treat all German-occupied territories in the same manner. Since supplies that went to occupied areas could eventually fall into the hands of the Germans, England refused to sanction economic relief. Although the English expressed sympathy for the populations under Axis domination, they stressed the scarcity of goods in the British Isles and pointed out that the Germans maintained sufficient supplies to avert a disastrous famine in occupied countries. In support of this, Winston Churchill cited a German broadcast of June 27, 1940, which stated that although the Hoover plans for relief in France, Belgium, and Holland deserved commendation, it was not necessary, for German officials had already begun preparations to insure the feeding of these populations.[10]

Despite other reports describing the economic plight of the French, the British remained adamant. Officials insisted that "France is well known to be self-supporting in essential foodstuffs and any willingness to allow relief supplies to enter would be an encouragement to Germany to remove supplies from France for her own use."[11] England's policy was to treat both areas of France alike.

Through the French ambassador, Gaston Henry-Haye, the state department was well aware of the deteriorating economic conditions within his country. The Germans continued to confiscate enormous quantities of food, ostensibly for the 1.5 million French prisoners of war, but as American, English, and French officials realized, these goods rarely found their way to the prisoners. The exploitation was so extensive that the French estimated that only the importation of thousands of tons of wheat and corn could alleviate severe shortages before the spring harvest.[12]

By the end of 1940 the situation became even more acute when over 4 million displaced persons in search of refuge arrived in unoccupied France. The multitudes that came from the Benelux countries and northern France consisted primarily of older men, women, and children. Once

in Vichy France they found it already heavily populated with escapees
from other political pogroms—anti-Nazis, anti-Franco Spaniards, and
Jews from Czechoslovakia, Poland, Germany, and Austria. Few of these
people possessed sufficient supplies of food, clothing or fuel. Housing
and sanitation facilities were virtually nonexistent, leaving the vast majority of refugees to live in squalid conditions.[13] Thus the Vichy government, whose area comprised roughly one-third of France, faced an awesome relief burden as winter rapidly approached.

The chief obstacle to the importation of supplies into France was the
British blockade. Both Roosevelt and Secretary of State Cordell Hull assured Henry-Haye that they would urge the British to relax their policy.
However, throughout 1940 the British relentlessly enforced the blockade
and consistently rejected American appeals to permit the passage even of
minimal requirements of food, vitamins, and clothing for unoccupied
France.[14]

American officials attributed English aggressiveness and obduracy to
Hugh Dalton, the minister of economic warfare. However, both Churchill
and Lord Halifax, the British ambassador to the United States, were cognizant of Dalton's policy, and in essence his directives reflected the position of the British government. The policy also received overwhelming
support in Parliament, which indicated the widespread acceptance of it
on the part of the public. The severe loss of civilian life in London, South-
ampton, Bristol, Birmingham, and Coventry had so hardened the British
that they readily rejected even humanitarian concessions.[15]

The situation in France did little to dispel British apprehensions and
suspicions. Admiral Darlan's vituperative anti-British rhetoric further
alienated the English. The policy of Marshal Pétain was at best ambiguous,
and the threat remained that the pro-German forces directed by the arch-
collaborationist Pierre Laval could, with the assistance of German pressure, seize power. Therefore, in 1940 the British felt that as long as the
potential for excessive collaboration existed, either through voluntary
or involuntary acquiescence, they had to maintain their rigid policy. They
interpreted close Franco-German cooperation as potentially disastrous
to the British cause.

Leahy found the situation in France more serious than even French
reports indicated. Relief was one of the foremost concerns of Pétain. The
marshal quoted figures of German confiscation and emphasized the necessity of harvesting the spring crops in North Africa. Vichy officials stressed

the necessity for immediate relief, arguing that a starving population posed a serious threat to the Pétain government. The marshal feared that the pro-Axis faction would capitalize on the food shortages, create a crisis atmosphere, and then promise provisions from German reserves. Admiral Darlan completely agreed with Pétain and expressed serious concern over the political impact of such an economic crisis.[16]

The French argument evidently impressed Leahy, who throughout his stay in France demonstrated considerable sensitivity to the deprivations of the French population. American Red Cross representatives assured him that their organization was capable of distributing any quantity of supplies in unoccupied France without danger of the materials either directly or indirectly falling into the hands of the Germans.[17] Both Pétain and Darlan expressed a willingness to receive aid under any reasonable conditions the Allies imposed. Consequently, in a series of reports Leahy advocated the necessity of retaining the goodwill of the French people and strongly recommended American approval of French requests for economic assistance in unoccupied France as well as North Africa. At the same time, he informed the French that assistance for the occupied area was out of the question.[18]

By the end of January 1941 efforts on the part of the United States to provide relief for the unoccupied zone met with limited success. In response to a direct appeal from Roosevelt, Churchill suggested that England would permit two vessels with relief supplies for Vichy France to pass through the blockade. Churchill's conditions were minimal: (1) the relief goods were to consist of medical supplies, vitamin concentrates, dried milk, and children's clothing; (2) the American Red Cross was to supervise the distribution closely; (3) press coverage was to note British cooperation. The prime minister, never known as one to shun publicity, sought to exploit the assistance to its fullest—"The impression which we should like to see created is that of Anglo-American co-operation for humanitarian ends."[19]

As the United States and England slowly edged toward a compromise, French leaders continued their anti-British tirades. Much to the dismay of Leahy, Pétain announced publicly that the British and in particular Churchill were responsible for starving the French people. Admiral Darlan threatened to employ the French fleet to sink English vessels that interfered with the deliverance of supplies.[20] However, Leahy himself began to exhibit utter disgust with the British policy. On February 24,

1941, he wrote to Undersecretary of State Sumner Welles that "the British blockade action which prevents the delivery of the necessary foodstuffs to the inhabitants of unoccupied France is of the order of stupidity as many other British policies in the present war."[21] Although Leahy's future criticism was less caustic, his impatience was clearly evident. On March 4 he cabled Welles that he was still "unable to understand why the British Ministry of Economic Warfare or any group in America should desire to acquire or maintain the ill will of the French people by forcing them on to starvation rations."[22]

Finally in March an agreement between the United States and England permitted the passage of two ships with relief goods for unoccupied France. Churchill's conditions provided the basis for the arrangement, which also stipulated that the goods were for the children of the area. Pétain accepted the conditions and guaranteed their enforcement.[23]

By this time the focal point of American, British, and French attention had shifted to North Africa, where Franco-American negotiations produced the most significant developments with long-range impacts. To counter German initiatives and to cultivate the friendship of the African natives, American officials assiduously worked to develop an economic program in order to prevent a complete collapse of the North African economy. In November 1940 Welles directed Felix Cole, the American consul general in Algeria, to confer with the French delegate general of North Africa, General Maxime Weygand. The purpose of the conference was to determine Weygand's views on the feasibility of establishing an economic assistance program. American officials were well aware of Weygand's loyalty to Vichy, yet at the same time they recognized his friendly disposition toward the United States. Thus, Welles instructed Cole: "Tell the General that we understand the difficult position in which he is placed, that we should like to assist him, at least from the economic point of view if that could be done without injury to Great Britain. . . ."[24]

The North African situation was extremely complex and required a delicate approach. On January 14, 1941, Murphy informed Hull that in the presence of Pierre Boisson (French Governor General of West Africa) Weygand told him, "Obviously I hope for an English victory. We all do. My primary job however is to keep North Africa intact—for France. . . ."[25]

The French North African officials were not dissidents; rather they pursued a policy sanctioned by the Vichy government. Both Weygand

and Pétain regarded French North Africa as France's final trump, which if skillfully exploited would benefit France as well as Africa. Economically, however, French North Africa was in a precarious position. Although in early 1941 food remained plentiful, business stagnated. There were already shortages of coal and gas; the transportation network and the agricultural equipment required extensive maintenance and repair. This became practically impossible, since the British blockade prevented North Africa from importing the necessary materials.[26]

For Weygand the situation could only become worse. He informed the American representatives that immediate economic assistance was imperative; he would grant whatever concessions the United States desired, including an American control commission. At the same time, he cautioned against an overly aggressive approach. Although he possessed the authority to enter into economic agreements, he warned that British broadcasts describing him as about to lead an independent movement in Africa aroused German suspicions and inhibited his freedom of action. Weygand described it as "a situation in which the greatest discretion must be exercised. It is a great misfortune that the British feel that everything must be shouted from the rooftops."[27]

As in the case of relief for France the United States and Great Britain clashed over the principle of economic aid for North Africa. Basically the United States was much more concerned over the inability of the French to maintain the North African economy than England. The Americans pointed out the deleterious effects that the blockade had produced in North Africa. The British replied that while they would enforce the blockade as much as possible, it was not their intention to strangle the French colonies. Rather, they argued that the application of a certain degree of pressure was an attempt to employ economic factors to drive the French colonies away from Vichy.[28] The British continued to hope that Weygand would establish an independent government, attract the fleet to Algeria, and continue the struggle against the Axis. This Weygand refused to do without massive support from the Allies. As Weygand told Leahy, "If the British come with four divisions, I will fire on them; if they come with twenty I will welcome them."[29]

American officials firmly believed that the British policy, rather than gaining French cooperation, tended to push the French colonies in the direction of the Axis.[30] They also pointed out that the blockade was at best imperfect. Cargoes continued to pass through Gibraltar and arrive

at Marseilles. At the same time, the United States emphasized the incon-
gruity of British policy that permitted them to trade with Morocco but
refused navicerts for American trade.[31]

By the end of January 1941 the United States desired to conclude
some arrangement for economic assistance. Since December, Robert
Murphy, as a special representative of President Roosevelt, had established close contacts with Weygand and other North African authorities.
However, the state department was reluctant to finalize any understanding without serious consideration of the English position. The basic conditions the British insisted on were for the most part acceptable to both
France and the United States. The British desired guarantees that the
goods were for consumption in Africa and not for reexportation to
France. They also required the assignment of American agents to ports
and railroads in order to prevent an accumulation of stocks and possible
seizure by the enemy. The approval of these stipulations did not pose
any problems, but the British also demanded the release of English vessels detained in North African ports.[32]

American officials regarded this prerequisite as virtually impossible
for the French to guarantee. On February 15 Welles told Halifax that
"after careful study of the armistice conditions, it did not seem to the
Department of State that the French authorities could possibly agree
to this condition." Beyond this Welles reported that he did not believe
"any useful purpose would be served by attempting to insist upon a condition which we knew the French Government and the French authorities of North Africa were not able to grant." Therefore, the United States
refused to make the release of the vessels a sine qua non and informed
the ambassador that at best Murphy would mention England's concern
over the ships.[33]

Although Halifax agreed with Welles, it was with considerable misgivings that the British viewed the progress toward an agreement. To the
Americans the major British shortcoming was their failure to realize that
a German takeover was imminent should French control break down as
a result of a native population bereft of supplies. It was also evident that
the British had far less confidence in Weygand than the Americans and
remained skeptical of the outcome of an economic accord. They also
felt that Weygand's loyalty to Vichy would result in the reexportation
of goods to France. Although American officials argued that a success-

ful program was possible, their assurance did little to assuage British trepidations. In a conversation with British representatives Assistant Secretary of State Adolf Berle pointed out that "the future course of the French authorities in Morocco was problematic; that the steps we were taking were experimental; that the policy had to be flexible and that its continuation had to turn on results."[34]

Despite British apprehensions over the experimental nature of the program, the United States concluded negotiations. On February 26, 1941, Weygand and Murphy initialed an agreement known as the Murphy-Weygand Economic Accord, which stipulated the conditions under which the United States would provide aid to French North Africa. As its basis the accord included the British requirements with the exception of any guarantee for the release of English vessels. The United States reserved the right to terminate the agreement if the French failed to enforce the conditions. The French were to make payment with dollar reserves held in North Africa and when exhausted the United States would release French funds frozen in this country.[35]

The agreement met no serious objections in Washington, and on March 10, 1941, Vichy completed the ratification process. With the approval of the accord the French transmitted a request for urgently needed supplies. The list consisted of:[36]

Sugar	30,000 tons
Gas for Trucks	15,000 tons
Petrol	6,000 tons
Gas oil, light fuel	12,000 tons
Lubricating oil	2,000 tons
Coal	60,000 tons
Pitch	750 tons
Coke	375 tons
Paraffin	700 tons
Binding Twine	2,700 tons
Iron Wire	1,000 tons
Agriculture Machinery Parts	300 tons
Medicaments:	according to needs

Unfortunately for North Africa the implementation of the program was fraught with controversy. On March 13, 1941, the British in a memorandum accused the French of permitting extensive German infiltration into North Africa and demanded that they take specific measures to halt such action. The British urged the United States to assign the largest number of vice-consuls possible to counteract the German influence. They also advocated discussions with the French on the possibility of armed resistance.[37]

Although the British accusation that six thousand German agents had infiltrated North Africa proved far from correct, nevertheless Pétain under German pressure had agreed to an increase of German personnel from fifty-six to two hundred. Hull in turn warned Pétain that if he were incapable of halting German penetration, the United States would abrogate the accord. To Leahy, Pétain appeared quite helpless against this German demand, and at best had extracted a promise that the number of German agents would not exceed two hundred. However, Leahy believed that Pétain's acquiescence should not result in curtailment of the programs for North Africa and unoccupied France. He still felt that although the marshal could not act in defiance of every German encroachment, he represented an effective obstacle to full military cooperation.[38] In a cable to Hull, Leahy argued that Pétain "will try to save the fleet from German hands and we cannot fairly say that North Africa is yet lost."[39]

Other support for retention of the accord came from the state department's Wallace Murray, chief of the Division of Near Eastern Affairs. Murray, a proponent of the economic aid, accused the British of confusing the entire issue by making economic aid to North Africa contingent upon a successful assistance program in unoccupied France. He stressed that it was imperative to move ahead with the African plans in order to emphasize the "distinct character" of that area. Furthermore, Murray argued that regardless of the outcome of the assistance program for France, it was essential that Weygand receive the aid promised him.[40]

On the French side Emanuel Monick, the secretary general of the French zone of Morocco, stressed the value of the accord in terms of the confidence and assurance it gave Weygand. Monick reported that on a recent visit to France Weygand deplored the idea of yielding to German demands and insisted on halting the sending of any more German agents to North Africa.[41]

On April 7, 1941, while government officials remained indecisive over the future of the accord, the first relief ship with food, medicine, and clothing for the children of unoccupied France docked at Marseilles. Admiral Leahy actively participated in supervision of the supplies and reported to Roosevelt that distribution proceeded efficiently and without leakage. He described the assistance in terms of a humanitarian contribution and cited the countless letters of appreciation. At the same time, Leahy pointed out that it provided an effective means of influencing public opinion, and at a cost that was negligible.[42]

Despite this initial success the British and American press castigated the United States for favoring France and pressuring England into a policy contrary to her wishes. The press denounced the American policy as "sentimentally humanitarian." Hull, evidently stung by the criticism, accused the British of inspiring such a reaction and countered that "sentimentalism plays but a little part. We believe we see an opportunity to benefit both the British cause and our own in a most practical way." Hull further contended that "the effect of the shipments on French public opinion—still a factor not to be ignored—is good from our point of view and that of the British." He also noted that the policy of the United States corresponded with Great Britain's and that the English had received credit and publicity for their concessions. At the same time, he added that the United States would not extend further assistance without British consent.[43]

The same month, the United States arrived at a decision on the aid program to North Africa. On April 24 Welles informed Murphy of the government's intention to proceed with the accord. After consultations in Washington Murphy returned to North Africa as the president's personal representative to assume a position that Murphy described "as a sort of High Commissioner for North Africa."[44] His duties entailed maintaining North African contacts, especially with Weygand, supervising the vice-consuls, and transmitting reports on African developments to the Department of State.

Murphy's background, experience, and performances made him the foremost candidate for the extraordinary assignment. A Foreign Service officer since 1917, he had spent several years in Germany and a decade in France where he had attained the rank of chargé d'affaires. Murphy, then forty-six years old, was thoroughly familiar with the politics, language, and personalities of both countries, and during the previous four months he had demonstrated his ability in negotiations with French leaders in North Africa. Moreover, Roosevelt believed that Murphy's religion—Roman Catholic—was a major asset. In fact Roosevelt informed

Murphy that this was one of the reasons he chose him to investigate North Africa and to maintain relations with Vichy. Religion aside, Murphy possessed the necessary skills for one of the most difficult wartime assignments. He demonstrated tact, intelligence, resourcefulness, and sensitivity. At the most crucial times he provided intrepid and dynamic leadership and commanded the respect and loyalty of those who served with him.[45]

One of the most immediate problems Murphy encountered was the inability of the Foreign Service to provide the necessary personnel to function as supervisors. The state department had very few men with any considerable African experience. A greater handicap was that while these men were ostensibly hired to supervise the distribution of goods, in practice everyone concerned with the program including Weygand and Pétain, knew that they would operate as intelligence agents. For such irregular and dangerous work the war department consented to assign reserve officers as the vice-consuls. The military discharged the men so that in case the United States became involved in the war, the Axis, at least theoretically, could not shoot them as spies.[46]

The French eagerly awaited implementation of the agreement, but difficulties within the Roosevelt administration delayed the departure of the vice-consuls. Weygand had granted the Americans unprecedented concessions by permitting them to use secret codes and the courier service. This enabled American observers to transmit uncensored, confidential material on events in North Africa. After considerable bureaucratic infighting over financing, the president's emergency fund provided the salaries for the observers, but much to the dismay of Murphy, in order to save a few dollars the vice-consuls crossed the Atlantic by ship so that the first did not arrive until June 10, 1941.[47] The entire recruitment and funding episode frustrated Murphy, who commented that the American intelligence organization was "primitive and inadequate. It was timid, parochial, and operating strictly in the tradition of the Spanish-American War. To the chiefs of the Army and Navy Intelligence groups, North Africa seemed something new, almost another planet. . . . The Departments of State, War and Navy had failed to produce a single American familiar with the Arabic language or with conditions in Moslem communities."[48]

While Murphy cultivated French relations the ubiquitous rumors concerning Vichy cooperation with Germany persisted. Consequently, on May 16, 1941, Hull cabled Murphy: "For your own confidential information pending further clarification of the situation, all activities in behalf of France and French North Africa are at a standstill."[49] According to Murphy the suspension resulted from false reports that emanated from the British embassy in Lisbon. The reports indicated that the Germans had massed sixty thousand troops in Spain for the purpose of seizing Gibraltar. However, Murphy's explanation barely touched a much more complex situation that unfolded in Vichy. In May, Admiral Darlan visited Germany and even the optimistic Leahy despaired: "The calling of Admiral Darlan to Berchtesgaden by Hitler is so reminiscent of the Schuschnigg and Hacha incidents as to indicate serious complications in the near future."[50] Despite Darlan's repeated assurances that he would not agree to any terms that went beyond the armistice, there was really nothing in what he said that would have prevented him from yielding to German demands.[51] The United States and Great Britain anxiously awaited the outcome of the Franco-German conversations. Fortunately, Adolf Hitler's Mediterranean "blind spot" persisted. By this time his chief concern was the Russian invasion and the Middle East. The Hitler-Darlan meeting produced serious repercussions in French-controlled Syria but did not alter the North African situation.[52]

The French in North Africa neither shared nor appreciated American and British concern over the potential Franco-German collaboration. Instead their reaction to the suspension of aid was that of sarcasm and cynicism. The French were critical of American vascillation. They questioned the seriousness of American intentions and noted that even if the United States was serious, the policy was at best ineffectual. A high-ranking official remarked to Murphy that "the Germans at least are able to make up their minds and having taken a decision act without months of delay and procrastination."[53] The French also continued to criticize the British. They blamed them for the continual breakdown of the aid program and accused them of having deliberately sabotaged the plans to bring supplies to North Africa.[54]

In conversations at Rabat, Murphy reported that British prestige had sharply declined since his visit in January. He discerned very little confidence or interest in the British effort; rather, the question of utmost importance was "what is the United States going to do. If the United States does propose to act, what is the timetable."[55] The most Murphy could promise was a possible resumption of the accord. In preliminary reports Murphy recommended the implementation of the understanding and the establishment of an effective control organization. In conversations with Weygand, Murphy made it clear that the United States would abrogate the accord if the situation in North Africa no longer remained intact. Weygand assured him that he foresaw no changes in North Africa. He deplored the increase in the number of German armistice personnel and noted that efforts to control their propaganda among the natives had met with some success. Weygand reiterated his promise to defend North Africa and pointed out that the necessity for economic assistance was now greater than ever.[56]

Impressed with Murphy's recommendations, the state department urged the British to withdraw their objections. In a meeting with Lord Halifax, Welles expressed satisfaction with Weygand's assurances and believed that "under these conditions, it seemed to me that this Government had nothing whatever to lose, nor did the British Government have anything to lose, by carrying out the terms of the North African agreement until and unless the situation changed in North Africa."[57] He informed Halifax that he had already approved the immediate departure of additional American agents. Welles emphasized the necessity of the aid to preserve French control and thereby prevent a situation from evolving that the "Germans would desire in order to insist upon increasing their own political and military control in that area."[58] Welles reported that Halifax appeared in agreement, but British disgruntlement over American policy continued. Yet as events proved, the British policy of "nothing for Vichy" lacked the farsightedness of the American approach. However, the United States found itself in the somewhat awkward position of having promised Weygand assistance and not delivering; as Welles told Halifax, "the time had now come for this Government either to 'put up or shut up.'"[59] Finally on June 16, 1941, the oft delayed, much criticized economic program moved forward, but with less than enthusiastic support from the British. Immediate plans called for two French ships to sail from New York to Casablanca in the very near future.[60]

The delays encountered in implementing the program alarmed French leaders. Economic conditions in North Africa had rapidly deteriorated, while the position of the British army in Egypt remained precarious. French representatives feared that this combination would produce serious consequences in North Africa. In conversations with the state department the French urged a substantial increase in the number of shipments, extensive propaganda efforts that concentrated on American production and power, and an extension of the program to include West Africa. French officials pointed out that the success of the accord was obvious, although in a negative sense; that is, the Vichy government had not granted any North African bases to the Axis, nor had Vichy surrendered the fleet.[61]

In North Africa one of the most important aspects of the accord—the activity of American vice-consuls—proceeded without major hindrances. On October 13 Murphy cabled Murray that the vice-consuls' reception was cordial, and although observed "like hawks" by members of the German and Italian armistice commission, their work and reports were exceptional. They investigated German and Italian infiltration, evaluated the military situation, and worked particularly hard at promoting American interests. Murphy reported that "individuals whose judgment I respect have insisted repeatedly that the very presence of our consular officers is a source of comfort and inspiration to the French."[62] In Oran, which adjoins Mers-el-Kebir, the officers encountered intense Anglophobia. Although two vice-consuls could not eradicate the animosity, Murphy believed that they had succeeded in altering the conviction that Germany could not lose the war. Along with their French contacts the agents also developed a valuable rapport with the Arab population. However, Murphy sarcastically commented that the work of the officers in control of the distribution of goods "has not provided a monumental task because only two tankers have arrived over a period of nine months of discussion. . . ."[63] With a population of over fifteen million the economic impact of these few deliveries on the lives of the people was inconsequential.

Despite the paucity of goods the United States supplied, the accord remained a controversial issue. In September Hull informed Leahy that new issues had arisen that were so serious that several government units, including the army and navy, had become intimately involved over the question of continuing the French assistance program. Specifically, the Board of Economic Warfare charged that large quantities of goods exported to France eventually arrived in Germany. The army and navy revealed considerable alarm over information that the French under German direction intended to fortify Dakar, thereby posing a direct threat to the security of the Western Hemisphere. The British did nothing to dispel American suspicions and in fact supported American critics of the programs. Although the British participated in the North African discussions and approved the program, the British Ministry of Economic Warfare spoke for those elements who merely accorded lip service to the agreement. In addition to the American charges, the British claimed that the Germans requisitioned trucks and other materials from Tunisia in order to reinforce the Axis army in Libya. They also accused the French in North Africa of planning a punitive campaign against de Gaulle's forces in French Equatorial Africa.[64]

Although the state department remained committed to the program, the charges required careful investigation. Both Murphy and Leahy closely analyzed and evaluated the reports for what they were worth. Neither Murphy nor Leahy denied that Germany was the ultimate destination for a large proportion of colonial products that arrived in Marseilles. However, this resulted from official agreements that specified that Germany was to receive between 12 and 50 percent of all colonial goods shipped to Marseilles. The French never concealed these terms, but it proved virtually impossible to obtain exact figures on the transactions. The Germans operated chiefly with the assistance of French intermediaries rather than through government requisitions.[65] However, actual deliveries fell far short of original estimates, and as Murphy observed, "Algerian and Tunisian ports are practially stagnant, and shipments out of Casablanca to Europe, I am informed, are far below what they were some months ago."[66]

Delivery of war material to Libya, Murphy stressed, was not a clandestine operation, nor did it reveal bad faith on the part of the French. Article VI of the armistice required France to maintain quantities of military equipment in unoccupied French territory as deposits for German use. Before Weygand ever arrived in North Africa, a census and designation of this material had been made. Thus, Murphy caustically criticized the English for interpreting the transfer of some 450 trucks to forces in Libya as aid furnished by General Weygand.[67]

The report on the military buildup in West Africa proved accurate except that the French were solely responsible for it. There was no evidence of German direction or supervision. The French military authorities believed that most of West Africa required additional fortifications in order to bolster its defenses. The other report concerning French military preparations proved erroneous. In a meeting with Murphy, Weygand ridiculed the charges that he planned a punitive military expedition against the

Free French. He described the physical characteristics of the area, which presented insurmountable obstacles, and he emphasized that such a mission "is furtherest from our minds."[68]

Once again Murphy and Leahy found themselves in opposition to the British and those Americans who clamored for an end to the assistance. Although Leahy did not place as much faith in Weygand as did Murphy, he nevertheless supported Murphy's position. On October 4 Leahy cabled, "I am in full agreement with Murphy's expressed opinion that our present policy of encouragement and material support should be continued with the purpose of maintaining such obstacles to German penetration into French Africa as at the present time exist."[69] As a result of these recommendations the accord remained in effect through October 1941.

As with the African agreement the relief program for unoccupied France was hardly immune from mounting criticism and required constant justification. By August 1, 1941, the Red Cross's distribution of the supplies that had arrived in the spring ended, and the organization either had to withdraw from the area or acquire more goods. The Red Cross strongly urged continuation of the program. To counter British objections Norman Davis, the chief spokesman for the Red Cross, carefully outlined the vast differences between relief for the children in unoccupied France and relief for the occupied zone. The Red Cross discontinued services in the latter and did not press for resumption, primarily because the organization had lost control over the operation. However, in the unoccupied area the situation differed considerably. There the Red Cross maintained control and exercised freedom of action that accounted for the success of the program. Although the Red Cross admitted its efforts lacked sufficient publicity, they stressed that there was sufficient evidence that the children received enormous benefits and that French morale had improved. The Red Cross felt that the strongest argument for renewal was that the program in no way benefited Germany and went a long way in countering German propaganda at a time when French opinion favored the Allies.[70]

Both Hull and Roosevelt requested British approval for resumption of the assistance on the same limited basis. The British again raised their usual objections to aiding a collaborationist country while other occupied areas that were much worse off resisted Axis domination. They contended that the two previous shipments provided no basis for an evaluation and that the Red Cross had failed to receive the publicity it deserved. Nevertheless, they consented to admit, as an exception, an occasional shipment of relief goods for the children of unoccupied France. Immediately the Red Cross began preparations for a shipment valued at $2.5 million to depart for France within a month.[71] However, events in Vichy and North Africa brought both plans for continued assistance to a rapid halt.

By the end of October, Weygand's close cooperation with Murphy, his anti-German attitude, and the continuation of the accord resulted in German pressure on the Vichy government for his removal. Leahy also discerned considerable friction within Vichy over Weygand. On October 28 he reported, "We believe that neither the General's person nor his policies in Africa enjoy the support either of Admiral Darlan or of his ambitious and even more 'collaborationist' rival Pucheu and that both would like nothing better than to 'eliminate' the General."[72] Hull instructed Leahy to impress upon Pétain and his associates that "should Weygand be removed, we might be obliged to revise our present policy as regards North Africa entirely. . . ."[73]

Despite Leahy's remonstrances, on November 18 Jacques Benoist Mechin, the French secretary of state in charge of Franco-German relations, arrived in Vichy with an ultimatum for Weygand's recall. Pétain informed Leahy that for over a year he had resisted such a move, but the German directive prevented him from retaining Weygand any longer in Africa. Consequently, on November 20, 1941, the United States suspended all plans for economic assistance and announced that American policy toward France would undergo extensive review.[74]

On November 15 Weygand, evidently aware of his impending dismissal, prepared a memorandum reviewing the entire North African situation since his arrival. In regard to the accord, he admitted that it had failed to produce the anticipated economic results. He attributed the failure to the British objections as well as the German reluctance to release more French merchant ships to engage in this traffic. However, he noted that from the political point of view the agreement offered important advantages. Weygand emphasized that "France, thanks to its Empire, remained the only European power retaining its economic relations with the United States. As long as French control of its own territories was not threatened, the Anglo-Saxons respected it."[75]

In addition the accord also offered the advantage of maintaining friendly relations with a power, which as Weygand noted, "will be one of the arbiters of the situation at the end of the war."[76] At the same time, he believed that the military situation in 1941 had evolved in such a manner as to increase the importance of North Africa. Weygand concluded that only through the control of the Mediterranean could a Germanized Europe emerge, and "opening Africa to Germany means in the last analysis giving to Germany a unique opportunity to be able to continue the war during 10 years and to impose without the possibility of any reaction its will upon France."[77] Following his official recall, Weygand wrote to Murphy on November 21, "Continue I beg of you to favor the supply program. As the Marshal told Admiral Leahy nothing is changed in French policy by my departure. Just suppose that I have passed to the other world."[78]

With Weygand's removal the British and Americans once again engaged in the seemingly endless considerations and reconsiderations of the economic accord. The United States' officials overseas continued in their support of the program. The American chargé at Tangier transmitted a message from the French consulate Pierre Lyantey, which pointed out that the accord had the incontestable advantage of assuring the United States the publicity that it never before had in Africa. Such a realistic policy, he added, "ought not to be eliminated by the sole fact of the disappearance of one man."[79]

The major argument presented for the retention of the accord emphasized the agreement's strategic and political advantages rather than its economic contributions. In fact much to the dismay of Murphy, his associates, and the French, the economic impact was virtually negligible. On November 20 Murphy cabled that Yves Châtel, Weygand's successor as governor general in Algeria, had informed him that "it is a great pity that during the 9 months of its operation actual deliveries have been restricted to a handful of products, that is to say, four small cargos and 3 tankers of petroleum products for the 30 millions of French African populations." Deliveries had amounted to a mere 7 percent of the authorized quotas.[80]

In Washington the state department concluded that if Pétain assured the United States and England that French policy in North Africa would not change and that the fleet would remain in French hands, they would resume the aid program. On December 12, 1941, five days after the United States entered the war, Leahy received such assurances from the marshal. The United States then decided to permit a vessel to sail for North Africa sometime in January.[81]

While preparations for assistance continued, reports from France and North Africa indicated that both areas had experienced further economic deterioration. At the same time, the press severely criticized the innocuous relief effort in France. On January 31, 1942, the *New York Times* charged that the Germans had confiscated a large quantity of Red Cross supplies at Marseilles. Hull and the Red Cross denied the accusation, and later asserted that it had succeeded in distributing without leakage almost $5 million worth of relief goods to unoccupied France.[82] In France Kenneth Austin, an American studying the country's food requirements, regarded the conditions there as extremely grave. He rejected the *Times* story as totally inaccurate and stressed that any cooperation with Germany "ameliorated very slightly the wretched conditions of the people in both halves of France."[83]

Austin attacked the administration for adhering too closely to the British policy of "nothing for Vichy."[84] He emphasized that the French urgently required milk, vitamins, soap, clothing, and shoes and recom mended all shipments of petroleum for maintenance of the transportation network. Austin took the position that since relief essentially promoted the defense of the United States, the lend-lease administration should absorb the project.[85] However, the agency regarded this as extremely unwise. In rejecting the proposal lend-lease officials cited the fact that the Germans continued to transport supplies to their forces in French vessels and that current negotiations between Vichy and the Japanese produced great concern within the state department.[86]

After conversations with the secretary general for French Africa, Murphy reported from North Africa the dire need for economic assistance. As in France, the shortage of fuel and lubrication undermined the entire economic structure; food distribution lagged and internal commerce stagnated. Algiers supposedly possessed only a three-day coal supply.[87] Murphy cited his French contacts who emphasized that "this area is wide open to American influence and that we are failing to take advantage of it."[88]

departed from New York harbor, and the United States indicated that the program would operate on a larger scale. However, once again events in North Africa brought such plans to an abrupt halt. In early February the United States confirmed the validity of British reports that the French in Tunisia had furnished General Erwin Rommel's forces with large quantities of gasoline and foodstuffs. The French attempted to justify the shipments on the basis of the armistice and further argued that such cooperation prevented the German occupation of Tunisia. Their case was extremely weak. Even a Francophile such as Murphy expressed skepticism over French intentions. Moreover, the French action infuriated the British. In a memorandum of February 7, 1942, the British emphatically stated that they did not regard "the stability and prosperity of North Africa as an end to be pursued for its own sake. If it is impossible to divert supplies from the enemy, then it is in the American and British interest that the territories should be poor."[89]

The British argued that the lack of critical supplies in North Africa had reduced production and decreased exports to France during the previous year. They further maintained that French resistance to German demands depended on the amount of military assistance England and the United States could furnish them and not on whether they were poor or prosperous. Therefore, they recommended that any shipments to North Africa include only the bare minimum to retain American influence. Anything beyond this would depend on the willingness of the French to support the Allies.[90]

The English policy basically advocated a separation of Africa from France by means other than force. In order to accomplish this they recommended some firm offer to the French, either in the form of a barter proposal or a positive military commitment. The British pointed out that throughout the war the French in Africa never received sufficient inducement to attract them away from the Axis.[91]

The British implication was that in some way the United States was responsible for this failure. However, in taking such a position the British failed to realize that the United States had only recently entered the war. Prior to this time, it was out of the question for the United States even to consider supplying the vast quantities of military equipment, let alone the manpower, that Weygand required before he would force a break with the Axis. Above all the assistance that the British could provide was virtually negligible. As Murphy cynically commented, "The British could no more provide adequate military support for the French African empire in 1941 than they had been able to provide for the French homeland in 1940."[92] In February 1942, the United States concentrated primarily on the economic accord. Commitments beyond that remained for the future.

As the United States reconsidered its economic policy relations with the French revealed signs of deterioration. In Washington, French representatives criticized the propensity of the United States to apply the economic program with political considerations. They believed that throughout the war's duration issues such as the supplies to Libya and German infiltration would continue to arise. The French recommended that the United States come to a decision on the program rather than commencing it and then suspending operations until they received clarification on some political question. In the final analysis the French evidently favored termination of the assistance rather than maintenance on such an indefinite basis. The present policy, they agreed, led only to distrust and questioning of the United States' sincerity.[93]

On March 3, 1942, the French submitted a memorandum that analyzed the results of the accord.[94] They claimed that the civilians received all of the goods and consumed them almost immediately. A careful check of the program clearly substantiated their contention, as well as Murphy's, that the meager quantity of goods actually delivered were of little consequence to the Axis, even if they had seized them all.[95]

Despite the dearth of goods the United States provided, the administration refused to resume assistance until Pétain halted the shipments to Libya. On March 14, 1942, after consultations with the Germans, Darlan informed the United States that Vichy had curtailed the assistance to Rommel.[96] The *New York Times* remained skeptical of French assurances. It cited past failures and emphasized that the French weakness still prevailed; that is, Vichy could not guarantee how it would react if the Germans forced the issue. The only meaning the *Times* could conjecture was that Vichy had conceded to pressure from the population, who demanded the retention of the last surviving link with the United States.[97] Nevertheless, on April 7, 1942, Hull, with British approval, announced the resumption of shipments of food, clothing, lubricants (petroleum products), and other supplies for North Africa.[98] At the same time, the French reaffirmed the value of the accord as the only effective argument they possessed to resist Axis economic pressure and to maintain their political position with the United States.[99]

Unfortunately, once again the spirit of economic cooperation collapsed. This time the disrupting factor was the power struggle within Pétain's cabinet. By April 1942 the arch-collaborationist Pierre Laval had consolidated his political power and with German assistance pressured Pétain to appoint him vice-premier. To the United States Laval was anathema. American officials interpreted the appointment of Laval or his close associates as confirmation that Pétain no longer possessed freedom of action. On

March 27, 1942, Welles instructed Leahy to inform the marshal that in
the opinion of Roosevelt, if Laval assumed power, "it would be impossible for this Government to maintain diplomatic relations with the French
Government at Vichy."[100]

Early in April the ubiquitous rumors concerning alterations in the Vichy
government circulated. However, information concerning Laval's position
was somewhat vague. On April 6 the secretary general for French Africa
informed Murphy that "Laval will not be returned to power in the near
future."[101] Within a week, however, Leahy cabled Welles of the distinct
possibility of Laval's return to the cabinet. In Leahy's opinion the Germans forced the issue. The only meaning the *Times* could conjecture was
ington and Berlin."[102] If this were true, it was hardly a contest. On April
15 Pétain confirmed Laval's appointment. Washington responded by recalling Leahy and suspended the accord. At the same time, the French
ambassador presented a rather anemic defense of Laval based on the premise that he was not as bad as the United States believed.[103]

Once again American officials reviewed and reconsidered their French
economic policy. However, this time the supporters of the accord in-
jected a new and significant consideration—the value of the American
vice-consuls. After a meeting with the Joint Intelligence Committee, Assistant Secretary of State Adolf Berle reported: "The view was expressed
that it would be desirable to go to considerable lengths to create a situation in which this representation could be maintained."[104]

Wallace Murray, chief of the Division of Near Eastern Affairs and an ar-
dent supporter of the accord, urged its continuation for the valuable
military, political, and economic information that the agents transmitted
to the United States and England. He pointed out that if the United States
terminated the agreement, German toleration of these officials would end,
thereby necessitating their withdrawal.[105]

At the end of May Assistant Secretary of State Dean Acheson also came
to the defense of the accord. He cited the virtual unanimous agreement
among British and American officials on the value of the control officers.
He also warned that from all indications the expulsion of the consuls was
imminent unless the United States resumed the aid program.[106]

Henry Stimson, in a letter to Hull, spoke for the war department. The
secretary of war commented on the significant contributions of the vice-
consuls in the past. He also emphasized their indispensability should the
military situation in North and West Africa radically change.[107]

In France the American chargé conferred with Charles Rochat, the secretary general of the French Foreign Office, who informed him that German pressure was so intense that unless the United States resumed the program, the French could no longer justify the presence of the vice-consuls. Rochat noted that the German Armistice Commission had scheduled a meeting within a week and that without guarantees for the implementation of the aid program, a German ultimatum for the removal of the control officers appeared inevitable.[108]

The argument for the retention of the vice-consuls proved decisive. On June 11, 1942, Hull announced the resumption of the economic assistance. Theoretically, two vessels were to sail from the United States within two weeks; simultaneously, two vessels at Casablanca were to depart for America with needed commodities such as cork, olive oil, and tartar.[109]

By the end of July plans for the invasion of North Africa had reached advanced stages and those with knowledge of it considered economic assistance more essential than ever before. Thus, on July 29 Roosevelt informed the British that service to North Africa would continue without interruption. At the same time, the Red Cross received permission to proceed immediately with a shipment of medicine, canned milk, and layettes for the children of unoccupied France.[110] Information indicated that the situation had become critical. The Quakers reported that in their two refugee internment camps approximately 16,000 men, women, and children faced starvation unless assistance arrived.[111]

By August the United States had finally impressed upon the British their determination to implement the economic aid programs. Consequently, the British suddenly launched a campaign to insure extensive publicity for "their share" of the North African economic arrangement. They requested publicity material to broadcast over the BBC into North Africa. Their attitude represented a culmination of the hypocritical approach the British achieved throughout the entire affair. In point of fact they had no share in the program; the goods were American and the ships French. The British had voiced objections from the very beginning and although ostensibly supporting the accord, the Economic Ministry consistently did its best to undermine it. Adolf Berle, evidently flabbergasted by the British request, replied that "examination of the papers fails to disclose a scintilla of 'British share,' unless it may be that, after finally examining many extraneous considerations they at length waived their objection—an objection, incidentally, which they were unable to enforce, except as we were prepared (as we were) to consider their views."[112]

Berle also felt that the British idea appeared somewhat foolish since the manufacturers conspicuously labeled the goods "Imported from the United States of America" in French and Arabic.[113] In fact the Office of War Information had spent considerable time and expense persuading cloth manufacturers to place a label every five or ten yards. As a result the producers had placed over 3.5 million labels on the goods.[114] Berle cynically concluded, "There is a fair chance that the BBC would look rather foolish if they proclaimed this as a British *démarché.*"[115]

From August until November the Board of Economic Warfare (BEW) replaced the British as the chief obstacle to implementation of the accord. In early August a directive from the president summarized the principles for supplying North Africa. The shipment of food and consumer goods was to continue as long as they had no value to the enemy; the main objective was the regular shipment of goods, not the quantity. Above all, Roosevelt insisted that a French guarantee to terminate trade with the Axis was not a prerequisite for assistance. For the most part this final stipulation was unacceptable to BEW. The agency raised many of the same objections that the British had; specifically, BEW rejected the principle of assistance on an unconditional basis. BEW officials pointed out that the French still supplied the Axis in North Africa and Europe. Like the British they argued that the decline in exports from North Africa was a direct result of an effective blockade and that providing goods would only increase the supplies available to the enemy.[116]

The agency cited the contributions of North Africa to the Axis. In a memorandum of August 12 BEW declared that during 1941 shipping under the French flag from North Africa to France's Mediterranean ports totaled 3,300,000 tons or 275,000 tons per month; during the first two months of 1942 the total amounted to approximately 500,000 tons. The memorandum also added that even if the shipments were for a German account, the French authorities cooperated and suppressed the real destination on the bills of lading.[117]

In practice BEW exerted considerable influence over the program. The agency scrutinized French orders and possessed the power to reject commodities. For the two ships scheduled to leave New York for Casablanca, BEW had refused to include French requests for binder twine, seed corn, and spare parts for farm machinery. The board based its negative action on the fact that the French continued to export agricultural products to the Axis.[118]

The board's refusal to approve farm machinery replacements precipitated a controversy between the United States and France as well as between the Department of State and BEW. The French apparently believed that the 15 tons of spare parts were in return for the shipment of 212 tons of olive oil. BEW contended that such parts were not consumer goods and were therefore excluded from the president's directive.[119]

To Admiral Leahy, who was appointed Chief of Staff on his return from France, the entire dispute over the aid program approached absurdity. Leahy, acting as a mediator between the two agencies, possessed the advantage of prior knowledge of the planned invasion. Consequently he argued that "if a good feeling could be induced in French North Africa at this time, it might save thousands of American lives, which might otherwise be lost through delays and quibbling over small amounts of economic supplies that could not change the course of the war."[120] Although BEW agreed to the parts' request, it emphasized that the United States should seize the opportunity to withhold larger quantities of goods in order to pressure the French to export strategic materials such as cobalt and molybdenum.[121] Frustrated over BEW's procrastination and suggestions, Leahy frankly stated, "This is an order from the President of the United States and is not a matter for discussion. . . . the President says 'Do it.'"[122]

For security reasons BEW remained uninformed of the scheduled invasion. Thus, when the French requested additional tonnage of leaf tobacco, used clothing, and coal, the agency approved the tobacco but rejected the clothing and coal; the latter on the basis that coal maintained the North African railroad that transported goods destined for Germany. When representatives of the state department suggested that the matter required referral to a higher level, the BEW representative replied that "BEW took its instructions from the Vice-President."[123]

The problem with BEW went beyond its lack of knowledge of the invasion. Basically the thinking at BEW represented the antithesis of those who supported the principle of economic aid. When the question of providing North Africa with petroleum arose, this difference became most evident. The board emphasized that even if the United States contemplated military action in the area, it was best to have an oil-starved country to conquer. The agency's justification was simple and specious: "This is not only because petroleum products may be used against us but because the lack of petroleum would tend to make the population welcome the occupying force, bringing with them the goods necessary for the maintenance of the economy."[124]

Evidently BEW gave little consideration to the disastrous effects of the blockade and the German exploitation of the North African economy. With this shortcoming the agency remained virtually oblivious to the fact that economic deterioration had progressed to such an extent that rehabilitation, especially under wartime conditions, might prove impossible.

Amid the protracted discussions concerning aid to North Africa and France, the question of economic assistance to French West Africa remained secondary. However, as early as the Murphy-Weygand conversations the participants considered extending the program to include West Africa. In May 1941, as a result of reports describing the severe economic depression in West Africa, the United States officially announced its support of the principle of economic aid to that area. Yet for well over a year this was as close as West Africa ever came to receiving assistance. The reason was simply that the British severely criticized the large-scale exportation of edible vegetable oil from West Africa to the Axis and refused to sanction aid to that area unless the French substantially reduced this exportation. French officials replied that they did not possess the authority to comply. They pointed out that the Germans permitted the operation of the Merchant Marine on the condition that the French delivered certain commodities, and edible oil was one of them.[125]

Those who supported the North African Accord also advocated its extension to West Africa. Murphy in particular bitterly resented the British obstruction. Although he conceded that their objections had a sound economic basis, he also interpreted the British position as a "narrow minded decision" that overlooked the more important political and military considerations. Furthermore, Murphy emphasized the impact of the lack of aid on Pierre Boisson, the governor general of French West Africa, who had succeeded in preventing the Germans and Italians from establishing a foothold in the area. Murphy reported that the reluctance of the United States to press for assistance to West Africa left Boisson bitter and disillusioned after "seeing the economy of French West Africa go to hell in a big way. . . ."[126]

In July 1942 American representatives informed the French and British that they intended to extend the North African Accord to West Africa.

The British as usual voiced considerable concern but agreed. Recent reports indicated a significant reduction in the exportation of edible oil and evidently made them more amenable to the proposal. They attributed the cutback to the shortage of material required for producing the oil and warned against the shipment of equipment that would once again stimulate production.[127]

The Board of Economic Warfare offered no objections, since by this time it recognized the potential value of West Africa. The board discussed the area in terms of the strategic position of Dakar as an air supply base as well as the region's vast untapped agricultural and mineral resources. The agency recommended the immediate establishment of a mission in order to organize the economy, stimulate production, and exploit the commercial possibilities.[128]

Despite the board's "enlightened" position on West Africa the clash between BEW and the state department continued unabated. Shortly after the North African invasion the sorry affair reached its culmination. On November 12 at a meeting between the two agencies Berle precipitated a heated controversy over the fact that two ships in New Orleans with orders for North Africa had not departed prior to the invasion. He held BEW responsible and contended that the failure of these ships to reach Casablanca produced bitterness and anger on the part of the French army and natives. He further maintained that this provided the explanation as to why the American forces encountered their strongest resistance in the Casablanca area. In conclusion Berle charged that BEW procrastination had cost hundreds of American lives.[129] Although BEW investigated the charges and denied them, it merely revealed the level to which discussions had degenerated.[130] Thus, the issue of economic assistance to the French concluded as it had begun, on a bitterly controversial note.

In the last few months preceding the invasion the frustration of the supporters of the program became even more evident as they vehemently denounced BEW and British policy. Yet their strong, aggressive attitude came much too late. The state department itself was not immune from responsibility for the failure to provide significant economic assistance. Their reluctance to embark on a program that the British claimed would have a disastrous effect upon their war effort was understandable in 1940 and 1941. However, once the United States entered the war, any adverse repercussions from American policy affected the United States as well as Britain. Yet until August 1942 the American position on the aid program remained virtually the same; it was ambivalent and vascillating. State department officials continued to overemphasize political considerations and hastily suspended the program. Consequently when the lend-lease administration assumed the task of providing economic aid to the civilian population, it faced the awesome task of restoring an economy that for over two years had deteriorated because of French and Axis exploitation.

NOTES

1. William D. Leahy, *I Was There* (New York: McGraw Hill, 1950). Leahy's work provides details of his career from 1940 through the first Truman Administration. *See also* William S. Langer, *Our Vichy Gamble* (New York: Alfred A. Knopf, 1947), 255; Robert D. Murphy, *Diplomat among Warriors* (Garden City, N.Y.: Doubleday, 1964), 93. For a detailed account of Leahy's activities *see* James H. Holmes, "Admiral Leahy in Vichy France, 1940-42," Ph.D. Thesis, George Washington University, 1974.

2. Roosevelt to Leahy, November 17, 1940, Leahy Diary. Library of Congress, Washington, D.C.

3. Murphy, *Diplomat among Warriors,* 53-63.

4. Roosevelt to Leahy, November 17, 1940, Leahy Diary.

5. Leahy Diary, January 21, 1941.

6. Leahy, *I Was There,* 444. The Appendix includes duplicates of some of Leahy's correspondence. This reference is to Roosevelt's letter containing the president's instructions, December 20, 1940.

7. Ibid., 445.

8. Ibid., 13.

9. United States Department of State, *Foreign Relations of the United States, 1940,* Vol. 2 (Washington, D.C.: United States Government Printing Office, 1957), 537 (hereafter referred to as *Foreign Relations 1940* 2); Langer, *Our Vichy Gamble,* 127. A copy of Langer's manuscript, "Our Vichy Policy and the North African Venture," can be found at the National Archives (hereafter DNA), Washington, D.C.

10. Ibid.

11. *Foreign Relations 1940* 2, 537.

12. Ibid., 555-56.

13. Ibid.; Murphy, *Diplomat among Warriors,* 63.

14. United States Department of State, *Foreign Relations of the United States, 1941,* Vol. 2 (Washington, D.C.: United States Government Printing

Office, 1959), 89 (hereafter referred to as *Foreign Relations 1941* 2).

15. *Foreign Relations 1940* 2, 553-54.

16. Leahy Diary, January 21, 1941; *Foreign Relations 1941* 2, 94.

17. Leahy Diary, January 21, 1941; Leahy, *I Was There,* 13.

18. *Foreign Relations 1941* 2, 95-96.

19. Ibid., 89-90.

20. Leahy Diary, January 21, 1941. Evidence of the British reaction is contained in a memorandum from Lord Halifax, March 13, 1941, State Department Document 851R.24/8-1/2, DNA. Halifax stressed that Darlan's attacks increased British reluctance to assist the American effort to aid France. The document also reveals the lack of British enthusiasm to accept American policy.

21. Leahy to Welles, February 24, 1941, Leahy Diary. This letter and another (*see* Note 22) are contained in diary number seven as part of a small but separate collection of correspondence between the ambassador and the undersecretary of state.

22. Leahy to Welles, March 4, 1941, Leahy Diary. *See* Note 21.

23. Leahy Diary, March 25, 1941.

24. *Foreign Relations 1940* 2, 616.

25. *Foreign Relations 1941* 2, 207.

26. Ibid., 207-08.

27. Ibid., 207.

28. Ibid., 242.

29. Leahy, *I Was There,* 23; Langer, *Our Vichy Gamble,* 86. Langer points out that Weygand's position represented the attitude of Pétain and other Vichy officials.

30. *Foreign Relations 1940* 2, 242.

31. Langer, *Our Vichy Gamble,* 130-31.

32. *Foreign Relations 1941* 2, 219, 253-54.

33. Ibid., 262.

34. Ibid., 261.

35. Ibid., 227-28.

36. Ibid., 238.

37. Ibid., 268.

38. Ibid., 293-94.

39. Ibid., 295.

40. Ibid., 273.

41. Ibid., 279.

42. Leahy to Roosevelt, April 21, 1941, Leahy Diary.

43. *Foreign Relations 1941* 2, 151.

44. Murphy, *Diplomat among Warriors,* 88.

45. Ibid., 27-81; interview with Lloyd Cutler, May 27, 1972, Washington, D.C. Roosevelt's emphasis on his religion somewhat puzzled Murphy: "The President seemed to have exaggerated ideas of the bond existing between Catholics because of their religion." In urging Murphy to establish intimate contacts with Weygand, who was also a catholic, the president winked and commented, "You might even go to church with Weygand." Murphy, *Diplomat among Warriors,* 66. Murphy's career reached its culmination in 1952 when Truman appointed him as the United States' first postwar ambassador to Japan.

46. Murphy, *Diplomat among Warriors,* 88-91.

47. Ibid.

48. Ibid., 90.

49. Ibid., 88; *Foreign Relations 1941* 2, 335.

50. *Foreign Relations 1941* 2, 170.

51. Langer, *Our Vichy Gamble,* 145.

52. Ibid., 156-60. For a detailed account of Darlan's visit and its potential as well as actual ramifications, *see* Langer, Chapter 4.

53. *Foreign Relations 1941* 2, 340.

54. Murphy, *Diplomat among Warriors,* 88-89.

55. *Foreign Relations 1941* 2, 340.

56. Ibid., 342, 344-46.

57. Ibid., 349.

58. Ibid., 350.

59. Ibid., 375.

60. Ibid., 380. Despite this decision, British criticism continued unabated. *The Economist* [141 (July 19, 1941), 76] supported British policy and credited it with weakening Vichy's bargaining position. At the same time it condemned American "friends of Vichy" and asked why Vichy apologists received such a warm reception in the United States.

61. Ibid., 386.

62. Ibid., 319.

63. Ibid., 318.

64. Ibid., 434-35.

65. Ibid., 436.

66. Ibid., 441.

67. Ibid., 442.

68. Ibid., 444.

69. Ibid., 445.

70. Ibid., 190-93.

71. Ibid.

72. Ibid., 455.

73. Ibid., 457.

74. Ibid., 464, 469.

75. Ibid., 462.

76. Ibid.

77. Ibid., 463.

78. Ibid., 472.

79. Ibid., 476.

80. Ibid., 471.

81. *Foreign Relations 1941* 2, 498-99.

82. *New York Times,* January 31, 1942, 4.

83. Austin to Stettinius, January 31, 1942, Foreign Economic Administration Records, Box 171, Record Group 169, Washington National Records Center, Suitland, Md. (hereafter referred to as RG 169).

84. Ibid.

85. Austin to Stettinius, February 9, 1942, Box 171, RG 169.

86. Cox to Stettinius, February 18, 1942, Box 171, RG 169.

87. United States Department of State, *Foreign Relations of the United States, 1942* Vol. 2 (Washington, D.C.: United States Government Printing Office, 1962), 236 (hereafter referred to as *Foreign Relations 1942* 2).

88. Ibid., 237.

89. Ibid., 243.

90. Ibid., 243-44.

91. Ibid., 245.

92. Murphy, *Diplomat among Warriors,* 87. Murphy maintained this evaluation and emphasized the unrealistic nature of the British position. (Interview with Robert Murphy, November 29, 1972, New York City.)

93. *Foreign Relations 1942* 2, 250.

94. Ibid., 261-63. *See* Appendix 3 for the entire list.

95. Ibid., 261. Murphy explained that the type of goods and the quantity shipped to North Africa could not have sustained or greatly assisted the Axis and certainly could not have influenced the outcome of the war. He emphasized that the criticism of the program was unnecessary and unwarranted. (Interview with Robert Murphy, November 29, 1972, New York City.)

96. Ibid., 149.

97. *New York Times,* March 25, 1942, 9.

98. Ibid., April 8, 1942, 10; *Foreign Relations 1942* 2, 280.

99. *Foreign Relations 1942* 2, 168-69.

100. Ibid., 160-61.

101. Ibid., 279.

102. Ibid., 169.

103. Ibid., 172.

104. Ibid., 294.

105. Ibid., 295-97.

106. Ibid., 302-03.

107. Ibid., 304. Further elaboration by Stimson can be found in "Summary of the United States Export Policy to North Africa," June 11, 1942, Box 363, RG 169, and in "Report of French North Africa as a Source of Supply for Nazi Germany," November 13, 1942, Box 969, RG 169.

108. *Foreign Relations 1942* 2, 306-07.

109. Ibid., 313.

110. Ibid., 348.

111. Kirshner to Bureau of Areas, July 14, 1942, Box 362, RG 169.

112. *Foreign Relations 1942* 2, 357.

113. Ibid., 358.

114. Fertig to Danielson, October 12, 1942, Box 1648, RG 169.

115. *Foreign Relations 1942* 2, 358.

116. "Summary of the United States Export Policy to North Africa," August 11, 1942, Box 363, RG 169.

117. Moats to Fagan, August 12, 1942, Box 364, RG 169.

118. Canfield to Villard, August 8, 1942, Box 756, RG 169. *See* Appendix 4 for a list of the goods sent.

119. Fagan to Canfield, September 6, 1942, Box 366, RG 169. Details of the controversy are in "Memorandum of Conversation with French Officials," August 11, 1942, State Department Document 851R.24/9-1/16, DNA.

120. "Record of Conversation, Leahy, Villard, and Canfield," September 7, 1942, Box 362, RG 169; *Foreign Relations 1942* 2, 369.

121. *Foreign Relations 1942* 2, 368.

122. Leahy, *I Was There,* 113. Murphy was extremely critical of BEW officials, whom he described as a group of "hostile economic warriors in Washington," (Murphy, *Diplomat among Warriors,* 105.)

123. *Foreign Relations 1942* 2, 386.

124. "Proposed Resumption of Petroleum Shipments to North Africa," October 20, 1942, Box 363, RG 169.

125. *Foreign Relations 1941* 2, 327-30, 392-93, 399; *Foreign Relations 1942* 2, 280, 341, 374-75.

126. *Foreign Relations 1942* 2, 341.

127. Ibid., 366.

128. Canfield to McCamy, August 29, 1942, Box 1101, RG 169.

129. Memorandum of North African Committee Meeting, November 12, 1942, Box 576, RG 169.

130. Stone to Perkins, December 4, 1942, Box 756, RG 169. Further detail and reports concerning Berle's charges can be found in State Department Document 851R.24/11-1942, DNA.

3.

Limited Lend-Lease for the Free French and a Controversial Arrangement with Darlan

In its relations with the Free French the United States appeared to be understanding and sympathetic but exercised caution and restraint. The administration was reluctant to adopt any policy toward the Free French that would jeopardize American relations with Vichy. Specifically, the policymakers considered an extension of direct lend-lease to the Free French potentially damaging to American ties with Pétain's government, so it rejected requests for such aid. Simultaneously incidents arose that undermined American confidence in de Gaulle. Consequently, the United States made few commitments to de Gaulle; it refused to inform him of the North African operation and exhibited little hesitation in supporting his adversary, Admiral Darlan.

During late 1940 the Free French movement achieved limited objectives in Central Africa. From July to November 1940 de Gaulle's followers succeeded in establishing Free French control over French Equatorial Africa, the Cameroons, and Gabon. However, on September 22, 1940, a combined British and Free French assault on Dakar encountered fierce resistance from the Vichy forces under the command of General Pierre Boisson. The aborted, ill-conceived venture intensified anti-British and anti-Free French sentiment in the Vichy territories of North and West Africa. While the United States applauded de Gaulle's accomplishments in Central Africa, it deplored his failure at Dakar. Churchill, who had informed Roosevelt of the operation, temporarily lost face, while American confidence in de Gaulle diminished considerably.[1]

Throughout 1941 the Free French directed their efforts at developing an effective movement within the United States. The purpose of this endeavor was to clarify de Gaulle's position, increase Free French propaganda, and above all counter the strong Vichy influence in America. The organization, which became known as France Forever, assembled chapters throughout the United States. By September 1941 it included nine thousand members grouped in twenty-four chapters in seventeen states. As a result, the press and the public exhibited a marked increase in interest in Free France. The impact of the movement, however, remained confined to the popular, rather than the official, level.[2]

In May 1941 Jacques de Sieyes headed the first official Free French delegation to the United States. But the organization lacked effective coordination and had so many other shortcomings that it failed to acquire any status. The basic problem was that the political affiliations of the numerous French politicians, who arrived as "representatives of the Free French," ranged from the extreme left to former servants of Vichy. These men possessed no coherent programs, no unity, or even trust for one another. The politicians lacked any stature or prominence; the delegation remained unimpressive.[3] The United States had no desire to endanger its Vichy contacts by embracing this motley French representation.

In June 1941 de Gaulle dispatched René Pleven to undertake the task of improving relations with the United States. Pleven, one of the most capable and astute Free French leaders, had previously succeeded in bringing Chad into de Gaulle's camp. In London he functioned as the head of the Free French Civil Administration; as such, he understood the entire movement. Above all Pleven possessed extensive knowledge of America and demonstrated diplomatic skill and tact.[4]

Pleven's instructions clearly revealed the magnitude of his assignment. De Gaulle authorized him to establish permanent relations with the state department, organize economic relations between Free French Africa, Oceania, and America, and direct purchases of needed war material. His duties also included refining the information and propaganda programs in order to improve the overall coordination of France Forever.[5]

To reinforce Pleven's position de Gaulle proffered inducements to the United States. In anticipation of American participation in the war the Free French cabled the Department of State that it would welcome in Equatorial Africa whatever military installations the United States desired to construct. They invited a commission to study firsthand the strategic value of such an outpost. At the same time, they requested a more definitive policy of economic aid through lend-lease.[6]

Economic aid was of vital importance to de Gaulle's followers, especially those in Oceania and Africa. Like North and West Africa the French colonies had relied on Metropolitan France for their manufactured products. The Free French estimated that they required approximately $6 million worth of assistance per year. They argued that announcement of such assistance would greatly encourage those brave men who opposed capitulation and were fighting alongside their British allies. Furthermore, the Free French believed that American economic support would demonstrate to the Vichy colonies that America had extended assistance to those who refused surrender.[7]

French persuasion, however, had little impact on official policy. Pleven progressed slowly, and his relations with various government agencies remained somewhat vague. Lend-lease authorities reported that they had no contact with the Free French government, "which is apparently represented as far as procurement goes by M. Pleven who makes his headquarters at the Willard."[8] Due to the unclear status of the Free French the state department declined to receive him. In a request for an interview Welles informed Pleven that he should contact the department's European section.[9] Evidently the state department had relegated Pleven to a secondary position.

During the late summer and early fall Pleven made inroads with other agencies. He managed to confer with Secretary of the Treasury Henry Morgenthau, Harry Hopkins, Secretary of the Navy Frank Knox, and Henry Stimson of the war department. Halifax lent British support by sending a memorandum to Welles requesting direct lend-lease for the Free French. But in August Welles told Halifax that "it was too early for the Free French to requisition articles directly and that Pleven should have the British requisition defense articles for re-transfer to the Free French."[10]

Finally, on October 1, Welles received Pleven. Welles emphasized that while the goals of both were identical—namely, the restoration of an independent France—their methods differed. Welles's reception was at best chilly, and he rejected Pleven's request for direct lend-lease. In so doing Welles stressed that lend-lease applied only to legally constituted governments and that the Free French lacked this prerequisite.[11]

Prior to Pleven's interview with Welles there was evidence of support among some officials for direct lend-lease to the Free French. Oscar Cox, the legal counsel for the Office of Lend-Lease Administration and an extremely influential adviser, urged Morgenthau to intercede with Roosevelt in support of direct aid. Cox felt that such assistance would clearly demonstrate American support for de Gaulle's fight against aggression and would strengthen the Free French position throughout the world. Moreover, Cox argued that direct aid would encourage the anti-Vichy forces in France and make the government less susceptible to all-out collaboration.[12]

Further support came from General J. H. Burns, an executive officer in the Office for Emergency Management, Division of Defense Aid Reports. In a letter to Hopkins, Burns commented that in his opinion Roosevelt "was missing a real opportunity in his battle against the Axis Powers in failing to aid the Free French forces." He cited riots in France as an indication of strong anti-Vichy sentiment. Burns believed that such a policy would lessen the possibility of Weygand's joining the Axis; it would also strengthen the Free French territories in Equatorial Africa in their resistance to German penetration. Direct assistance, he noted, qualified as lend-lease since the defense of these areas was clearly vital to the defense of the United States. He asserted that in the eyes of other Frenchmen the retransfer system relegated the Free French to mere secondary allies of the British.[13]

Cox continued to pursue the issue and on September 4 informed Hopkins that a recent Gallup Poll revealed that 74 percent of those polled favored direct lend-lease to the Free French while only 16 percent opposed it.[14] Cox appealed to Edward R. Stettinius, director of the lend-lease administration, to exert his influence on Hopkins and Roosevelt, since the president had not as yet arrived at a decision on the matter. Cox also described the retransfer system as giving de Gaulle's followers the appearance of "poor relatives." Furthermore, Cox insisted that continued recognition of Vichy represented a separate problem, unrelated to the question of direct aid; as such, Cox concluded, Leahy could continue his battle to prevent extensive Vichy collaboration.[15]

The decision on such aid proved more complex than its advocates realized. Hopkins replied to Stettinius that direct aid to the Free French "is a very touchy subject and must be explored only through the State Department. It gets into the matter of foreign policy and the decisions must finally rest there."[16] Under the circumstances the state department proceeded very deliberately. The agency's chief concern was maintaining the influence that Murphy and Leahy had cultivated with the representatives of Vichy France. Furthermore, American authorities feared that the Free French might in some way construe direct economic assistance as implying recognition of de Gaulle's forces as the official French government. Therefore, the United States adhered to the position that Welles had explained to Halifax: "It would be difficult for the United States to maintain diplomatic relations with Vichy and, what was far more important, cooperative relations with the authorities in North Africa if anything in the nature of official recognition were to be given by this Government to the Free French Committee."[17]

As a result of British support and Pleven's efforts the status of the Free French increased. Thus, the question of economic assistance required official clarification. On November 11, 1941, in a directive to Stettinius Roosevelt declared, "I hereby find the defense of any French territory under the control of the French Volunteer Force (Free French) is vital to the defense of the United States." However, the president stipulated that such assistance would operate "by way of re-transfer from His Majesty's Government in the United Kingdom or their Allies."[18] The Free French territories at this time included New Hebrides, Chad, New Caledonia, French Equitorial Africa, the Cameroons, Gabon, and Syria.[19] The president's decision had more significance than was immediately evident. It indicated that only a month before Pearl Harbor he was still attempting, despite isolationist pressure, to aid the Allies in some way short of intervention—at a time when he appeared to have exhausted his possibilities.

Although the announcement represented a step forward in improving Free French relations, in essence the declaration merely made public a policy that the United States had pursued for the past year. The retransfer system still provided the basis for Free French assistance. Hull fully supported the arrangement, since the United States had already stationed consular representatives in Free French areas. However, he carefully pointed out that "the distinction in our treatment of the Free French was thus clear. We would give them material assistance wherever necessary in their efforts to combat the Axis. We would keep in touch with them through our consular representatives. But we would not recognize them as a Government."[20]

Despite the state department's qualifications, the Vichy ambassador, Gaston Henry-Haye, presented a formal protest against such assistance.

He also criticized the presence of the American military mission that had arrived in French Equatorial Africa.[21] The most significant feature of Henry-Haye's objection was its mildness. In most respects it confirmed the innocuous nature of Roosevelt's directive, which neither altered American relations with Vichy nor eroded the influence of Murphy and Leahy.

Despite the unfortunate St. Pierre and Miquelon incident the entrance of the United States into the war considerably assisted the Free French cause. On December 24, 1941, under the command of Admiral Emile Muselier, de Gaulle's followers seized St. Pierre and Miquelon, two small French fishing islands off the coast of Newfoundland. The United States and England wanted the islands to pass to the control of the Allies, but de Gaulle regarded the islands as a strictly French affair. His initiative resulted in the Free French taking the islands without firing a shot. A plebescite that followed disclosed that approximately 98 percent of the population preferred Free French control to that of Vichy.[22]

Although the American public overwhelmingly approved the action, de Gaulle's move precipitated a bitter and hostile reaction within the state department. Hull, who feared that the Axis would use the incident to occupy all of France and North Africa, severely criticized de Gaulle and threatened to restore the islands to their former status. Hull's position, however, incensed the American public. With this in mind and Vichy's apparent unwillingness to sever relations over the issue, Roosevelt and Hull permitted the affair to die.[23]

Although the impact of the seizure diminished, Hull never forgave de Gaulle for his coup. Both he and Roosevelt questioned the Free French leader's integrity and mistrusted his motives. As Hull stated, "Our relations with de Gaulle's movement were not helped by the incident." The president and Hull held de Gaulle personally responsible for violating what they considered his commitment to England. They also accused him of acting contrary to the wishes of the United States and Canada and "regarded him as more ambitious for himself and less reliable than we had thought him before."[24] Hull later reported that Roosevelt cited this incident as justification for refusing to include de Gaulle in the North African invasion.[25]

Yet whatever Washington felt toward de Gaulle, cooperation with his forces appeared essential. In the Pacific the strategically located Free French islands assumed major significance. Some were already in use as landing fields and supply bases, and New Caledonia's nickel deposits were of great importance for the manufacture of armaments. Assistance to these areas and to those in Africa increased the importance of the Free French.[26]

In the United States the Free French delegation developed into a more cohesive organization. American officials agreed to discuss with the delegation matters of Free French interest but did not accord it official diplomatic recognition. Pleven returned to London and de Gaulle replaced him with Adrien Tixier. The new chairman was a militant syndicalist and assistant director of the International Labor Office in Geneva. In February 1942 the Free French completed their delegation by assigning a military mission to Washington.[27] The delegation performed the duties normally discharged by consular officers, such as renewing passports and registering those persons who swore allegiance to Fighting France. It also coordinated the war effort with the United States and supervised the training of French aviators on American fields. On February 4, 1942, Tixier authorized Jean-Paul Levi to secure aid under the Lend-Lease Act. Levi informed Roosevelt that the Free French in compliance with Section IV of the Lend-Lease Act would not without presidential consent transfer any goods or articles received through lend-lease.[28]

While the retransfer system operated, American officials debated long-range plans for lend-lease to de Gaulle. On April 10, 1942, the president approved a memorandum that rejected negotiations for a more formal lend-lease agreement. When the time came for such talks, the state department recommended that the agreement should in general correspond to the British model. At the same time, the United States insisted that coordination with the Free French and aid to them constituted an integral part of American policy.[29]

The American position that economic cooperation in no way represented political recognition remained unaltered. On June 11, 1942, in an aide-mémoire to the British embassy the state department once again expounded its policy. Hull asserted that the United States agreed with the British and French National Committee "that the destiny and the political organization of France must, in the last analysis, be determined by the free expression of the French people under conditions giving them freedom to express their desires unswayed by any form of coersion."[30]

As the war progressed, the need for a more definitive understanding on economic matters between the United States and the Free French increased. In London the French National Committee and a United States mission

coordinated their common war objectives. In July 1942 Admiral Harold
B. Stark and Brigadier General Charles L. Bolte arrived for discussions with
the Free French on all matters concerning the war, including lend-lease.
On recommendations from the OLLA, BEW, and the Departments of War,
Navy, and Treasury, Roosevelt agreed that the United States should not
at that time conclude a formal lend-lease agreement of the British type
with the Free French.[31] Instead he authorized the signing of a reciprocal
aid agreement. The French drew up a letter to General Bolte outlining the
principles of reciprocal aid, and on September 3, 1942, Roosevelt approved
the exchange of notes between de Gaulle's representatives and the United
States. On the same day, the United States concluded similar agreements
with the United Kingdom, Australia, and New Zealand.[32]

The first two articles embodied the basic principles of the agreement.
Article I stated: "The United States of America will continue to supply
Fighting France with such defense articles, defense services and defense
information as the President shall authorize to be transferred or provided."
In Article II the Free French agreed to supply American forces with "such
aricles, services, facilities or information as it may be in a position to supply."[33] By this time the Free French in Africa and New Caledonia had
furnished American forces with services and materials.[34]

American officials regarded the reciprocal aid agreements as essential
to the establishment of economic cooperation throughout the war. In his
report to Congress on lend-lease operations Stettinius pointed out that
countries abroad had provided American troops with supplies and services
without dollar payment; consequently "millions of tons of shipping space
and hundreds of millions of dollars have already been saved in this way."[35]
Furthermore, Stettinius added that since no one could predict when the
war would end, it was impossible to estimate total savings. However, he
drew a comparison to the previous war, in which "the United States' War
Department spent more than $2 billion in the United Kingdom and France
for supplies, equipment and services for our troops of the kind that are
being provided in this war as reciprocal aid."[36]

During the course of negotiations over reciprocal aid the question of
direct lend-lease to the Free French once again surfaced. By this time Allied plans for the invasion of North Africa had reached the advanced stages.
Although the United States still carried on diplomatic relations with the
Pétain government, these were almost certain to dissolve with the invasion
of Vichy territory. Therefore, the state department recommended to

Roosevelt that he amend his directive of November 11, 1941, in order to permit the direct presentation of Free French requests for lend-lease.[37] On October 6, 1942, Roosevelt instructed Stettinius "to arrange for Lend-Lease aid directly to the authorities of the French National Committee."[38] The new arrangements were to take effect as of November 2, but until that time the British offices prepared the requisitions and directed the shipping procedures as in the past.[39]

In general the retransfer system had served its purpose and functioned fairly well. As of July 1942 the British had requisitioned for the Free French civilian goods valued at $3 million.[40] And a final report revealed that the British had filed seventy-nine requisitions for de Gaulle's organization. The United States had supplied the Free French with military and civilian materials valued at roughly $7 million.[41]

In light of subsequent military events the announcement of direct aid had no practical affect. In the early morning hours of November 8, 1942, the Allies launched the invasion of North Africa. The invading force, which numbered 83,000 Americans and 26,000 British troops, anticipated a welcome by the French, or at worst token resistance.[42]

Roosevelt informed Pétain of the action and appealed to the French leader for assistance in defeating the Axis. Roosevelt emphasized that America would provide the French with modern military equipment "in our mutual fight against the enemy." The president further added: "My clear purpose is to support and aid the French authorities and their administration. That is the immediate aim of these American armies." He disavowed any territorial aggrandizement and in a conciliatory manner concluded, "I send to you, and through you, to the people of France my deep hope and belief that we are all of us soon to enter into happier days."[43]

Unfortunately Roosevelt's approach failed to persuade the aged French leader. Pétain immediately replied, "It is with stupor and sadness that I learned tonight of the aggression of your troops in North Africa." He made it quite clear that he considered such an attack a flagrant violation of French territory and condemned the Allied action as a cruel initiative. Pétain concluded that "France and her honor are at stake. We are attacked, we shall defend ourselves; this is the order I am giving."[44]

Because of Pétain's reaction Allied troops encountered stiff resistance at Oran and Casablanca. In Algiers only the timely intervention by French dissidents brought hostilities to an abrupt halt. On orders from the president American leaders were to negotiate with whatever administration they found in North Africa. At the time, Admiral Darlan was visiting his ill son in Algeria; as commander in chief of all the armed forces of Vichy France he represented the highest authority in the area. As such, he assumed the leadership of the opposition forces.[45] Convinced by Murphy that a massive force of over 250,000 Allied troops had descended on North Africa, Darlan concluded that further resistance was useless. On November 9, 1942, he ordered a cease-fire in the Algiers area and expressed a willingness to negotiate with the Allies. On November 10 he conferred with General Mark Clark and Robert Murphy and the following day issued orders for a general cease-fire. The directive arrived just in time to prevent a destructive attack on Casablanca.[46]

With the termination of hostilities negotiations progressed toward a satisfactory political arrangement. On November 13 Murphy, Clark, Darlan, and other French representatives arranged a pattern for French military and political organization. By this understanding Darlan became high commissioner of North Africa and Commander in Chief of the naval forces; General Henri Giraud assumed the position of chief of the ground and air forces; General Alphonse Juin served as commander of the eastern sector; and General Auguste Nogues and Yves Châtel filled the offices of resident general of Morocco and governor general of Algeria, respectively. The French assured the Allies of immediate cooperation and participation in the forthcoming campaign to liberate Tunisia. Negotiations continued over the specific details of the relationship between the French and the Allies. On November 22 after protracted discussions the talks concluded with the signing of the Clark-Darlan Agreement. The understanding outlined the basic principles for cooperative action in expelling the Axis from North Africa, for liberating Metropolitan France, and for restoring the French empire.[47]

The collaboration with Darlan precipitated some of the most bitter tirades against American wartime policy. For many Darlan represented the most reprehensible aspects of Vichy France. Opponents regarded him as an arch-collaborationist, pro-German, and anti-British. Critics accused the United States of abandoning principle for expediency and in so doing raising to power a former servant of Vichy.[48] In defense of its action the United States stressed that the negotiations with Darlan in no way committed the country to perpetuating his control. Spokesmen for the government pointed out that the understanding merely represented an agreement by a field commander to arrange for appropriate civilian and military functions in a theatre of operations.[49]

Despite the administration's deemphasization of Darlan the opposition persisted to such an extent that Roosevelt felt compelled to issue a statement. On November 17 the president described the understanding as "only a temporary expedient, justified solely by the stress of battle." At the same time, he noted that the agreement had accomplished two military objectives—"the first was to save American and British lives on the one hand, and French lives on the other. The second was the vital factor of time. The temporary arrangement has made it possible to avoid a mopping up period in Algiers and Morocco, which might have taken a month or two to consummate. Such a period would have delayed the concentration for the attack from the West on Tunis, and we hope on Tripoli."[50] To alleviate suspicions that the United States intended to extend Darlan's control, the president added that "the temporary arrangements with Admiral Darlan apply without exception to the local situation only."[51] This statement succeeded in quelling the agitation in the United States and made possible the Combined Chiefs' approval of the Clark-Darlan Agreement.[52]

In England adverse reaction to Darlan's appearance as the man of the hour continued. With him as high commissioner any agreement with the Free French was out of the question. On November 16 de Gaulle issued a statement that the Free French would take no part in or assume any responsibility for the negotiations taking place with the Vichy delegates. Furthermore, de Gaulle insisted that "if these negotiations lead to the establishment of the Vichy regime in North Africa, they obviously cannot be accepted by Fighting France."[53]

In Washington Roosevelt outlined the North African arrangements to the French delegation, and Tixier voiced the objections of the Free French. He told the president that Free France would never accept Darlan, "whose authority must end, as soon as possible."[54] However, American policy remained unaltered, and on December 8 Tixier cabled de Gaulle that "the position of the State Department has not changed fundamentally. One cannot say how long they will continue to make use of Darlan. Everything depends on the military situation. . . ." He further commented that Hull obviously had arranged a meeting in order to improve relations with the Fighting French and that "we will also work toward this indispensable end."[55]

Fortunately the issue over Darlan was of short duration. On Christmas Eve an assassin's bullet took the life of the enigmatic admiral. General Giraud replaced him as high commissioner and received British approval. The Free French on the other hand exhibited mixed reactions over Giraud.

Originally, as Tixier had explained to Roosevelt, de Gaulle's followers welcomed him "until he felt it to be his duty to accept Darlan's command." Nevertheless the Free French believed that an agreement with him was possible whenever he terminated his association with Darlan.[56] Although de Gaulle and Giraud had open differences, his ascendency helped establish a basis for a reconciliation between the Fighting French and the French in North and West Africa.

The vehement denunciations of American associations with Darlan had represented extreme narrowmindedness. Those who opposed collaboration with the admiral had overlooked the vital necessity of dealing with the man who possessed the most power at the time. The military and civilians in North Africa still proclaimed loyalty to Pétain's government and therefore respected and obeyed the decisions of its foremost military authority. Above all, the critics had ignored Darlan's ability to make good on his promises. As a result of his decisions French resistance terminated two days after the invasion. In the abbreviated fighting American casualties totaled 1,404, including 526 killed.[57]

Darlan also had undertaken immediate steps to provide for French cooperation in the Tunisian Campaign. Perhaps his most significant contribution was his success in persuading General Pierre Boisson to lead West Africa into the Allied camp. Boisson had previously prevented the Axis, the Fighting French, and the British from occupying West African territory. Through Darlan he had offered West Africa as a supply base, and on December 7 the combined chiefs had approved an agreement with Boisson that was similar to the Clark-Darlan understanding.[58] Ironically, Darlan had failed where his strength was greatest. His power and influence within Vichy had always rested on his position as commander of the French Navy. Yet his attempts to attract the fleet to Algeria had proved unsuccessful. The Germans occupied all of France following the African invasion, and French officers in accordance with a Darlan directive of June 1940 scuttled the fleet in Toulon harbor.[59]

At a point when criticism of the United States had reached its peak, Stalin provided what was perhaps the best assessment. In a communication to Churchill the Russian leader commented, "It seems to me that the Americans used Darlan not badly in order to facilitate the occupation of Northern and Western Africa. The military diplomacy must be able to use for military purposes not only Darlan but, 'Even the Devil himself and his grandma.'"[60]

NOTES

1. "Summary of Fighting French Policy Relative to Lend-Lease, 1941-1942," March 26, 1943, Box 3187, RG 169.

2. Dorothy Shipley White, *Seeds of Discord* (Syracuse: Syracuse University Press, 1964), 227-37. Although White did not have access to state department files, at present this is one of the best descriptions of the Free French in the United States. She does not consider in any detail attempts to acquire lend-lease or to distinguish between direct and indirect assistance. *See* also Arthur Layton Funk, *Charles de Gaulle: The Crucial Years, 1943-1944* (Norman: University of Oklahoma Press, 1959), Chapter 1.

3. Langer, *Our Vichy Gamble,* 174; Fighting French, *Fighting French Yearbook* (New York: Fighting French Commission, 1943), 81.

4. Charles de Gaulle, *War Memoirs: The Call to Honor, 1940-1942* (New York: Viking Press, 1955), 211 (hereafter referred to as *War Memoirs 1940-1942*): White, *Seeds of Discord,* 263.

5. de Gaulle, *War Memoirs 1940-1942,* 211.

6. *Foreign Relations 1941* 2, 572; de Gaulle, *War Memoirs 1940-1942,* 211; White, *Seeds of Discord,* 263.

7. *Foreign Relations 1941* 2, 578.

8. Williams to Young, June 28, 1941, Box 159, RG 169.

9. White, *Seeds of Discord,* 264.

10. Cox to Morgenthau, August 11, 1942, Box 59, RG 169.

11. de Gaulle, *War Memoirs 1940-1942,* 211; White, *Seeds of Discord,* 274.

12. Cox to Morgenthau, August 11, 1941, Box 59, RG 169.

13. Burns to Hopkins, August 20, 1941, Hopkins Papers, Roosevelt Library, Hyde Park, N.Y. (Hereafter referred to as Hopkins Papers)

14. Cox to Hopkins, September 4, 1941, Hopkins Papers.

15. Cox to Stettinius, September 24, 1941, Box 144, RG 169.

16. Hopkins to Stettinius, September 25, 1941, Box 144, RG 169.

17. *Foreign Relations 1941* 2, 574.

18. Roosevelt to Stettinius, November 11, 1941, Box 160, RG 169.

19. "Chronological Summary of Events in Africa," n.d., Box 971, RG 169.

20. Cordell Hull, *The Memoirs of Cordell Hull,* Vol. 2 (New York: Macmillan, 1948), 1042.

21. *Foreign Relations 1941* 2, 582-83.

22. Robert E. Sherwood, *Roosevelt and Hopkins: An Intimate History* (New York: Harper Brothers, 1948), 479-82; de Gaulle, *War Memoirs 1940-*

66   The Politics of Wartime Aid

1942, 215-16; White, *Seeds of Discord,* 282-93; Hull, *Memoirs of Cordell Hull,* II, 1127-38.

23. White, *Seeds of Discord,* 294-313; Hull, *Memoirs of Cordell Hull* 2, 1127-38; Sherwood, *Roosevelt and Hopkins,* 283-89.

24. Hull, *Memoirs of Cordell Hull* 2, 1137.

25. Ibid., 1133; Sherwood, *Roosevelt and Hopkins,* 283-89.

26. de Gaulle, *War Memoirs 1940-42,* 217.

27. White, *Seeds of Discord,* 272-73; de Gaulle, *War Memoirs 1940-1942,* 213.

28. Fighting French, *Fighting French Yearbook,* 81; Tixier to Roosevelt, February 4, 1942 and Levi to Roosevelt, February 4, 1942, Box 59, RG 169.

29. George Fennemore, "The Role of the State Department in Connection with the Lend-Lease Program," unpublished manuscript, Historical Division, Department of State, 1943, DNA, 121.

30. *Foreign Relations 1942* 2, 523.

31. Charles de Gaulle, *The War Memoirs of Charles de Gaulle: Unity, 1942-1944. Documents,* trans. Joyce Murchie and Hamish Erskine (New York: Simon and Schuster, 1959), 20 (hereafter referred to as *War Memoirs 1942-1944*); Fennemore, "Role of the State Department," 121-23.

32. Fennemore, "Role of the State Department," 121-23.

33. Fighting French, *Fighting French Yearbook,* 84. This is a duplication of the entire agreement. Other copies are in Box 160, RG 169 and *The Department of State Executive Series,* No. 273.

34. Fighting French, *Fighting French Yearbook,* 84.

35. *Report to Congress on Lend-Lease Operations from the Passage of the Act March 11, 1941 to December 31, 1942,* Box 896, RG 169, p. 49.

36. Ibid., 50.

37. Fennemore, "Role of the State Department," 121-23.

38. Roosevelt to Stettinius, October 6, 1942, Box 59, RG 169.

39. Orchard to Franks, October 23, 1942, Box 59, RG 169; Tixier to Stettinius, October 27, 1942, Box 171, RG 169.

40. Graham to Young, "General Report on Free French Requisitions," July 28, 1942, Box 59, RG 169. *See* Appendix 5 for a complete list.

41. "Summary of the Retransfer System," February 28, 1943, Box 59, RG 169.

42. Marcel Vigneras, *The United States Army in World War II: Rearming the French* (Washington, D.C.: Office of the Chief of Military History, Department of the Army, 1957), 16 (hereafter referred to as *Rearming the French*).

43. Samuel I. Rosenman, ed., *The Public Papers and Addresses of Franklin Delano Roosevelt,* Vol. 11 (New York: Random House, 1950), 456.

44. Ibid., 457.

45. Vigneras, *Rearming the French,* 16; George F. Howe, *The United States Army in World War II. Northwest Africa : Seizing the Initiative in the West* (Washington, D.C.: Office of the Chief of Military History, Department of the Army, 1957), 267-69.

46. *See* Note 45 above. For details, *See* Langer, *Our Vichy Gamble,* Chapter 9.

47. Ibid.

48. Langer, *Our Vichy Gamble,* 368-75; Sherwood, *Roosevelt and Hopkins,* 651; James MacGregor Burns, *Roosevelt: The Soldier of Freedom* (New York: Harcourt, Brace, Jovanovich, 1970), 265.

49. *Foreign Relations 1942* 2, 453.

50. Sherwood, *Roosevelt and Hopkins,* 651; Rosenman, ed., *Public Papers of FDR* II, 480.

51. Ibid. Darlan informed Murphy that he would abdicate whenever the Americans felt it necessary. (Interview with Robert Murphy, November 29, 1972)

52. Langer, *Our Vichy Gamble,* 272. Of the Cabinet members Henry Morgenthau expressed the greatest concern over the "Darlan deal." Roosevelt assured him that the arrangement was only a military convenience after Morgenthau had expressed his bitter opposition to it. Although he remained disturbed, Morgenthau wrote in his Diary: "I believe the President when he says he won't tie up with the Darlans and Flandins. . . . McCloy says that both Eisenhower and Clark are soldiers and have no political ideas, that Eisenhower is a farm boy, and that it is merely a matter of military strategy. I hope they are right. . . ." (Quoted in John Morton Blum, *Roosevelt and Morgenthau* (Boston: Houghton Mifflin, 1970), 497-98)

53. De Gaulle, *War Memoirs 1942-1944,* 92.

54. Ibid., 97.

55. Ibid., 113-14.

56. Ibid., 97. The assassination of Darlan remains a controversial issue. For an interesting conspiratorial interpretation *see* Peter Tompkins, *The Murder of Admiral Darlan* (New York: Simon and Schuster, 1965).

57. Howe, *U.S. Army in WW II,* 173.

58. Ibid., 271.

59. Langer, *Our Vichy Gamble,* 375.

60. Quoted by Robert Sherwood in *Roosevelt and Hopkins,* 651.

4.

November 1942-January 1943: Organizing Civilian Lend-Lease

American policymakers regarded North Africa as a crucial area, where it was imperative for the Allies to demonstrate their benevolence. Since North Africa represented the first liberated area, Roosevelt considered it essential to demonstrate the goodwill of the United Nations. The president cited the necessity of employing extraordinary measures to insure the welfare of the North African civilians and publicly proclaimed that "no one will go hungry if without other means of livelihood in any territory occupied by the United Nations, if it is humanly within our power to make the necessary supplies available to them."[1] From a military standpoint a pacified population behind the lines was a prerequisite for successful operations. Sullen, semi-starved, rebellious civilians posed a serious threat to the campaign in Tunisia, which depended on unprotected supply lines stretching over 1,500 miles.

The United States' commitment to a civilian economic assistance program through the mechanism of lend-lease forced the government to act quickly to provide the administrative apparatus required for such an undertaking. Since the French in North Africa possessed little understanding of lend-lease, lacked effective local organization, and had no representative purchasing commission in the United States, the organization problems proved exceedingly complex. From November 1942 until January 1943 in Washington, London, and North Africa, the Allies designed bureaucratic structures that with some minor alterations provided the basic administrative pattern for the duration of the civilian program. At the same time, the United States attempted to clarify the role of the military in civilian affairs. Directives on the subject, however, were often contradictory, so that during the first few months a satisfactory solution remained elusive. Since there was no formal lend-lease agreement with the French, the state department approved a temporary arrangement in order to expedite the distribution of the urgently needed supplies.

The North African invasion necessitated major alterations in the French lend-lease arrangements. The state department and OLLA concluded that Roosevelt's directive of October 6, 1942, was inadequate to cover the North African situation. Advisers pointed out that the announcement applied only to territory under the control of the Free French, and it overlooked the very real possibility of the absense of the Fighting French from a role in the newly occupied French areas.[2]

Policymakers recommended a revised presidential order that would proffer assistance to all French territories desiring aid, including Metropolitan France.[3] As a result on November 13, 1942, Roosevelt declared: "I hereby find that the defense of any French province, colony, protectorate, mandated area or other territory not under the control of the Axis is vital to the defense of the United States."[4]

The invasion prompted a tremendous effort from the civilian agencies to cope with the inherent problems in keeping the civilian population contented. Moreover, a Nazi broadcast from Toulouse confirmed American reports of the enormous supplements that North Africa had contributed to the Axis economy.[5] Thus, the Allies encountered a desperate situation; one observer reported that "the local population had been reduced to almost starvation."[6] But military requirements demanded a populace that contributed to the war effort. The army relied on the civilians to function as miners, stevedores, farmers, and road builders. Consequently the assistance America furnished them had to consist of supplies beyond the mere subsistence level. At the same time, the problems that the Americans confronted in North Africa convinced them that similar conditions existed elsewhere. Therefore, they not only recommended minimum requirements but also requested materials for the rehabilitation of the North African economy. The purpose was to restore the area to its former role as a producer of surpluses in order to provide goods for future liberated areas.[7]

To undertake such an ambitious program required immediate and unique adjustments in lend-lease procedures. All of the countries that received lend-lease had representative governments that demonstrated knowledge, organization, and efficiency in presenting their requirements. They also had established missions in the United States. With North Africa, such was not the case.[8] Prior to the invasion the United States had not designated North Africa as a requisitioning area; therefore, it lacked a representative purchasing commission in America. Furthermore, North Africa had remained out of the war for almost three years, and the local governments exhibited little comprehension of wartime conditions and no knowledge of the methods to present lend-lease requisitions. Consequently during the weeks immediately following the landing the Civilian Affairs officers attached to the British and American military forces dealt with the problem of civilian supply.[9]

The American civilian representatives functioned under the direction of Robert Murphy, who Roosevelt assigned as operating executive head of the Civil Affairs section and adviser for Civilian Affairs under General Dwight David Eisenhower.[10] On November 11 Hull had recommended to Roosevelt that "all political and economic personnel activity in North Africa be centered under Mr. Murphy's control."[11] However, before reaching a decision on civilian control Vice President Henry Wallace urged extensive consideration of the role of civilians, "since the entire structure of the post war world may depend in considerable measure on the way in which this matter is handled in North Africa."[12]

The president's directive of November 13, 1942, had clearly designated the OLLA as the agency responsible not only for financing civilian aid but for procurement as well. As a result of inter-agency conferences, on November 24 the war department informed Eisenhower of its decision to assign the responsibility for civilian activities in occupied areas to the state department. General Geroge C. Marshall, Chief of Staff, instructed Eisenhower that state's representative "will act as the Commanding General's civil adviser, but when civil activities affect or are affected by military operations he will be subject to your decisions." At that time the war department failed to understand the numerous problems that civilian supply presented. Had the military leaders possessed such knowledge, they would not have surrendered so readily to the high degree of control given the civilian agencies.[13]

Marshall also informed Eisenhower that the two departments, war and state, would closely coordinate their efforts in support of the North African operation. He explained to Eisenhower that although the military campaign continued, Murphy remained the general's subordinate. More-

over, Marshall assured Eisenhower that a decision of the final divorce of
civil affairs from his control would "be based on recommendations from
you at the time that the military situation permits such action."[14]

The directive from the Chief of Staff evidently confirmed Eisenhower
and the military as the possessors of the ultimate authority. Roosevelt,
however, remained wary of military influence and uncertain as to the degree of responsibility the army assumed. Consequently, on December 18
he informed the war department: "Today I am appointing Robert Murphy
to be my personal representative in North Africa with the rank of Minister. He will continue on General Eisenhower's staff in his present capacity as Civil Affairs Officer until such a time as consultation with the War
Department suggests a change." The appointment permitted Murphy direct access to the president, and as such his influence surpassed that of
Eisenhower. However, one of Murphy's outstanding contributions was his
ability to adopt the political point of view, which he represented, into the
framework of military affairs.[15]

The organization of military and civilian affairs during the first few
months proved exceedingly difficult. Confusion and chaos prevailed among
American officials, while an apathetic populace contributed little. For
Eisenhower in particular the task amounted to a frustrating experience.
His associations with Darlan proved complex; he informed Marshall: "I
have kept my relations with Darlan on a military basis and he clearly un-
derstands this. But our military situation has continued to be such as to
make all these civil matters an essential part of active operations." Eisenhower reported the situation had not improved and that "we are trying
to make a system work here which is admittedly full of defects from every
standpoint both at home and here."[16] He described local French officials
as straddling the fence and antagonistic, and he found that the population
exhibited little enthusiasm for the war. Due to the campaign in Tunisia
Eisenhower realized that tight control was necessary in order to prevent
a total breakdown in civilian affairs. The reports reaching him that indicated that measures were underway to separate military and civilian matters "delighted" him. In exasperation he cabled Marshall: "The sooner I
can get rid of all these questions that are outside the military scope the
happier I will be! Sometimes I think I live ten years each week, of which
at least nine are absorbed in political and economic matters."[17]

In Washington the lend-lease administration placed considerable emphasis on North Africa. On November 17 Murphy cabled Hull that it was

imperative for the civilian departments in England and the United States
to reinforce his skeleton staff. He recommended recruiting experts from
the OLLA and BEW.[18] Oscar Cox also stressed the significance of the
liberated area and urged the appointment of the most competent people
possible because "the relationships and patterns for Continental Europe
are likely to be established in Africa, chiefly because the same top Army
people are going to be involved." Cox pointed out that North Africa had
suddenly become the focus for relief, reoccupation, and rehabilitation
and suggested dispatching Stettinius to indicate the importance that the
government attached to the operation.[19]

Stettinius presented the case for additional personnel to Assistant
Secretary of State Dean Acheson. He argued that a mission composed of
American technicians was essential since French North Africa lacked any
supply organization in the United States. The state department accepted
the recommendations, and Hull cabled Murphy of the decision to send additional personnel to assist him in economic matters.[20] The functions of
these experts included: supplying essential materials to the population as
well as industry; purchasing, exporting, and storing materials for future
use by the United Nations; handling currency and all financial problems,
including the evaluation of Axis firms; supervising and maintaining all
vital transportation systems; insuring public health through estimates of
the pharmaceuticals necessary to prevent epidemics; and conducting surveys of pertinent industries to provide for increased production of civilian
and military materials for North Africa and elsewhere.[21]

By the end of November the only formal arrangement applicable to
North Africa was the Clark-Darlan Agreement, which dealt primarily and
directly with military and political cooperation; indirectly it implied the
necessity for a civilian assistance program. Article XIX provided for the
immediate formation of a Joint Economic Commission to analyze the requirements of North Africa. It also authorized the commission to suggest
measures for increasing agricultural production, expanding the import and
export facilities, and improving the general prosperity of the area.[22] The
understanding contained no provisions or directives for means to achieve
such ends. Murphy, aware of the complexities involved in dealing with
the North African colonies individually, required that Darlan's representatives to the commission act as spokesmen for all the North African colonies. He also insisted on the appointment of technical personnel and added
that the United States had experts available. At the same time, the British

endorsed a proposal to coordinate civilian affairs under a North African economic board, to be supervised by Eisenhower. Furthermore, the British anticipated dispatching supply, censorship, communications, and technical personnel to the area in the near future.[23]

By mid-December the Allied bureaucracy in North Africa began to assume a more definitive structure. On December 18 Livingston Short and Lloyd Cutler arrived as the first official lend-lease representatives. The twosome presented a sharp contrast. Short, at fifty-two and a member of an old, well-established family, had achieved status as a director of the General Motors Acceptance Corporation. A veteran European traveler, Short was also one of the few American business leaders with previous experience in North Africa. On the other hand, Cutler appeared as the agency's bright young man. A 1939 graduate of the Yale Law School, he had served as an administrative assistant in the OLLA before his assignment to North Africa.[24] Short and Cutler formed part of a special mission, headed by Paul Culbertson of the state department that included administrators from the departments of treasury and agriculture. The Americans joined their British counterparts, and on December 19 Eisenhower officially organized the North African Economic Board (NAEB), which combined the two groups into a central organization. Murphy as Chief Civil Administrator and (the English) General H. M. Gale presided over the board as joint chairmen. The NAEB functioned as the chief instrument for the civilian supply program. It maintained communications with the French through Murphy and established headquarters in Algiers and later in Oran, Casablanca, and Dakar.[25]

On January 8, 1943, Eisenhower amended his earlier directive and created the Civil Affairs Section of the NAEB, which assumed responsibility for all civilian and industrial matters. The Civilian Affairs Section consisted of five divisions: The Procurement and Development Division, headed by a BEW representative, was responsible for economic intelligence work, the purchase of commodities, and the development of local resources. The Famine and Control Division operated under army auspices and closely supervised all local functions to prevent disorder. The Public Health and Relief Division received direction from an administrator in the Office of Foreign Relief and Rehabilitation Operations. The Coal Division's chairman was a British coal expert, since this was the only product that the United Kingdom could supply in quantity. Of utmost importance was the Import Division under the direction of Short; it served as the focal point for the entire lend-lease operation. The divisions' field personnel analyzed and determined North African requirements, coordinated with the OLLA the procurement and shipment of supplies, and supervised distribution, pricing, and other lend-lease functions. In all, British representation amounted to approximately 20 percent. Thus, the responsibility for civilian supply rested with the American agencies whose field personnel dominated the Civil Affairs Section of the NAEB.[26]

Since North Africa served as a military theater for American and British forces, any central organization required the participation of the Combined Chiefs as well as delegates from the supply agencies of both countries. On November 29 officials announced the creation of the Committee of Combined Boards, composed of representatives from the state department, the British embassy, the Combined Raw Materials Board, the Combined Shipping Adjustment Board, the Combined Food Board, and the secretariat of the Combined Chiefs of Staff. Thomas Finletter of the state department served as chairman. The function of the committee was to determine the necessities that each country would provide for North Africa and designate which materials would come from other sources.[27] Unfortunately most committee members lacked direct involvement with the operational aspects and were of little assistance in resolving the related difficulties. Consequently the committee transferred its authority to an executive secretariat designed for the purpose of meeting with operational administrators. Authorities further reorganized the secretariat into the Combined Committee for North and West Africa. This consisted of personnel from OLLA, BEW, the secretariat of the Combined Chiefs of Staff, the Combined Shipping Adjustment Board, the British embassy, and the Departments of State, Army, and Agriculture.[28]

The Combined Committee for North and West Africa functioned as the focal point in Washington for the Northwest African Civilian Affairs Operation. It reviewed and answered all cables from the North African Economic Board, directed assignments to the appropriate agency, and scrutinized the action taken or proposed. American officials also created the Combined Committee for North Africa, composed solely of representatives from United States agencies for the purpose of resolving the various problems each encountered.[29]

To provide for relief in the newly liberated areas, on November 21 Roosevelt established the Office of Foreign Relief and Rehabilitation Operations (OFRRO) under the direction of Former New York Governor

Herbert Lehman. The instructions on the function of OFRRO and its relation to other government agencies were extremely vague, and almost immediately many citizens and members of Congress erupted with criticism of the new agency. They interpreted OFRRO as a harbinger of international relief without consideration of costs or termination.[30]

The OFRRO formed the Division of Health and Welfare of the North African Economic Board for the purpose of distributing goods to civilians without payment. The agency derived its funds from OLLA, which also placed its orders for goods. In January the OFRRO assigned a mission to North Africa. But until there was some clarification as to where relief began and lend-lease terminated, the functions of the two agencies often overlapped. The early development of Lehman's organization was fraught with open and bitter interagency controversy. Lend-lease authorities interpreted assistance to North Africa as an economic and political necessity, whereas the OFRRO viewed much of it as a relief project. Time was needed to define the roles of each and to bring about a reconciliation between the two agencies.[31]

In London the Harriman Mission, engaged in coordinating the British and American war effort, established contact with de Gaulle's French National Committee. The OLLA instructed the delegation to impress upon the French a number of factors governing economic assistance. The most important of these were: the amount of material transferred to them depended on the availability of supplies and requirements for similar goods in other areas; the French were to cooperate in such a manner that the process would not entail playing off the Americans and the British in order to acquire goods; the British and Americans considered the French North African territories as a single unit, not separate areas; for ordering purposes the French were to include all materials, whether they were acquiring them on a cash basis or through straight lend-lease. The English, French, and Americans also formed a Tripartite Committee in London to scrutinize the French program. The committee reviewed French requests on their reasonableness, availability, and requirements for other areas. The American members recommended to Washington the percentage of goods that the United States should provide, but the final decision on this remained in the hands of the OLLA.[32]

As the bureaucratic pattern developed, the most immediate problem involved the shipment of goods urgently needed in North Africa. With the civilian supply agencies unprepared to assume such a task, the situation became serious. Fortunately the Vichy government had requisitioned goods with a high priority in North Africa, under the terms of the Murphy-Weygand Accord. Officials located approximately 15,000 tons of these various supplies awaiting shipment to North Africa. They consisted of cotton piece goods, used cloth, condensed and powered milk, matches, tea, nails, sugar, and pharmaceutical products. The four Vichy vessels in New Orleans scheduled to transport the goods proved unfit, but the War Shipping Administration found space on army transports in New York.[33]

The OLLA allocated $5 million to the treasury department for the purchase of duplicate items. The goods served as filler cargo on military vessels, and on December 11, 1942, over eight thousand tons of lend-lease supplies sailed for North Africa. In the same convoy the war department transported about two thousand tons of goods for barter purposes in areas where the army relied on native labor. The actual shipment of the goods relieved lend-lease administrators, who feared the military would omit the lend-lease cargo or replace it with similar cargo procured by the army. Under these circumstances the civilians insisted that the army would gain control of civilian supplies.[34] But before the goods were on their way Stettinius commenced an extensive publicity campaign. He proclaimed that "a program has been prepared for the purchase of additional supplies of many times that value to be sent as shipping space becomes available." The *New York Times* reacted to the announcement by expressing concern over the enormous task that confronted the United States. It cited North Africa as an example of the necessity to provide food in all liberated areas. This meant the feeding of an estimated 500 million people. The paper questioned the ability of the country to perform such a feat and therefore lent support to the argument of economic rehabilitation of North Africa for the purpose of providing surpluses for Europe.[35]

Reports from North Africa indicated that virtually every newspaper gave prominence to the fact that $5 million worth of goods was on its way. In a radio broadcast from the area Charles Collingwood pointed out that there was much less food in North Africa than in London and emphasized that "when we say we are going to send these things to them we are making the best propaganda we can." He urged the continuation of the assistance and more publicity on its origin and described the aid as more important "than any devious political maneuvering we may undertake."[36]

Eisenhower, however, regarded the publicized tonnage as totally inadequate. In a cable to the war department he declared, ". . . I cannot overemphasize the adverse political effect of not meeting minimum needs of the civilian population where it is possible to do so in view of public assurances in the United States which have been given prominence in the press here. . . ." In stressing the close connection between civilian pacification and military success, Eisenhower insisted that unless there was an increase in the tonnage, ". . . I shall be compelled to decide between reducing the size of the total forces or causing disaffection with the French by failing to supply essentials which they are expecting to receive."[37]

After conferences with the civilian representatives Eisenhower informed the war department that in order to satisfy local requirements, the Allies would have to export to North Africa approximately 30,000 tons of goods per month. He stressed that any significant reduction below this figure would produce serious political and military consequences. In Washington the war department and the OLLA accepted the general's recommendations. Eisenhower also clarified shipping priorities by excluding all non-military goods from primary consideration. Thus the quantity of civilian supplies in any shipment depended on space made available through the reduction of ballast and the use of broken stowage not utilized by the military.[38]

On December 5 American officials in Washington received a first-hand account of the North African situation. General Arthur Wilson, who participated in the landings at Morocco, returned with a vivid description of conditions there. He assessed Darlan as an opportunist but defended the agreements with him as essential to saving lives and to preventing the garrisoning of the area. He insisted that the military, the civilians, and the press supported Darlan, and although he remained anti-British, he indicated no pro-German leanings. His evaluation of the natives was totally negative. He admitted there was a genuine need for cotton goods, tea, candles, soap, and sugar, but he argued that the United States "must insist on payment for such goods and thereby not give the North Africans any idea that we are going to let them have the goods for the asking." Moreover, he warned officials against publicizing Roosevelt's message concerning assistance to the impoverished, as this would destroy their work incentive and disrupt the native labor markets. He characterized the native practice of exhuming American soldiers to obtain clothing as deplorable and pointed out that natives were responsible for stabbing fourteen Americans in the back. In typical military fashion Wilson advocated firm treatment of the natives and commended the French practice of a "good strong kick" as the best method. Wilson concluded by reviewing the supply situation and asserted that military requirements necessitated the relegation of civilian shipping to a secondary consideration. The general estimated that the area required only about 1,250 tons of civilian goods per convoy.[39] This hardly approached the figure advocated by Eisenhower and revealed a serious shortcoming in Wilson's comprehension of the overall African situation.

Following his appointment as head of the Import Division, Livingston Short asked Stettinius for additional personnel. He stressed the uniqueness of the North African operation and pointed out that "the military situation and relations existing between our government and the local government in North Africa present Lend-Lease in North Africa with an entirely different problem than it faces in other lend-lease territories." Short described the local government as a de facto organization of recent origin, and "for this reason the confidence and efficiency of its personnel can only be judged over a period of time." He advocated a large staff "to do the work which in other territories can be turned over with full confidence to the local government." Short argued that the acute shortage of shipping made the recruitment of skilled, technical experts imperative. These men had to determine the minimum needs and submit the requirements and specifications in proper form, especially since Short felt that the French "do not grasp or are unwilling to grasp the tightness of the shipping situation." He requested a staff of 108 of the following specialists: Requirements—24; Pricing and Distribution—16; Record Keeping—8;[40] General Supervision—9; Stenographers and Clerical—36; Port Clearance and Shipping—7; Inland Transportation—8.

To Short the success or failure of the entire operation depended on shipping and port handling. In his request for personnel Short urged the assignment of port-clearance experts to handle the large volume anticipated in the near future. These specialists, Short asserted, "could supply the drive, direction and imagination needed at each port, and could utilize military personnel to do most of the work on the docks." He reported that all facilities, including trucks and labor, operated at capacity levels, "but unless we whip the unloading and dock clearance problem, it will eventually become the big transport bottleneck."[41]

By the end of December goods had arrived in North Africa, but no lend-lease agreement existed with the French. In order for the distribution of the much needed supplies to commence, Murphy proposed an interim arrangement. On December 27 in a letter of Commandant André Bataille, the Haut Comissariat of French North Africa, Murphy stated that the goods that had reached North Africa "should be available for distribution as soon as possible to the local population." Murphy outlined the conditions and procedures for distribution: the price of the goods remained subject to a later agreement; the margins or markups permitted by wholesalers, retailers, and handlers depended on the rates previously established; the wholesalers and retailers were to receive the same percentage of business they had in prewar years. Murphy strongly recommended as wide a distribution as possible and requested permission for American and British representatives to visit the groupements, wholesalers, and retailers in order to report on the progress of distribution.[42]

On January 2, 1943, Bataille replied to Murphy and agreed to begin distribution without waiting for price settlements or a final sum. He assured Murphy that the prices would remain at their November 8 level but pointed out that price ceilings were dependent on American charges for consumer goods and heavy items. He accepted Murphy's directives and cited the temporary nature of the arrangements and the necessity for eventual modification.[43] The Murphy-Bataille Agreement provided the basis for pricing and distribution of lend-lease goods.

By the middle of January the OLLA reviewed the first two months of its North African operation. The agency had sent approximately 26,000 tons of goods, while the army shipped 5,000 tons and Great Britain provided 25,000 tons. Of the contemplated 30,000 tons for January, two-thirds consisted of sugar and flour. The other materials included soap, milk, tea, sugar, new and used clothing, cotton piece goods, tobacco, matches, drugs, and copper sulphate. The monthly coal supply from the United States was set at 7,500 tons, while Britain contributed 189,000 tons per quarter.[44]

In answer to a request from the British on lend-lease policy to the area the state department replied that it was the intention of the United States to provide military aid on a straight lend-lease basis through the army. Civilian assistance, however, was to proceed through the Civil Affairs staff, which sold the goods directly to the French for resale through normal commercial channels. The state department also agreed to recommendations of Murphy and Eisenhower to include West Africa under the jurisdiction of Eisenhower and the Civil Affairs section.[45]

NOTES

1. *New York Times*, November 14, 1942, 3.

2. Cardozo to Cox, November 12, 1942, Box 3189, RG 169; Stettinius to Acheson, November 13, 1942, State Department Document 851R.24/7 psTL, DNA.

3. Ibid.

4. Roosevelt to Stettinius, November 13, 1942, Box 59, RG 169.

5. Office of War Information, November 13, 1942, Edward R. Stettinius, Jr., Papers, University of Virginia, Charlottesville (hereafter referred to as Stettinius Papers).

6. "Report on French North Africa as a Source of Supply for the German Empire," November 12, 1942, Box 969, RG 169.

7. Ibid.

8. Office of the Lend-Lease Administration (hereafter referred to as OLLA) History: "Ships and Shipping," unpublished manuscript, 1947, Box 3219, RG 169, 33-36. The lend-lease administration compiled a history of its operations following the war. The project is arranged topically into special subjects including histories of the programs in specific countries. It is very inconsistent—some sections are well done and documented while others are very sketchy. None of the subjects are described in depth, but a chronological approach serves as a useful guide.

9. Ibid. An example of French shortcomings was their request for 300,000 tons of flour. There was nowhere near the shipping available for such an order. In the end the United States shipped 89,000 tons.

10. *Foreign Relations 1942* 2, 379.

11. Hull to Roosevelt, November 11, 1942, President's Secretary File (hereafter referred to as PSF), Roosevelt Papers.

12. Wallace to Roosevelt, November 11, 1942, PSF, Roosevelt Papers.

13. Harry L. Coles and Albert K. Weinberg, *The United States Army in World War II, Civil Affairs: Soldiers Become Governors* (Washington, D.C.: Office of the Chief of Military History, Department of the Army, 1964), 38 (hereafter referred to as *Civil Affairs*). This is an invaluable source consisting solely of documents and in particular war department communications that describe the problems the army had coordinating military and civilian affairs.

14. Ibid., 44.

15. Ibid., 40. For more detail of Eisenhower's situation, *see* Alfred D. Chandler, Jr., ed., *The Papers of Dwight David Eisenhower.* Vol. 2, *The War Years* (Baltimore: Johns Hopkins, 1970).

16. Ibid., 47.

17. Ibid., 45.

18. *Foreign Relations 1942* 2, 443-44.

19. Cox to Hopkins, November 16, 1942, Hopkins Papers, Roosevelt Library, Hyde Park, N.Y.

20. Stettinius to Acheson, November 18, 1942, Box 272, RG 169.

21. *Foreign Relations 1942* 2, 450.

22. Ibid., 457.

23. Murphy to Darlan, November 24, 1942, Box 32, RG 169; Coles and Weinberg, *Civil Affairs,* 40; *Foreign Relations 1942* 2, 463.

24. Stettinius to Department of State, November 28, 1942, State Department Document 851R.24/8, DNA.

25. Eisenhower to War Department, December 19, 1942, Box 512, RG 160; Coles and Weinberg, *Civil Affairs,* 40-41, 53.

26. Coles and Weinberg, *Civil Affairs,* 40; OLLA History: "North Africa," Box 3219, RG 169, 21-22; Bureau of Areas "Report," January 20, 1943, Box 361, RG 169.

27. Fennemore, "Role of the State Department," 124-25.

28. Ibid.; OLLA History: "Ships and Shipping," 39-42.

29. Fennemore, "Role of the State Department," 124-25.

30. OLLA History: "Liberated Areas," Box 3219, RG 169, pp. 14-16.

31. Ibid.; OLLA History: "Ships and Shipping," 40.

32. Orchard to Stettinius, December 5, 1942, Box 171, RG 169.

33. Appelby to Stettinius, November 17, 1942, Stettinius Papers; "Progress Report on North Africa," December 2, 1942, Box 272, RG 169.

34. Stettinius to Morgenthau, November 16, 1942, Stettinius Papers; Coles and Weinberg, *Civil Affairs,* 39; OLLA History: "Ships and Shipping," 33; Thayer to Knollenberg, January 4, 1943, Box 970, RG 169.

35. *New York Times,* December 1, 1942, 14, 33; Press Release, December 1, 1942, Stettinius Papers.

36. "Excerpt of Radio Talk from North Africa by Charles Collingwood," December 4, 1942, Box 272, RG 169.

37. Coles and Weinberg, *Civil Affairs,* 50.

38. Ibid.

39. "Report of Address by General Arthur Wilson," December 6, 1942, State Department Document 851R.24/21, DNA; Vieg to Stettinius, December 6, 1942, Box 272, RG 169.

40. Short to Stettinius, January 1943, Box 3189, RG 169.

41. Ibid.

42. Murphy to Bataille, December 27, 1942, Box 3189, RG 169.

43. Bataille to Murphy, January 2, 1943, Box 3189, RG 169.

44. "Civilian Supplies Shipped to North Africa, November 8, 1942-January 15, 1943," State Department Document 851R.24/27, DNA.

45. Appelby to Sir Frederick Phillips, January 11, 1943, State Department Document 851R. 24/12, DNA; Hull to Murphy, January 16, 1943, State Department Document 851 R.01/75, DNA.

5.

Bureaucracies at Loggerheads

A few months after the North African operation it became evident that substantial modifications were essential to ameliorate difficulties in shipping procedures, identification of goods, military and civilian arrangements, and coordination between Washington and North Africa. The lend-lease representatives, especially those abroad, appeared to be very sensitive to the problems and constantly recommended improvements, including assigning to the French a greater role in the program. The efforts on the part of the lend-lease administration succeeded in eliminating the most obstructive entanglements. Of utmost importance the French had assumed more responsibility for and involvement in the operation by the end of 1943. However, one problem remained beyond American control—the Black Market. It directly affected the civilian lend-lease program, and despite civilian and military intervention, continued practically unabated throughout the war.

From the point of view of the lend-lease administration officials the civilian program exhibited serious shortcomings. Their major complaint was the inadequate performance by the army in loading the civilian goods on military transports at American docks. On the convoys that had sailed between November and early January, American civilians charged that each convoy could have included approximately 47,000 more tons of civilian supplies. They pointed out that in one specific instance poor planning had resulted in a 38 percent loss in tonnage and a waste of 42 percent of cubic space. On one convoy the OLLA asserted that the military's carelessness with the civilian material caused the cargo to shift and thereby necessitated the return to port of some of the vessels. Consequently over 1,000 tons of civilian lend-lease goods from the convoy remained on army piers.[1]

In response to the accusations the army insisted that there was simply no space available for all the civilian items. The explanation proved totally unacceptable. The OLLA interpreted the matter differently and severely castigated the military for its ineptitude. The civilian agency described army methods as constituting "an utter waste of what we have the least of—shipping space."[2]

In North Africa the situation was far more chaotic. Under the established procedure of shipping civilian supplies as filler cargo on military vessels, the lend-lease representatives could not assume the responsibility for the goods until they left the dock area without interfering with the army's port procedures. Along with this a lack of adequate records further hindered operations. Military shipments under army control did not require the detailed paper work such as signed bills of lading, the ship's manifest, invoices mailed in advance, or a careful receipting system. These, of course, were all an integral part of transporting commercial goods.[3] Due to the absence of such procedures during the early stages of the program the civilians in North Africa possessed no reliable information on what the shipments contained until they arrived. Furthermore, Cutler admitted that neither he nor Short had any practical experience in shipping matters. Yet even if they had, the task of carefully receipting and recording goods on a dock where the military convoy discharged its cargo as rapidly as possible would have proved virtually impossible. Specifically the job consisted of clearing an average of approximately 600,000 separate packages, which in some harbors the army loaded directly into trucks in order to eliminate dock congestion.[4] The identification of the goods, once the lend-lease agents acquired them, presented another problem. The packages arrived labeled only with code numbers representing a general category of goods. Since the shipments lacked documentation, identification proved time-consuming. In the case of bulky materials such as sacks of wheat and flour the recipients encountered little difficulty. But for shoes, clothing, auto parts, and cotton piece goods neither the French nor the Americans could identify the goods without opening the crates. Since the Americans required payment for the civilian supplies, the French often insisted on such a procedure. On many occasions cotton piece goods arrived with each crate containing a number of bolts of different length, color, and grade. The French literally tore open such packages, sorted the goods, unrolled the bolts on the docks, measured them, and with a magnifying glass counted the threads. The ensuing congestion at dockside and the warehouses defied description.[5]

The aggravation over the loading and identification of the materials served to intensify a more far-reaching controversy over the quantity of goods the French received. The OLLA had based their total requisitions on the 30,000 ton-per-month estimate that Eisenhower and Washington had agreed upon in December. The French, however, argued that at the Casablanca conference they had obtained a written agreement that guaranteed them 65,000 tons per month. Lend-lease officials were cognizant of the understanding but interpreted it differently. They insisted that the promise at Casablanca merely meant that North Africa might require a specific allotment of 50,000 tons of flour or wheat, 12,000 tons of sugar, and 3,000 tons of other goods. However, following the conference and after extensive analysis Short reported, "We pointed out to the French that the promise had been made on the basis of 50,000 tons of flour and they didn't need that much, but only 14,000 tons for a few months, and that 30,000 tons would cover their needs."[6] The American position remained unaltered and further embittered the already disgruntled French. The French expressed considerable dissatisfaction over the fact that after three months only 66,000 tons of civilian supplies had reached them. In comparison the Germans, they claimed, had permitted an importation of 77,000 tons per month.[7]

Whether the French point was valid or not, remedies for the civilian program were essential. Realizing that the shortage of civilian personnel had a deleterious effect on the operation, Short concluded arrangements with the army whereby the responsibility for unloading, receipting, and transporting civilian goods to the warehouses rested with the base commander. On February 26, 1943, Deputy Theater Commander General E. S. Hughes directed that "base commanders must receive, unload, store and account for all supplies received whether they be for the American Army, the French military or French civilians."[8]

An important civilian function was the supervision of the process of distribution. When Short had settled in North Africa, he discovered that the colonial commercial operations functioned through the groupements. "The Groupements," Short reported, "represented a sort of cross between an Italian Fascist cooperative and one of our trade associations, more like the former because although all members are commercial dealers all the officers are government officials and all the decisions are made by government representatives." After discussions concerning distribution with the economic section of Giraud's government, Short concluded "that if we are going to get the goods distributed we would have to use the existing organizations."[9] Cutler concurred and averred that the groupements were essential, because they provided the best source of data possible on the economic requirements of the various regions.[10]

The distribution procedure entailed a number of organized steps. Once the groupements acquired the goods, they established contact with the wholesalers, who received allotments based on their share of the commercial operations in the prewar years. The retailers operated through a "bon" or purchase warrant received from the service municipal, which was under the control of the "chef de la region" or controleur civilian. The purchase warrants indicated the retailer's allotment as well as the wholesaler supplier.[11]

The entire distribution arrangement reflected the inveterate French colonial discrimination. In February 1943 John O'Boyle, a lend-lease observer, reported that the large native population was receiving a rather small share of the goods. Since the French refused to sell European goods to native retailers, any Arab or Jew who desired European clothing could only purchase such materials through the flourishing Black Market. Some of the more influential members of these groups, however, could obtain such goods through bribery or political favors. Although the high comissariat, the British, and the Americans all possessed the authority to inspect the system, it proved virtually impossible to eliminate irregularities.[12]

The atmosphere in North Africa sustained and perpetuated the Black Market. Prior to the invasion meat, foodstuffs, and locally produced soaps comprised the majority of the market. But after November 8 the list of items on the Black Market expanded considerably. The purchasing power of the Allied soldiers combined with the ever present shortage of goods created an ideal situation for such an operation. At the same time, the native had acquired unaccustomed purchasing power; but with few goods to select from, he readily sold his ration card, which provided a large source of goods for illegal resale. The wholesaler exploited his position and also contributed to the market. By withholding certain items he sold them for double the price without coupons.[13] Extensive stealing at docks and warehouses, which resulted from the problems with landing, storage, and transportation, provided the Black Market with its major source of supply. Although the military attained some success in curbing theft by the Arabs, it was unable to effectively curtail the impetus given the market by its largest supplier—the American soldier. Truck and jeep gasoline appeared most frequently for illegal sale, but civilian lend-lease articles such as sugar, flour, shirts, and women's hosiery served as valuable additions to the thriving and lucrative Black Market. Reports from the areas indicated that eradication of it was impossible.[14]

The arrangements completed to eliminate dock congestion and to expedite distribution would have become somewhat meaningless if the United States could not maintain a sufficient supply of goods. Throughout 1943 controversy arose between the civilians in North Africa and their counterparts in Washington over the quantity of goods received. Lend-lease representatives in North Africa argued that the 30,000 ton-per-month supply was no longer adequate and that it represented 40,000 tons less than the Germans had permitted. Furthermore the Allies had failed to consistently maintain even this minimum amount. They noted that by the end of January 1943 only 43,000 tons had arrived, and by the end of March there was no indication of any considerable improvement.[15] The OLLA, acutely aware of this serious shortcoming, sought a remedy through an alteration in the shipping procedures. Consequently a debate began as to whether lend-lease cargo served best as "filler" or deadweight. In March the military personnel in Africa, who had originally sponsored the filler concept, concluded that military supplies could provide adequate filler. In Washington, however, the military officials who had originally opposed the use of civilian lend-lease cargo as filler now favored it.[16]

As the discussions progressed the civilians concluded that only the employment of separate ships would provide an adequate solution to the problem. In April J. E. Slater, the War Shipping Administration's (WSA) regional director in North Africa, cabled Washington that the advantages to such a system were clearly evident: civilians could load goods at commercial piers as ordinary cargo; it would simplify the marking procedure and assure proper identification; the separate handling of civilian material would eliminate interference with military supplies; it would permit the assignment of a "commercial berth" as its destination and thereby permit unloading independent of military cargo. "Advantages would be obtained in the complete segregation of civilian supplies from the military," Slater concluded. Under such an arrangement the WSA would allot a certain number of ships for the handling of civilian supplies in each convoy depending on the general policy laid down by the military and civilian authorities.[17]

Slater's position gradually received endorsement from other officials, in particular those in Africa. In June a report on the port operations in Oran and Casablanca further revealed the weakness of the existing system. Although the Short-Hughes arrangement continued to be in effect, officials experienced difficulty in its implementation. Civilian goods still competed with military equipment, and the army continued to unload the civilian items carelessly and last. On one occasion the report described huge losses of flour, sugar, copper sulphate, cotton goods, and parts for farm machinery. Flour and copper sulphate from broken bags accumulated in piles as high as ten feet while "cotton piece goods were piled loose in a jumbled mass on the dock."[18]

The patience of the personnel in North Africa wore thin. In utter frustration Murphy informed Hull on July 12 that during a three-month period the total amount of civilian cargo amounted to less than forty thousand tons, despite Eisenhower's demand for sixty thousand. Murphy described the supply situation as critical and advised that in the opinion of experts in the area, without the thirty thousand tons per month it was impossible to sustain the essential conduct of military affairs. Resources had rapidly diminished and an industrial breakdown appeared imminent unless the minimum shipment arrived.[19]

While officials considered the question of separate shipping, Cutler challenged the basic principle upon which the filler system rested. He argued that the concept of "spreading the risk" by combining civilian and military goods no longer had any validity. Cutler cited statistics that indicated that losses to North African shipping from sinkings averaged less than 3 percent, whereas the operating losses from military transfer ran as high as 10 percent for some convoys. Thus he rejected the security argument based on unlucky sinkings. Furthermore, Cutler pointed out that a recent study revealed that military and civilian officials recommended the employment of separate ships for the 1943 program as well as for future liberated areas.[20]

In Washington the OLLA realized that the shortcomings of the system left the agency vulnerable to criticism. The OLLA confirmed reports of a number of discrepancies between the amount of goods shipped and those on the receipts. Stettinius strongly advocated separate shipping after the army had proposed to eliminate civilian cargo from two convoys. It was only after forceful protests, Stettinius noted, that the military placed the goods on the vessels.[21]

The persistence of the OLLA officials in North Africa and Washington resulted in a minor success that served as a harbinger for later modifications. In July Lewis Douglas, the deputy administrator of the War Shipping Administration, directed that the steamer *Charles W. Hall* transport only civilian goods to North Africa. On July 8, 1943, the vessel carrying 7,000 tons cleared New York harbor along with the military ships that transported the remainder of the civilian goods as filler cargo. Stettinius hailed it as a definite improvement over past procedures but added that much remained to be accomplished.[22] Finally in August, after discussions between the OLLA, the WSA, and the war department, officials concluded that civilian lend-lease shipping would operate more effectively under a different arrangement. Thus the agencies adopted a procedure whereby the WSA designated one vessel in each convoy as a carrier of lend-lease civilian supplies to North Africa. Despite the alteration the army still had to transport approximately 8,000 tons of civilian cargo per month.[23]

While the authorities had worked to resolve the shipping issue, other problems emerged that continued to produce friction between Washington and North Africa. Of utmost importance was the controversy that arose over the processing of import division requests. The matter became more serious in March 1943, when the NAEB determined that it was unsatisfactory to file requisitions on a month-to-month basis. Instead they established a procedure whereby the import division submitted six-month-period requests for the three areas.[24] Consequently the new orders were huge and complex in comparison to those that had arrived on a monthly basis.

Officials in Washington claimed that the information they received on the end use of the products in many cases did not justify meeting the requests.[25] The agencies defined the end use as "a clear statement of the relation of the stated end use to the war effort."[26] They cited a specific example in which the import division cabled, "We are in need of one ton of non-congealing oil." The return cable noted that the oil industry in the United States did not use such a term. Consequently the home-front bureaucrats inquired, "Do you wish oil of 500 viscosity and minus-ten coal test? For what purpose is it to be used? Also, advise the port it is to be sent."[27] Such oversights supposedly were common and confused those in procurement.

Stettinius attempted to alleviate the growing animosity between the field representatives and administrators in Washington. In a letter to Short he pointed out that in order to appease the OLLA and especially those agencies involved in the procurement process, it was vital to present as clear a description as possible of the requested articles. This involved the inclusion of all the necessary details and an emphasis on the end use of the items. The last stipulation he considered most important, since it provided the required justification for sending the material. During the early stages of the operation, while the military campaign continued, Stettinius asserted that the agencies disregarded the lack of clarity. But since the program operated for over seven months, the procuring agencies indicated that unless they received more extensive documentation, they would not send the goods to North Africa. In particular, Stettinius noted, the import division's orders contrasted sharply with the detailed British and Russian requests for scarce material and preferential placement on schedules.[28]

More specifically, Stephen Mitchell, the chief of the French North and West African branch, informed Short of the difficulty they encountered due to lack of information. "In face of WPB [War Production Board] insistence that an allocation must be greatly limited, without such information we are drawing heavily on our imagination," Mitchell wrote. "We are drawing up statements of end use and justifications which have no basis in fact other than our own broad knowledge of the North African situation."[29]

The explanations from Washington evidently had only a slight impact on those in the field. In July Murphy, in a cable to Hull, once again criticized the dearth of supplies as well as the returned orders requesting more detail on end use. He pointed out, however, that the arrival of the French technical mission should help eliminate these problems, but he caustically added, "And if possible a realistic recognition by the WPB regarding the difficulties of operations under field conditions where we must rely on a makeshift and inadequately staffed provisional authority for information should also lessen these difficulties."[30]

The constant criticism from North Africa prompted a state department reaction. Acheson responded to Murphy by describing the difficulties with the French requests and blamed the delays in the program on the failure of officials in North Africa to furnish adequate data for their requirements. Without this it was impossible to assign the allocations and priority ratings. Furthermore he urged the mission to consider the time required to manufacture the products and to show some toleration for the general shortage of shipping. Specifically Acheson cited the confusion over the congealing oil requirement and explained that the much needed calcium chloride also failed to arrive because of a lack of information as to its intended use. The product, he noted, had at least seven special purposes, yet the NAEB submitted an order without any information as to its end use; for similar reasons other orders that had arrived in April had not sailed until July.[31]

While Acheson replied to Murphy, Mitchell responded to Cutler. He cited a cable from Cutler that depicted the low morale afflicting the mission in Africa and indicated that the agency had obtained a much clearer picture of the problems that the mission encountered. At the same time he pointed out that the division personnel in Washington worked over sixty hours a week. He took umbrage, however, over the criticisms of Cutler's colleague, Paul Sturm, and branded his charges as unnecessary and untrue.[32]

Sturm's attack had clearly revealed the frustration plaguing those overseas. "I have come to the conclusion," Sturm wrote, "that the people who receive our cables willfully misunderstand them, for the net result of our operation has left much to be desired. Still we go on as best we can hoping rather wistfully that some of the industrial goods we want so much will one day arrive." Moreover, Sturm added, "Man cannot live by textiles, sugar, milk, and flour. I wish you would spread that rumor in the office. Our cables do not seem to have conveyed that impression."[33]

By midsummer the antagonisms reached their peak. Following the arrival of a large shipment Cutler informed Short that the criticisms were not a reflection on the French North and West African branch; rather, he and Murphy felt that such pressure was necessary to underscore the dire need for goods. In retrospect Cutler firmly maintained that the responsibility for the situation rested with the agencies in Washington. He expressed satisfaction over the fact that in North Africa the various agency representatives, though often in disagreement, managed to achieve compromises on the area's requirements. Most of the credit for this success he attributed to the adroit leadership and guidance of Murphy.[34] Cutler expressed dismay, however, that in Washington the agencies often failed to agree on the African compromises, despite the fact that they had established the Combined Committee for North Africa in order to resolve such difficulties. From Cutler's point of view the ability of authorities in North Africa to compromise represented a significant achievement, whereas the lack of agreement in Washington was uncalled for and responsible for the frustration revealed in Sturm's remarks.[35]

On May 13, the campaign for Tunisia terminated with the capitulation of the German and Italian armies. Roosevelt, commenting on the Allied success, stated, "Our Lend-Lease operations in French North and West Africa—the first of the liberated areas—have demonstrated how a freed people can aid in the defeat of the Axis. In this victory our military operations have been backed up by the friendly support of the peoples behind the lines."[36] With the cessation of hostilities the area no longer required an enormous quantity of military supplies. Therefore, the civilians looked forward to some alleviation of the port congestion that plagued the entire operation. Moreover the reduction of military requirements lifted the burden on the inland transportation network that the army had not only utilized but monopolized. To a great extent the problem of goods accumulating at the docks and warehouses stemmed from the military's employment of over 80 percent of the rail transportation along with all the vehicles it could confiscate. Once this necessity passed, the civilians envisioned much more rapid inland distribution and extensive rehabilitation of the transportation system.[37]

For the French and the Allies the resolution (at least temporarily) of the French military and political controversies represented a significant advancement. On June 3 Giraud and de Gaulle announced the creation of the French Committee of National Liberation (FCNL). The committee emerged as a compromise between the two rival generals and functioned under their combined leadership. In publicizing the committee de Gaulle proclaimed that "the National Committee thus constituted is the Central French Authority."[38]

With the creation of the FCNL the separate French missions in the United States representing the Giraud and de Gaulle factions combined into a single mission. Prior to this, the state department had not authorized the OLLA to deal directly with either of the missions. Consequently the OLLA had prepared, signed, and submitted the requisitions for North and West Africa to the procuring agencies. When the OLLA received the goods, it signed the receipts for them, thereby releasing the procuring agencies from any further responsibility. The French did not acquire the goods until they reached North Africa. This represented a radical departure from standard lend-lease procedures. The other major recipients, England, Russia and China, developed organized representative missions that had direct contact with the OLLA. These missions assumed the responsibility for their goods at American ports.[39] With the new political arrangement the head of the French mission received all the privileges accorded the Free French under Roosevelt's directive of October 6, 1942. Stettinius incorporated the various activities of the OLLA relative to the French supply program into the France branch under the direction of Stephen A. Mitchell. The branch serviced the major French territories not under Axis control as well as those formerly referred to as Fighting France. The new office functioned in the same manner as other foreign liaison branches, clearing requisitions for lend-leasability, policy, and supply. At the same time there was a growing feeling within the OLLA that the French should assume more responsibility for the development of data and requirements.[40]

In order to improve and refine the French operation lend-lease officials considered significant modifications. Ralph J. Watkins, who in August 1943 succeeded Short as chief of the import division, recommended major alterations. He argued that with the establishment of the French Purchasing Mission in Washington, it could assume most of the functions performed by the requirements section of the NAEB. Moreover, he urged that the OLLA transfer the goods destined for Africa to the French at dockside in the United States. Such a procedure benefited the United States. The bargaining over goods already in French territory, Watkins pointed out, only led to resentment and friction. If the United States desired to withhold items, it was much better to do so at the source and not in a warehouse overseas. Along with this such a system was more effective, cheaper, and more satisfactory to the French. Watkins believed that it would also relieve the overseas personnel of the complex accounting problems; reduce the number of agents in the African mission, and eliminate the constant civilian military conflicts.[41]

Bernhard Knollenberg, the acting lend-lease administrator, concurred with Watkins' suggestions and informed him that Washington had also adopted his other recommendation to eliminate the thirty-thousand-ton-per-month requirement. Instead the OLLA would send what it believed the area actually needed rather than attempting to meet an arbitrary fixed tonnage. Knollenberg also advised Watkins to assist the French in establishing supply organizations in North Africa. As time passed, Knollenberg emphasized, the desire within the OLLA to reduce and curtail the functions of the import division increased.[42]

In October Watkins informed the OLLA that in talks with the French he had made considerable progress. The French, he found, were willing to accept more of the burden of responsibility for the program. He reported that they had agreed with the dockside transfer proposal and that the requirements section of the NAEB had thoroughly instructed the French on the proper procedures for the presentation of their requirements.[43]

In Washington on November 15, 1943, Christian Valensi, as chairman of the French Supply Council, officially announced the existence of the organization. Its purpose was "to coordinate and direct activities of the various French Missions, Departments, and Organizations dealing with the supply of goods to French territories." The council required that all correspondence on general policy pass through the chairman and that any additional divisions become an integral part of the council. Therefore no organization could take up any matters with the American government on behalf of the FCNL without authorization from the council.[44] This represented a vast improvement over the previous French attempts to achieve centralization.

With the establishment of the French Supply Council, the modifications for the civilian lend-lease program based on Watkins's proposals proceeded through the necessary bureaucratic channels. The war department raised no objections, and on December 27, 1943, Mitchell informed the War Shipping Administration and the army, navy, treasury, and agriculture departments that the French would sign the required receipts for the transfer of goods to North and West Africa. On January 3, 1944, Mitchell cabled Watkins that the FCNL had agreed to accept delivery at ports in the United States for all civilian material destined for North or West Africa.[45]

The new French procedures conformed to the practices of England and other major lend-lease recipients. With the French accepting delivery at American ports, the FCNL relieved the OLLA of accountability for the goods, and assumed all the risks involved in the shipping—including sinkings. Mitchell advised Watkins to impress upon the French the necessity of maintaining close cooperation with the council in Washington, since it possessed full knowledge of all shipments. The new arrangement also provided for more efficient documentation. One set of documents accompanied the vessel, another went directly to the NAEB in North Africa and Dakar, another went to the French Supply Council, and another was retained by the OLLA. From this the OLLA prepared a formal invoice that represented the landed cost of each item on the ocean bill of lading as well as the total landed cost. This the agency presented to the French in Washington as the formal bill. Once the French completed the checking process, American officials expected payment.[46]

NOTES

1. Thayer to Knollenberg, January 7, 1943, Box 3189, RG 169.

2. Ibid.

3. OLLA History: "Ships and Shipping," 44; Cutler to Thayer, March 28, 1943, Box 970, RG 169.

4. Ibid.; Interview with Lloyd Cutler, May 26, 1972, Washington, D.C.

5. OLLA History: "Ships and Shipping," 43-44; John O'Boyle, "Summary Report of Lend-Lease in North Africa," February 19, 1943, Box 234, RG 169.

6. Livingston Short, "Report on North Africa to the OLLA Executive Staff Meeting," July 5, 1943, Stettinius Papers.

7. O'Boyle, "Summary Report of Lend-Lease."

8. General E. S. Hughes to Commanding Generals, February 26, 1943, Box 3189, RG 169.

9. Short, "Report on North Africa to the OLLA."

10. Interview with Lloyd Cutler, May 26, 1972. Support for retention of the groupements also came from other sources. *See:* Vice Consul Ridgeway Knight in Algiers to State Department, January 12, 1943, Box 969, RG 169; Jean Bleyfus to Maxwell Foster, March 3, 1943, enclosed copy of "The Official Defense of the Groupements in Morocco," written by an aide to General Auguste Nogues.

11. Goldman to Short, April 5, 1943, Box 975, RG 169.

12. Ibid.; John Cowles, "Rough Notes on North Africa," July 1943, Stettinius Papers; O'Boyle, "Summary Report of Lend-Lease"; Interview with Lloyd Cutler, May 26, 1972.

13. Charles S. Davis, "Report on the Black Market in Oran," June 5, 1943, Box 160, RG 169; Lloyd Cutler, "Manual of Operations for the Importation and Distribution of Civilian Supplies in Liberated Areas,"

July 19, 1943, Box 173, RG 169; Munroe to Watkins, September 17, 1943, Box 171, RG 169.

14. Ibid.

15. "NAEB Meeting," January 21, 1943, Box 973, RG 169; Thayer to Knollenberg, February 10, 1943, Box 970, RG 169; Cutler to Thayer, March 28, 1943, Box 970, RG 169.

16. Cutler to Thayer, March 28, 1943, Box 970, RG 169; Slater to Douglas, April 16, 1943, Box 3189, RG 169.

17. Slater to Douglas, April 16, 1943, Box 3189, RG 169.

18. Myers to Watson, June 16, 1943, Box 273, RG 169.

19. Murphy to Hull, July 12, 1943, Box 3189, RG 169.

20. Cutler, "Manual of Operations."

21. Stettinius to Short, June 17, 1943, Box 159, RG 169; Simmons to Orchard, June 25, 1943, Box 273, RG 169.

22. Stettinius to Douglas, July 15, 1943, Box 3189, RG 169.

23. Keating to Myers, August 10, 1943, Box 3189, RG 169.

24. "Report on the Activities of the Import Division, NAEB Meeting," March 11, 1943, Box 973, RG 169.

25. Mitchell to Short, July 3, 1943, Box 970, RG 169.

26. Catlett to Huber, October 29, 1943, Box 420, RG 169.

27. Smith to Short, March 3, 1943, Box 59, RG 169.

28. Stettinius to Short, June 17, 1943, Box 59, RG 169.

29. Mitchell to Short, July 3, 1943, Box 970, RG 169.

30. Murphy to Hull, July 12, 1943, Box 3189, RG 169.

31. Acheson to Murphy, July 28, 1943, Box 970, RG 169.

32. Mitchell to Cutler, July 28, 1943, Box 59, RG 169.

33. Mitchell to Cutler, July 28, 1943, Box 59, RG 169.

34. Cutler to Short, August 13, 1943, Box 59, RG 169; Interview with Lloyd Cutler, May 26, 1972.

35. Interview with Lloyd Cutler, May 26, 1972.

36. *New York Times*, May 26, 1943, 15.

37. Ibid., July 12, 1943, 3; Henry Morgenthau Diary, March 29, 1943, Roosevelt Library.

38. De Gaulle, *War Memoirs 1942-1944*, 179-81. Newspapers and journals throughout the world carried stories on the de Gaulle-Giraud agreement. For two of the most interesting articles *see: The Economist* 144 (June 12, 1943), 747-48 and 144 (June 26, 1943), 816.

39. OLLA History: "Ships and Shipping," 54-55.

40. Orchard to Stettinius, August 10, 1943, Box 171, RG 169; Stettinius to Acheson, August 30, 1943, Box 146, RG 169.

41. Watkins to Stettinius, September 24, 1943, Box 970, RG 169.

42. Knollenberg to Watkins, October 21, 1943, Box 972, RG 169.

43. Watkins to NAEB, October 29, 1943, Box 272, RG 169.

44. Christian Valensi, "Organization of the French Supply Council," November 15, 1943, Box 971, RG 169.

45. OLLA History: "Ships and Shipping," 56; Mitchell to Watkins, January 3, 1944, Box 3189, RG 169; Browne to Lorwin, January 4, 1944, Box 997, RG 169.

46. Mitchell to Watkins, January 3, 1944, Box 3189, RG 169.

6.

The Army Takes Control and Assistance Continues Throughout the War

One of the most important lessons that the Roosevelt administration learned from the North African experience was the deleterious effect that divided authority had on the operation. Roosevelt's assignment of responsibility for civilian affairs to the state department produced ill-defined directives that served to undermine any possibility of a smooth operation. The control given to the civilian agency frustrated the war department, whose chief spokesman, Henry Stimson, argued that only the army possessed the machinery and administrative force to undertake such a task. Despite strong evidence that military control would provide for more efficient administration, Roosevelt's misgivings over the role of the military in civilian affairs prevented him from officially sanctioning such an arrangement at an early date. It was not until a final, futile effort at maintaining civilian control collapsed that Roosevelt instructed the war department to assume the responsibility. In November 1943 Roosevelt informed Stimson that military control over civilian affairs in liberated areas would extend for a period of six months.

On January 8, 1943, in a letter to Assistant Secretary of War John McCloy, Roosevelt justified his decision by stressing that the occupation of North Africa was distinguishable from the ordinary occupation of a conquered territory. He pointed out that the United States was not at war with France and that the population of the French possessions had extended assistance in the effort to liberate France and her empire from the Axis. The president reinforced this distinction by noting that Eisenhower had not declared martial law, nor had he established a provisional government for the area. "On the contrary," Roosevelt asserted, "the situation has been one of cooperation between the American and French authorities. Local French governmental personnel have been allowed to continue in the performance of their functions in the customary manner, under an injunction of loyalty to the Commanding General and his forces."[1] The chief executive viewed the North African occupation as a friendly, cooperative venture and distinguished from occupied enemy areas with an unsympathetic population.

The war department, however, failed to share Roosevelt's point of view. In particular Henry Stimson, the secretary of war, disagreed and insisted that Eisenhower and the military cope with the problems of civilian administration in North Africa. In a memo to the president Stimson cited the historical precedents in Cuba and the Philippines, where the army performed this function. He argued that "no power exists in North Africa today except the military power of Eisenhower which is competent to deal with them without danger of a military defeat by the Germans." The secretary emphasized that the colonial arrangement made it unlike France in 1917, which possessed a homogeneous population and established traditions. "North Africa is subdivided into jealous factions and races susceptible to dangerous insurrections," Stimson contended, "unless they are held in check by the actual or potential power of the American Army." He asserted that such problems required Eisenhower's attention, and "he should not be by-passed by American agents reporting to separate agencies in D. C."[2]

At a meeting on February 11, 1943, with those immediately concerned with North Africa, Stimson's exasperation became most evident. The group consisted of Acheson from the state department, Lehman of OFRRO, and representatives from BEW, the treasury, and agriculture. They rejected the war department's point of view and confirmed Roosevelt's decision on the control of civilian affairs in North Africa. To Stimson the number of civilian agencies present attested to the "folly" of the entire arrangement. The state department, he claimed, had no machinery for this type of assignment and he predicted that "inevitable confusion will attend this bad administration of the President."[3] In Stimson's opinion no other agency except the military possessed a ready-made administrative force to handle such affairs.[4]

Within the civilian agencies there appeared some disagreement over the arrangement. On February 6 James Webb, the director of the Bureau of the Budget, had warned Roosevelt that the first sizable relief program encountered had demonstrated the possibility of a breakdown in American international operations. In summarizing the roles of the various agencies Webb pointed out: "BEW plans to rehabilitate and may develop; Lend-Lease plans, procures, finances and distributes; the Department of State plans and attempts to direct; the Army plans, administers and directs; all with respect to the same geographic area." The end result of this, Webb concluded, "is the confusion in the basic war jobs—the multiplicity of operating agencies—which complicates the task."[5]

At the meeting on February 11, however, Acheson defended the procedure while Lehman, still uncertain over the role of the OFRRO, saw nothing but chaos. Stimson had supported Lehman and described Hull as completely "at sea" as to what Lehman's duties included. The civilian agencies evidently had given little consideration to the army's role during the initial stages and did not discuss military government for such areas.[6]

The confusion that Stimson had described also became evident during congressional hearings, even to those not directly involved with North Africa. On February 26 in testimony before the House Foreign Affairs Committee Cox revealed that the OLLA had not as yet determined the amount of supplies to assign as relief. Their only decision on the matter was that Lehman's mission would collaborate with Murphy and Eisenhower, while the lend-lease staff dictated whether it was wise as a political and military necessity to make any supplies available on a relief basis. Should they reach such a decision, Cox informed the committee, Lehman's staff would supervise the distribution probably in coordination with the Red Cross.[7]

That conflicts would occur became apparent to Representative James W. Wadsworth of New York. In querying Stettinius he struck the fundamental issue: "It will be pretty difficult, Mr. Stettinius, won't it, to differentiate between military and political determination and relief determination in the same territory among the same people?" But Stettinius felt that such a sharp differentiation was unnecessary. "There is no clear line between sending such supplies in order to persuade the people to work for the Army and sending them in order to prevent public disaster of an epidemic or famine," he replied. Although Stettinius further described the close working relationship between the civilian representatives and the military, he actually evaded the basic issues that emerged with the divided responsibility.[8] Wadsworth's question revealed that he had quite accurately envisaged difficulties involved with two or more staffs dealing with the same problems.

The debate over the responsibility for civilian affairs continued unabated. Roosevelt, the OLLA, and the state department vigorously defended the arrangement, while the war department expressed bitter opposition. On March 28 Stimson wrote of Roosevelt: "He distrusted the Army (on such matters) and thought he could do it himself through other agencies."[9] At a conference on April 10 General Lucius Clay described the relationship between the OLLA and the army as a "mess." Clay contended that Murphy's political and military activities created confusion, and his interest in the political rather than the economic aspects of the operation handicapped it. Although Murphy was responsible to Eisenhower, Clay pointed out that the latter possessed no definitive directive to assume control over civilian affairs. Consequently Eisenhower focused his attention primarily on military operations. Moreover, Clay predicted that lend-lease would play no role in Tunisia, Italy, or any other enemy country distinguished from friendly liberated territory. In these areas, he argued, a military governor would control all the affairs and would remain in power with perhaps some civilian agency cooperating in relief and rehabilitation work.[10]

The campaign for Tunisia revealed the strength of the war department's position. In Tunisia the military assumed control over civilian affairs during the initial stages of the occupation. The assignment to the military, however, evolved by default rather than through an official presidential directive. At a meeting between the civilian agencies and the war department it became clear that the civilian agencies had determined that they could not at that time cope with civilian affairs in Tunisia. The OFRRO representative outlined the relief and rehabilitation task in Tunisia and concluded: "I assume that the initial operation of the program would be that of the Army, and in the next phase that of the French and North African Economic Board." Finletter of the state department and chairman of the Combined Committee for North Africa concurred that "the initial chaotic phase will be an Army problem."[11]

On March 18 Eisenhower received confirmation that "final determination by the War Department and United States governmental agencies is that planning and initial stages of operation of civilian relief in Tunisia will be strictly military responsibility. . . ."[12] The agreement set a period of ninety days for military control, although this "will of course vary with circumstances of each operation."[13] In order to handle civilian matters the army created a Civil Affairs Division under the direction of General John H. Hildring.[14]

Despite the acquiescence by the civilian agencies neither they nor Roosevelt favored military control as a permanent policy. In particular Stettinius objected to extensive or prolonged military control. Shortly after the fall of Tunisia he pointed out to Hopkins the "undesirability of separating Lend-Lease's responsibility for getting the funds for supplies to be used in liberated areas from the responsibility for distributing them." Furthermore he argued, "Tunisia is also likely to demonstrate that the concept of having the military control the distribution of civilian supplies for any length of time is a basic fallacy."[15] Stettinius also believed that future operations would duplicate the Tunisian experience of the enemy capitulating sooner than anticipated. Under such circumstances, he asserted, in terms of civilian supplies the procedure became less complex than in Algiers, Dakar, and Casablanca; such operations "can be more efficiently handled by the Lend-Lease Administration dealing with foreign governments than by the military."[16]

Still unwilling to accept military authority the president devised a scheme to insure overall civilian control. In a letter to Hull on June 3 Roosevelt enclosed a detailed plan for a new civilian organization. "Our civilian agencies," he asserted, "must be adequately prepared to assist our military forces in performing those services and activities in which they are expert. We must harness together the military and civilian efforts."[17]

The plan established within the state department the Office of Foreign Economic Coordination (OFEC) under the direction of Acheson for the purpose of facilitating interagency cooperation. To coordinate the civilian operations in each theater the secretary of state appointed an area director. The director functioned under two chains of command, Acheson and the military theater commander. The arrangement recognized the principle applied in Tunisia of the authority of the military during the early stages of operations.[18] But Roosevelt insisted, "It is equally essential that the transition from military to civilian operations in liberated areas be consummated as speedily and as quickly as possible."[19]

The OFEC Area Director Plan had little practical effect. Although they favored the principle of civilian control in their own operations, the British dealt it the first blow. They objected to the introduction of American civilians, who they felt might react in a more sensitive manner than army officials to controversial British political or economic policies. British opposition did not in itself destroy the plan. Rather, the OFEC failed because it proved incapable of fulfilling its purpose of improving and coordinating relations among the various agencies. Its only achievement was an agreement that extended the period of military responsibility from ninety days to six months.[20]

The president undertook a final effort to centralize civilian responsibility for foreign economic matters. On September 25 he created the Foreign Economic Administration (FEA) and appointed Leo Crowley as its director. The FEA represented a consolidation of OLLA, BEW, OFRRO, and OFEC into a single administrative unit. Yet from its inception the FEA fared little better than its components had. The FEA depended on the state department for policy determination, the War Shipping Administration for transportation, the War Production Board, the War Food Administration, and the treasury department for procurement.[21] But such an arrangement still failed to resolve a number of important difficulties. These became more complex with the increased necessity for organizing a common pool with the British and with the development of plans for postwar relief and international rehabilitation. In order to implement the latter Lehman became head of the newly founded United Nations Relief and Rehabilitation Administration in October 1943. However, since the organization possessed no funds and no machinery and concentrated its efforts on the postwar period, it offered no solutions to any immediate problems.[22]

By November it became evident to Roosevelt and his advisers that no civilian agency existed that could successfully cope with the expected relief burden once the Allies invaded the continent. Therefore on November 10 the president informed Stimson that while other agencies continued planning for liberated areas, "it is quite apparent that if prompt results are to be obtained, the Army will have to assume the initial burden of shipping and distributing relief supplies."[23] This official authorization delighted Stimson, who interpreted it as a vindication of the position he had upheld for over a year.[24] "His [Roosevelt's] experience with the

French Commission in North Africa," Stimson wrote, "has been so un-
favorable that he has come to the decision that the Army must be relied
on entirely." In regard to the French Stimson considered the president's
decision as timely and significant. He viewed the rivalry that had developed
between de Gaulle and Giraud as a "mess" and agreed with Hull's rejec-
tion of their requests for official recognition. Under such circumstances
Stimson deemed it vital for the military to deal with the French civilian
population.[25]

Despite Stimson's eager acceptance of the assignment, the army made
it quite clear that it intended to limit the scope of its assistance. During
the first six months the army asserted that it would provide food, fuel,
soap, and medical supplies, that is, only those items necessary to prevent
disease and unrest.[26]

The civilians with experience in the North African program severely
criticized the "disease and unrest formula." Harold Stein of the import
division noted that the army had derived its limited program from the following considerations: it was too inconvenient for the army to procure
standard goods; supplying other goods would pamper the population;
and civilian goods would compete with military procurement. He rejected these premises as utterly fallacious and argued that the experience
in North Africa revealed that such items as pots, pans, matches, and especially clothing were essential for the maintenance of minimum levels
of health and living conditions. In regard to possible competition between
military and civilian procurement Stein pointed out that excluding food,
civilian materials accounted for only 3 percent of the military program.
The omission of items such as agriculture and industrial equipment he regarded as "nothing short of catastrophic." In North Africa the food, textiles, and medical supplies arrived in sufficient quantities, but the delays
in the shipment of farm and industrial equipment produced such an adverse effect that in order for European programs to succeed, officials had
to eliminate this shortcoming. To do so Stein recommended that "the
planning and procurement of industrial and agricultural supplies must begin at the earliest possible moment." The North African experience, Stein
insisted, provided the justification for such supplies. Eisenhower had
created the NAEB and sanctioned the procurement of such goods in order
to achieve security, attain a certain level of production for the immediate
war effort, and conserve American and British supplies and shipping. Despite constant delays Stein felt that the NAEB had achieved partial suc-

cess in meeting these objectives. However, Stein concluded, had the Allies imposed limitations on imports during the first six months to include only the minimum army rations, standard medical units, and fuel, they would have failed to meet any of the objectives. The North African experience proved invaluable, and Stein recommended that the army's Civil Affairs Division include representatives from the NAEB. These men had acquired knowledge of French requirements and types of equipment that were more similar to European models than to American products.[27]

The civilian argument had only a slight impact on the military. After conferring with the civilian agencies the war department agreed in December to initiate plans for liberated areas in close collaboration with the FEA and the state department. Civilian officials desired to broaden the military program to include transportation equipment, utility repair items, clothing, shoes, seeds, fertilizer, and other agricultural supplies. Rehabilitation equipment for industry remained excluded from the military operation, and the civilians retained the responsibility for planning and procurement during the postmilitary period.[28]

Although Cutler expressed doubt that the military did a better job than the civilians, this appraisal seemed somewhat irrelevant.[29] Transferring the responsibility for the distribution of civilian supplies to the military eliminated the duplication and confusion that plagued the North African operation. Moreover it enabled the civilian agencies to spend more time planning and organizing their assistance. These agencies were not privy to secret strategic decisions; therefore, they never knew where the next invasion would take place until the actual attack began. The "military period" allowed the civilians to begin procurement and stockpiling of needed goods and thus to commence operations on a much more efficient level.

During the summer of 1943 France and the United States negotiated an arrangement to replace the hastily conceived Murphy-Bataille Agreement. Concluded on September 25, the *Modus Vivendi on Reciprocal Aid in French North and West Africa* provided the basis for the French lend-lease program for over a year. The accord officially confirmed the principle of French cash payment for civilian goods and stipulated that the French would pay the landed cost of such items. Despite the agreement and continued French payments it became evident that the French only reluctantly accepted the cash reimbursement arrangement. Nevertheless the United States presented regular billings and insisted on payment. By the end of 1943 the French owed more than $40 million. At the same time a controversy within the Roosevelt administration arose over the French program. A movement developed that proposed to transfer the French military lend-lease assistance from a credit to a cash basis. The money for this, its supporters argued, could come from the frozen French government funds. The state department opposed such a move and prevented its acceptance. The decision of the United States to demand cash payment for civilian goods was based on several considerations. As Livingston Short commented, "Before we went over we were instructed that the French had plenty of money so that the goods should be sold."[30] The United States argued that France, unlike England, possessed sufficient funds to pay for the goods. France's participation in the war was brief, and she had not incurred a huge financial debt. The immediate areas of concern, namely North and West Africa, had remained out of war almost entirely. Aside from this the United States acted on the assumption that the expenditures of the Allied forces, including the purchase of strategic and other materials, coupled with North African exports to other countries, would have a greater value than the French purchases of civilian lend-lease goods. The United States exempted military equipment from cash payment and provided this on a straight or credit lend-lease basis.[31] Such a policy placed a premium on the accuracy of pricing civilian goods. The Murphy-Bataille Agreement had fixed the price levels at those of November 8, 1942. Both the French and the Americans, however, regarded this as only temporary, and the United States sought to establish prices on a different basis. The "reasonable price" that they favored was "the landed cost of the goods including all charges borne by the seller up to and including delivery to the French purchasers in North Africa."[32]

Since the recommendation came during the early, unsettled stages of the program, the United States merely urged acceptance of it in principle. Obviously its application had to await the evolution of a more sophisticated and orderly shipping and documentation process. American officials believed the policy to be fair, provided that the costs contained no unusual factors. The United States also expressed a willingness to modify prices in individual instances should economic or political factors warrant it. If the French agreed to the landed cost as the basis for price determination, the United States informed them that they would furnish a list of prices for each commodity at the outset, subject to modification at fixed periods.[33]

American officials rejected the dollar exchange rate as a basis for the determination of price policy. Instead the United States preferred to determine pricing from the impact of inflation on the area, the standard of living of the natives, and the possibility of future economic fluctuations.[34] American policymakers desired that prices for goods be fair to the consumer and also emphasized a fundamental lend-lease principle that no country would garner excessive profits from the sale of lend-lease goods. In order to insure this the treasury periodically prepared financial statements that clarified the foreign exchange position of lend-lease recipients. From this analysis a committee composed of the vice-president, the secretaries of war, state, and treasury and representatives from the OLLA recommended the dollar exchange rate, which the countries should maintain. The committee's decision determined whether a country received civilian goods on a cash or credit basis.[35]

Even in the early stages of the program the cash-payment arrangement prompted serious objections. On March 3 Cox informed Cutler that he had presented a proposal to place all aid to North Africa on a straight lend-lease basis. He argued that the United States could furnish assistance on this basis with an understanding that the French would reciprocate with aid from their resources. "If transactions are allowed to get too financial, we are apt to end up by virtually paying rent for the trenches as in the dealings with France in the last war," Cox asserted. This he felt would do irreparable harm to the present and future programs, both publicly and politically.[36] Cox's position received little support, and as time passed the antithetical view that France should pay cash for both the military and civilian programs became more prevalent.

In the spring of 1943 the French payment arrangements went into effect. For the first six convoys the Murphy-Bataille Agreement provided the basis for pricing and payment. Instructions from Washington dictated that the French could provide payment through a franc check payable to the Bank of Algiers or to the treasurer of the United States for the OLLA account. The other approved method entailed the depositing of francs with the Bank of Algiers, which was a depository for American funds.[37]

In April Giraud presented American officials with a check for $15 million for civilian goods received during the period of November 8 to March 31. This first payment represented partial reimbursement for goods valued at $26.25 million. The French had not as yet distributed all the articles to the wholesalers, and a small portion of the supplies, in particular those for the children, had been distributed by the OFRRO through the Red Cross. The rest of the goods had proceeded through the normal commercial channels. In publicizing the assistance and the payment the administration purposely emphasized the hundreds of tons of seed provided to produce food for the Allied armies. The publicity aimed at maintaining close relations with the French but also at bolstering American public morale, which had already questioned the massive food program.[38]

In North Africa the civilian agents cooperated in publicizing the American effort and the French reimbursement. Even Murphy in his report for publication tempered his sarcasm: "It can now be revealed that the arrival of large shipments of flour and sugar from the United States helped to avert a food shortage which otherwise might have reached critical proportions in North Africa during the winter and early spring." Despite this achievement Murphy could not entirely refrain from a critical evaluation. "It should be emphasized," he added, "that imports have not yet reached North Africa in sufficient quantities to meet the population's industrial and agricultural demands."[39]

Other payments followed. On May 27 Stettinius informed Hopkins that he had received another $10 million from Giraud for civilian supplies valued at approximately $35 million.[40] The *New York Times* described the payment and pointed out that "Giraud is the only customer making cash payments."[41] From North Africa, however, Short reported that the French only reluctantly accepted the principle of cash reimbursement. His impression was that despite the American insistence on cash payment, the French continued to hope that the Americans would eventually transfer civilian supplies to a straight lend-lease basis. Short believed that his explanations as to why the United States required the French to pay cash were not entirely convincing. He reported that the French "still feel other nations are receiving more favorable treatment than they are." Short also pointed out that the failure to receive complete information on the landed cost of goods prevented any transfer form the Murphy-Bataille price basis.[42] Short informed Washington that the French had agreed to pay landed costs and to maintain a satisfactory price level provided the NAEB quoted them prices of the goods upon arrival. But the French were unwilling for the NAEB to continue to control retail prices if it failed to inform the French of their cost of the items. In the case of industrial equipment, price difficulties were not as complex. The NAEB knew upon arrival the landed cost of such items, and the French agreed to pay on this basis.[43] As a re-

sult of the difficulties over landed cost and the temporary nature of the
Murphy-Bataille Agreement, the United States and France commenced
negotiations for a more definitive understanding. In June 1943 representatives from the state, treasury, and OLLA opened discussions in Algiers
with a French delegation headed by Jean Monnet to sign a *modus vivendi*
or informal reciprocal aid agreement.[44]

Until the capitulation of France Monnet had served as the Allied chairman of the Anglo-French Coordinating Committee. Since then he had col-
laborated with the British Supply Mission in Washington and therefore was
thoroughly familiar with the activities of the combined boards. In February 1943 Roosevelt encouraged him to visit Algiers "because Monnet
knows a great deal about the whole problem of supply throughout the
world." Furthermore, the president commented, "I am sure also, that he
can be helpful to Murphy and Macmillan as well as Giraud in understanding the whole North African situation as viewed from here."[45] With the
formation of the FCNL in June, Monnet functioned as the commissariat
for armament, supplies, and reconstruction, and as the committee's chief
negotiator on such matters.[46]

Early in the discussions the United States drafted a statement outlining
the basic principles for any proposed agreement. In the final draft officials
amended it slightly, but did not alter its substance. In final form it stated,
"The provisions of this modus vivendi correspond to a desire to reduce
to an appropriate minimum the need of either party for currency of the
other party." The payment principle corresponded to the American position on France's ability to pay: "The provisions which call for payments
in dollars have been decided upon in view of the special situation arising
form accumulated dollar balances and availability of dollar funds due to
the presence of United States troops in French North and West Africa."
The United States made the payment principle conditional by providing
that "revision of the payment provisions of this modus vivendi will be
made should the situation require."[47]

During the discussions, however, the British had raised serious objections over the conditional nature of the cash payment. In their agreements to supply civilian goods to Allies the payment provision was unconditional and not intended to vary with the financial resources of a particular country. The American negotiators countered that their position
represented the keystone of lend-lease policy. They emphasized that it
was on this basis that the United States did not require the British to

make cash payments for civilian goods lend-leased to them. The Americans insisted that it was essential to treat the French on the same basis, especially since they requested an explanation as to why they had to provide cash reimbursement for civilian goods, while the British did not. American officials pointed out that the United States furnished assistance to both countries on the basis of need and contribution to the war effort. The conditions of payment, they insisted, varied according to the exchange balances of the recipient country. The Americans assured the French that should their exchange position deteriorate and decline to the level of the British, they would receive the identical treatment accorded the British.[48]

Although the negotiations progressed satisfactorily, a few issues caused a delay in the signing. The state department and the Combined Committee for North Africa insisted upon more discussion of the *Modus* in order to avoid future misunderstandings. These considerations took time since the overall agreement, they claimed, appeared complex. On this point there was little argument. The understanding covered five different arrangements: credit lend-lease, cash reimbursable lend-lease, reciprocal aid in kind, reciprocal aid in francs, and payment in francs as well as dollars. Aside from this, American policymakers insisted on including with the *Modus* a supplemental document stipulating "that nothing in the agreement shall be interpreted as precluding the early resumption of private trade when conditions permit."[49] Since the French presented no serious objections to this, the final issue settled was the French proposal to eliminate paragraph six from the *Modus*. The French had vigorously protested the six-month time limit that the paragraph placed on the agreement. Although the French expressed confidence that both sides could conclude a more inclusive and permanent agreement within that time, they argued that the limitation could raise serious questions. "Once the agreement is made public as it necessarily will be," Monnet warned, "the six month limitation upon the Modus for North Africa cannot escape attention. People will ask, for example, if, in case the general agreement is not concluded in a period of six months, the furnishing of material to the French Army would cease at this date." Furthermore, Monnet protested that similar American agreements with other countries contained no such time limitation.[50]

Murphy informed Hull of the determined stand the French had adopted and recommended acceptance of their proposal.[51] Consequently the United States agreed but stipulated, "Our government's willingness to proceed in this way is not to be taken as an indication that the terms of the Modus Vivendi can be completely incorporated in any ultimate overall Lend-Lease and Reciprocal Aid Agreement."[52] Thus, the United States adhered to its fundamental principle that until it recognized the FCNL as the official government of France, any agreement was temporary.[53]

The exclusion of paragraph six had significant ramifications. Evidently the perspicacious Monnet realized that due to the French political situation the refusal of the United States to recognize the de Gaulle government might continue indefinitely. This eliminated the possibility of an early conclusion of a permanent agreement. With a six-month limitation the French would have faced the possibility of losing assistance. Monnet's judgment proved accurate. It was not until February 1945 that both sides agreed to a permanent Master Lend-Lease Agreement.

On September 25 the American representative Robert Murphy initiated the *Modus Vivendi,* while René Massigli and Jean Monnet signed for the French Committee of National Liberation. The *Modus* satisfied both parties and provided the basis for United States-French lend-lease arrangements for over a year. The *Modus* officially confirmed the American policy of supplying military aid on a credit or straight lend-lease basis, while the French paid for their civilian goods. In return the French agreed to supply reciprocal aid or reverse lend-lease on both the military and civilian levels. The assistance consisted of military equipment, munitions, military and naval stores, and other services such as general materials and the use of railway and port facilities. The Americans paid cash for the civilian goods that they imported from North and West Africa. Two other important supplementary understandings, insisted upon by the United States, completed the accord. By these the French agreed to pay the landed cost for all civilian goods and also promised to maintain strict control over prices. They gave assurances of equitable distribution of imports, reasonable margins of profits, and prevention of speculation.[55] Thus, in theory at least, the French accepted the basic principle of lend-lease that no country should profit from it.

Although the agreement on landed cost represented a realistic approach based on the North African experience, much of the *Modus* revealed a naive idealism. "The desire to reduce to an appropriate minimum the needs of either party for the currency of the other" was virtually impossible to achieve. By September the United States had already begun to withdraw troops en masse for the campaigns in Sicily and Italy and thereby removed the major source of the North African dollar supply. It was also evident by this time that the value of reverse lend-lease would not approach the amount of assistance rendered by the United States. Moreover, the attitude of the United States toward continuing the cash reimbursement arrangement prevented any alteration in the liberal provisions of the *Modus*, which provided for cash payment on a conditional basis. Consequently the payment for civilian goods in cash depleted the French dollar supply.

Within the Roosevelt administration the question over the French financial position assumed major importance. The issue arose as to whether the French could continue to pay cash once the Allied troops had left. Also the prospect of Metropolitan France becoming a theater of operations necessitated a close examination of French assets, particularly the French funds frozen in the United States. It became evident that in order for the French to provide payment for civilian goods shipped to France and Northwest Africa, they would have to draw on these funds. This was no simple matter, however, since it brought up the question of the recognition of the FCNL as the official government of France. The state department argued that the funds belonged to France and not to the FCNL.[56]

The question over the use of the funds erupted into an interagency controversy between the state department and those who supported releasing the funds. On November 4 Secretary of the Treasury Henry Morgenthau proposed to the president that the French not only pay for the civilian goods but for their military supplies as well. He pointed out that the present arrangements rested on the assumption that the dollar and gold resources of the Central Bank and government of France were unavailable to the FCNL. "In our opinion," Morgenthau argued, "the use of these assets of France to pay for the equipping of a French Army on a credit lend-lease basis could easily be justified." Furthermore Morgenthau asserted that through September 1943 the United States had lend-leased $220 million worth of military goods and services to the French along with $74 million in civilian goods. According to Morgenthau's information the French held over $2.5 billion in gold and American dollars. The United States held all but $7 million of this amount for residents of Metropolitan France. In view of such large holdings Morgenthau recommended a reexamination of lend-lease to the French "with the idea of placing the entire program for the time being on a cash reimbursable basis." The secretary of the treasury believed that his proposals would

strengthen the United States' bargaining position with the French. Furthermore Morgenthau insisted that not only were his suggestions consistent with the objectives of lend-lease, but they also would assist in fulfilling congressional demands for a reduction of government expenditures.
Such a procedure was feasible, he noted, since the *Modus Vivendi* included
a provision for the payment of military supplies.[57]

Support for Morgenthau's position sprang from a number of sources.
Lauchlin Currie, an influential presidential adviser, wrote, "It would seem
silly to keep these assets locked up while we give them the goods. State
may object to recognizing the French Committee as owning the gold, but
a formula can be worked out."[58] On November 30 Crowley informed
Morgenthau that "we concur in the general policy outlined in your memorandum to the President." Crowley, like Currie, recognized that state
presented an obstacle but assured Morgenthau that "we are prepared to
join with you in presenting this position to the Secretary of State at the
appropriate time."[59] The support for such a drastic modification in the
French program proved extremely interesting, especially in light of Cox's
proposal in March to transfer the entire civilian program to a credit lend-
lease basis.

The discussions and considerations of Morgenthau's proposal by the
state department proved tedious and protracted. Nevertheless, whether
state accepted Morgenthau's suggestions or not, it was clear by this time
that Hull and his advisers had gravitated toward one basic principle of
Morgenthau's—the application of pressure on the French in order to insure payment. As of November 19 the French had paid a total of
$56,340,000. A month later Hull advised Watkins to consider a recent
reimbursement of $25,000,000 as partial payment for goods that had
arrived on the convoys through July. He also informed Watkins that
the agency had reached an agreement with the French on the value of
articles shipped between July and November. For North Africa this
amounted to $24,525,596, while for those goods sent to West Africa
the French owed $15,469,000. As of November 23, 1943, the French
debt for the civilian lend-lease supplies reached $40,000,000.[60] Hull
urged Watkins to present these costs to the French and asserted, "I see
no reason why the French should not pay immediately."[61]

Thus, by the end of 1943, the payment arrangement emerged as the
foremost controversial issue of the program. As Cox had accurately envisaged, the program approached the danger point of becoming "too

financial." And with the support for Morgenthau's recommendations the French could hardly look forward to relief from what they considered the burden of cash payments. Following the German collapse in Tunisia, the attention of the Allies shifted from North Africa to Europe. However, the need for civilian materials in North Africa continued, and the programs operated throughout 1944 and 1945. Robert M. Ferguson, chief of the American Economic Mission to North Africa, described the situation: "Although North Africa from a strictly strategic point of view has lost its importance in the war now going on, the Allied Economic Mission in North Africa has not lost sight of the fact that the civilian economy of this country must be maintained and supported."[62]

In November 1943, the French submitted their complete civilian requirements program for 1944, indicating the specific needs of each of these North African territories. The programs concentrated primarily on industrial and electrical equipment, which included internal combustion engines, compressors, motors, transformers, batteries, mining machinery, and household appliances. The requirements also included large quantities of agricultural equipment such as planting, seeding, and fertilizing machinery, plows, cultivators, grain binders, tractors, and various types of combines. The programs made no provision for textiles or wearing apparel other than shoes. Items such as cotton piece goods, toweling, and various types of clothing, including socks, underclothing, and suits for men and boys, were handled separately by the FEA through a textile expert stationed in North Africa.[63]

Although the North African operation had improved considerably, difficulties with the French continued. The French objected to the common-pool concept and insisted on employing North and West African goods solely for use in Metropolitan France rather than for the entire war effort.[64] However, the major controversy erupted over the failure of the French to keep their payments current. The issue also precipitated considerable interagency friction. The FEA felt that its discussions with the French failed to culminate in the desired conclusions. Thus, the agency urged the state department to impress upon the French the necessity of payment if the United States were to continue the program. On April 5, 1944, Cox reminded Eugene Rostow of the state department that the French had not furnished any payment since early January. He exhorted Rostow to initiate some measures for securing additional payments, as the gap between the amount of supplies provided and the payments received had widened enormously.[65] Rostow, evidently upset by the pressure, replied, "Stop needling me about this; they are about to accept our general plan, and what difference does it make."[66]

Generally, Rostow expressed the point of view of the state department— that it was unwilling to coerce the French at that time. Monnet had assured them that the French would mobilize their resources to meet the payments.[67] Moreover, Hull informed Morgenthau that he had not discussed with the French the disposition of the frozen funds of Metropolitan France. Furthermore, Hull had no intention of doing so unless the French raised the issue. "We are not prepared," Hull wrote, "to agree to the use of such funds in preference to other assets held in territories under the jurisdiction of the French Committee of National Liberation."[68]

The FEA authorities, who discussed the payments issue with representatives of the French Supply Council, continued to express alarm over the failure of the French to maintain a payment schedule. Following a meeting in April 1944 they described the French as "less than energetic and enterprising" in totaling and collecting their assets to meet obligations. They noted that such shortcomings seriously damaged American-French relations. By the end of April the FEA considered the French debt to have reached enormous proportions. As of April 31, 1944, the United States had transported 484,152,000 tons of civilian supplies valued at $127,317,340 to French North and West Africa. The French had provided payment for slightly less than half that amount and therefore owed approximately $65 million.[69] While the French promised to mobilize their resources and continue payments, American authorities grew impatient over French procrastination. In July Acheson expressed his displeasure to Valensi over the failure of the French to provide payment for over six months. He cited the *Modus Vivendi,* which stipulated that the French were to make payments "currently at convenient intervals." The outlook, however, for French reduction of their debt appeared bleak. In August, the FEA estimated that during 1944 the United States would export goods to North Africa valued at approximately $121 million while North Africa could export only $7 million worth of goods. In October, the French promised to pay $50 millionand on December 15, 1944, the French turned over this $50 million, which reduced the unpaid French balance to $50 million.[70] In early 1945 the French presented another payment. On March 12 the Office of War Information announced that the French Provisional Government had paid $40,000,000 against outstanding billings. This brought the total French payments for goods shipped between February 1943 and January 31, 1945, to $153,668,907, leaving approximately $31,000,000 unpaid and subject to future negotiation.[71] It represented the last French payment for North and West African goods prior to the termination of the program in July 1945.

Although civilian lend-lease assistance to North Africa sustained the economy, it never succeeded in fulfilling the more grandiose plans that American officials had designed. The most significant shortcoming was the failure to transform North Africa into the "breadbasket of Europe." In 1943 the United States exported thousands of tons of seed in order to restore agricultural production. In 1944 and 1945 the import programs revealed the concentrated effort to rehabilitate North African agriculture through the importation of farm machinery and spare parts. Unfortunately, these products were also in short supply in the United States. Thus, when the American farming interests became aware of plans to restore North African agriculture, the FEA found itself constantly pressed to justify its program. Crowley defended such assistance as essential to the war effort. He pointed out that "it is equally imperative that this food be produced to the fullest extent possible in areas where it is needed. This enables us to save valuable shipping space and to diminish the demands upon limited United States food supply."[72] Crowley also noted that the amount of agricultural supplies never reached the level that reports or rumors indicated. He considered it a very modest program and reported that as of June 30, 1944, the United States had provided only $2,000,000 worth of farm machinery and parts. This consisted of $1,236,000 of spare parts along with 514 combines and 112 tractors. To Crowley the extent of the assistance and the necessity of developing the area as a food producer for liberated Europe provided ample justification for the program.[73]

Despite a rather auspicious beginning North African agricultural production never realized its potential. Until December 1943 all the wheat shipped to Italy came from North Africa; but the 1943 harvest failed, and during the winter of 1943 to 1944 famine conditions threatened. Disaster also struck in 1945; natural conditions destroyed the grain crop, leaving a huge deficit for local requirements. However, by 1945 Europe had become the focal point for economic assistance, and there was little shipping available for North Africa. But in August 1945 the North African situation had deteriorated to such an extent that Monnet and the shipping authorities diverted six ships to North Africa from a convoy

destined for Metropolitan France.[74] Thus, after three years of economic
assistance, in the critical areas of food supply, North Africa appeared little better than when the Allies had arrived.

Although the North African Economic Board provided a satisfactory
working arrangement and had helped alleviate many of the early difficulties, in 1944 the Allies dissolved it. On May 31, 1944, the Allies created
the North African Joint Economic Mission (NAJEM) under the direction
of American and British joint chairmen, whose powers approximated
those of the former NAEB chairmen. The Policy Committee of the NAJEM
assumed the responsibility for the overall direction of operations and consisted of the joint chairmen, the heads of the North African Shipping
Board, American and British treasury representatives, and various economic advisers. The NAJEM functioned until December 31, 1944. The reasons
for its dissolution were twofold: First, the NAJEM had completed the
field work for the 1945 programs and could no longer justify a large staff.
In August the mission had submitted the entire North and West African
civilian programs to the French Division of the FEA. Secondly, the United
States believed that the closing of the mission would increase the pressure
on the French to restore private trade. The French expressed strong opposition to the move, but American authorities remained adamant.[75]

In order to maintain some economic assistance in the area the Americans and British created independent missions. The American Economic
Mission provided direction and advice, but as time passed its functions
lessened and the FEA began recalling its personnel. On October 25, 1945,
the mission closed and the few remaining FEA representatives fell under
the jurisdiction of the state department and became responsible to the
American consul.[76]

In relation to the war effort, the administration interpreted the North
African operation as a success. The essential North African services contributed heavily to the Tunisian Campaign and the invasions of Sicily,
Italy, and France. The French transferred to American and British forces
control over all the major ports, which the army claimed functioned with
an efficiency unknown even in prewar years. Military priorities governed
the railroads, telephone facilities, and power plants. The Allies converted
to military use other major industries, such as cement, cable, oxygen,
and welding plants. Furthermore, the Allies requisitioned innumerable
shops, garages, warehouses, hotels, larger stores and schools for billets
and headquarters. "The North African operation must be called a success," a state department expert commented. "As a vital link in our lines

of communications, particularly for Air Transport Command, and as a terminus for our sea lanes, North Africa more than lived up to expectations." Few would argue with his conclusion that "partly as a result of the civilian population sacrifices, our military forces were able to achieve a really outstanding efficiency in utilizing to the utmost North Africa's limited facilities."[77]

Yet only in a very qualified sense was the North African operation a success. The civilian supply program never attained its objectives. The sacrifice of the population, especially by the Arabs, was too great. As the same author pointed out, "the local population was left to shift for itself in a restricted economy which scarcely surpassed the subsistence levels."[78] But American civilian officials had planned and worked to achieve a higher level of economic well-being than merely subsistence. It was this obvious failure to provide for the population that frustrated men such as Murphy, Cutler, Short, and Watkins. Yet perhaps the civilians had expected too much from the first such endeavor, especially in territories where French domination, even during peacetime, had produced unhealthy economic conditions.

Nevertheless, the North African civilian program, under the cash reimbursement arrangement, cost the French millions of dollars, often embittered relations, and in the end produced minimal results. Moreover, the presence of American troops and civilian advisers with the introduction of American economic assistance loosened French colonial ties. Throughout the war the French regarded the Americans as a threat to their political and economic domination in Northwest Africa. But for the many Americans in North Africa sympathetic to the Arab cause, one of the more outstanding achievements of lend-lease—the rearming of the French—resulted in a tragic irony. Lend-lease military equipment in French hands thwarted Arab uprisings, and for a time at least, contributed to the preservation of French hegemony in North Africa.

NOTES

1. Roosevelt to McCloy, January 8, 1943, PSF, Roosevelt Papers.
2. Henry Stimson Diary, February 1, 1943, Sterling Library, Yale University, New Haven, Connecticut (hereafter referred to as Stimson Diary).
3. Ibid., February 11, 1943.
4. Ibid., March 28, 1943.

5. Coles and Weinberg, *Civil Affairs*, 60.

6. Stimson Diary, February 13, 1943.

7. Testimony before the House Foreign Affairs Committee, 78th Congress, 2nd Session, February 26, 1943, 43.

8. Ibid.

9. Stimson Diary, March 28, 1943.

10. Arthur Von Buskirk, "Meeting with General Lucius Clay," April 10, 1943, Box 145, RG 169.

11. Coles and Weinberg, *Civil Affairs*, 53-54.

12. Ibid., 54.

13. Ibid., 75.

14. Ibid., 63-64; Robert W. Coakley and Richard M. Leighton, *The United States Army in World War II: Global Logistics and Strategy, 1943-1945* (Washington, D. C.: Office of the Chief of Military History, Department of the Army, 1968), 743 (hereafter referred to as *Global Logistics and Strategy 1943-1945*).

15. Stettinius to Hopkins, May 24, 1943, Cox Papers.

16. Ibid.

17. Roosevelt to Hull, June 3, 1943, Official File 20, Roosevelt Papers.

18. Coles and Weinberg, *Civil Affairs*, 92; Coakley and Leighton, *Global Logistics and Strategy 1943-1945*, 746.

19. Roosevelt to Hull, June 3, 1943, Official File 20, Roosevelt Papers.

20. Coles and Weinberg, *Civil Affairs*, 93; Coakley and Leighton, *Global Logistics and Strategy 1943-1945*, 746.

21. Ibid.; Rosenman, ed., *Public Papers of FDR* 12, 406-11.

22. Coles and Weinberg, *Civil Affairs*, 93; Coakley and Leighton, *Global Logistics and Strategy 1943-1945*, 746.

23. Roosevelt to Stimson, November 10, 1943, Box 918, RG 169.

24. Stimson Diary, November 12, 1943.

25. Ibid., November 29, 1943.

26. Coles and Weinberg, *Civil Affairs*, 150-54; Coakley and Leighton, *Global Logistics and Strategy 1943-1945*, 754-55.

27. Stein to Reed, September 22, 1944, Box 2946, RG 169. Some of Stein's recommendations are also included in Coles and Weinberg, *Civil Affairs*, 151.

28. Coles and Weinberg, *Civil Affairs*, 150-54; Coakley and Leighton, *Global Logistics and Strategy 1943-1945*, 754-55. The civilian agencies, however, did little more than make suggestions, and the final decision on supply rested with the military. Stimson insisted that the army had no intention of developing assistance programs that went much beyond the disease and unrest formula.

29. Interview with Lloyd Cutler, May 26, 1972. Murphy felt that the decision was a wise one and agreed that only the military had the facili-

ties and means to carry out the civilian program during the early stages of liberation. (Interview with Robert Murphy, November 29, 1972).

30. Short, "Report on North Africa to the OLLA."

31. Hull to Eisenhower and Murphy, March 19, 1943, State Department Document 851R.24/46A, DNA; "Summary of the Activities of the Price and Distribution Section of the Import Division, March to November 1943," Box 59, RG 169.

32. Hull to Eisenhower and Murphy, March 19, 1943, State Department Document 851R.24/46A, DNA.

33. Ibid.; Eisenhower to War Department, April 21, 1943, Map Room, Roosevelt Papers.

34. Eisenhower to War Department, April 21, 1943, Map Room, Roosevelt Papers.

35. "Dollar Position of Lend-Lease Countries as of March 23, 1943," Box 211, RG 169. As of March 1943 Morocco and Algeria possessed a total of $80 million worth of gold and dollars. This consisted of $12 million in gold, $64 million in official dollars, and $4 million privately held dollars. At that time the United States had no information on the amount of gold in Fighting French territories but estimated that the areas had roughly $11 million.

36. Cox to Cutler, March 3, 1943, Box 87, RG 169.

37. "Statement of Lend-Lease Policy with Respect to Lend-Lease Aid and Prices at Which Civilian Goods Furnished Under Lend-Lease Shall Be Sold to the French Government in North and West Africa," April 24, 1943, Box 324, RG 169.

38. Office of War Information, Press Release, April 19, 1943, Stettinius Papers; Import Division to Brigadier General R. A. McClure, April 28, 1943, Stettinius Papers; New York Times, April 30, 1943, 4; NAEB "Report," May 21, 1943, Map Room, Roosevelt Papers.

39. Murphy to State Department, May 10, 1943, Stettinius Papers.

40. Stettinius to Hopkins, May 27, 1943, Box 144, RG 169.

41. New York Times, June 3, 1943, 4.

42. Short to Stettinius, May 24, 1943, Box 274, RG 169.

43. Short to Mitchell, July 31, 1943, Box 59, RG 169.

44. Oscar Cox, "American and British Lend-Lease Reciprocal Aid Negotiations with the French Committee of National Liberation," 1943, Cox Papers.

45. Roosevelt to Eisenhower, February 22, 1943, Hopkins Papers. Macmillan served with the rank of Minister on Eisenhower's staff.

46. Monnet to Royce, September 24, 1943, State Department Document 851R.24/138, DNA.

47. Cox, "American and British Lend-Lease"; Modus Vivendi for Reciprocal Aid in French North and West Africa, September 25, 1943 (here-

after referred to as *Modus Vivendi*). Copies of the agreement are in Box 59, RG 169, State Department Document 851R.24/138, DNA, and the Stettinius Papers.

48. Cox, "American and British Lend-Lease."

49. Frank Coe to Thomas Finletter, September 8, 1943, Box 763, RG 169.

50. Monnet to Royce, September 18, 1943, State Department Document 851R.24/138, DNA.

51. Murphy to Hull, September 18, 1943, State Department Document 851R.24/138, DNA.

52. Royce to Monnet, September 24, 1943, State Department Document 851R.24/138, DNA.

53. Combined Committee for North Africa, August 6, 1943, Box 973, RG 169; Ben W. Heineman, "Report on Reciprocal Aid Negotiations with the French," August 19, 1943, Box 973, RG 169.

54. *Modus Vivendi.*

55. Massigili and Monnet to Murphy, September 25, 1943, State Department Document 851R.24/138, DNA.

56. Stettinius to Roosevelt, November 4, 1943, Stettinius Papers; Lauchlin Currie to Crowley, November 23, 1943, Box 763, RG 169; Crowley to Morgenthau, November 30, 1943, Box 763, RG 169.

57. Morgenthau Diary, November 4, 1943. For a breakdown of these assets and their location, *see* Appendix 6.

58. Currie to Crowley, November 23, 1943, Box 763, RG 169.

59. Crowley to Morgenthau, November 30, 1943, Box 763, RG 169.

60. *New York Times,* November 19, 1943, 6. Hull to Ralph Watkins, December 17, 1943, Box 361, RG 169.

61. Hull to Watkins, December 17, 1943, Box 361, RG 169.

62. "Statement of Robert Ferguson," June 30, 1944, State Department Document 851.24/444, DNA.

63. OLLA History: "France and the French Empire," Box 3219, RG 169, 62-66; "French North African Supply Program for 1944," November 20, 1943, Box 3220, RG 169. The program comprised 576,661,270 tons with a value of $94,657,178.80. The NAEB also submitted the program for West Africa. *See* "French West Africa Program for 1944," n.d., Box 3221, RG 169. This program totaled 84,259 tons valued at $42,420,375. Both of these programs included all the required detail and afford an excellent insight into the magnitude of the assistance.

64. There is extensive correspondence and reports on the stockpiling issue. The most revealing are: FEA, "Conversation with the French," December 7, 1943, Box 763, RG 169; *New York Times,* March 27, 1944, 5; FEA, Information Bulletin, "Stockpiling Discussions in North Africa," Box 763, RG 169; Hull to Chapin, December 24, 1944, Box 461, RG 169.

65. Cox to Rostow, April 5, 1944, Box 1169, RG 169; James McCamy to Currie, April 7, 1944, Box 763, RG 169.

66. Rostow to Cox, April 6, 1944, Box 1169, RG 169.

67. Emerson to Currie, April 6, 1944, Box 975, RG 169.

68. Hull to Morgenthau, April 6, 1944, Morgenthau Diary.

69. Emerson to Thayer, "Meeting between Valensi, Beaulieu, Hannigan and Kahn," April 30, 1944, Box 969, RG 169; FEA, "Recapitulation of Shipments and Payments as of April 31, 1944," Box 969, RG 169.

70. The records are replete with correspondence and reports on the matter. The following are of most interest: Valensi to Acheson, June 28, 1944, Box 813, RG 169; Robert Ferguson, "American Aid to North Africa," June 30, 1944, State Department Document 851.24/444, DNA; Acheson to Valensi, July 17, 1944, Box 813, RG 169; FEA, "Economic Progress with Reference to French North Africa," August 8, 1944, Box 808, RG 169; Crowley to Morgenthau, September 18, October 5, 1944, Morgenthau Diary; Morgenthau to Crowley, October 6, 1944, Morgenthau Diary.

71. Office of War Information, Press Release, March 12, 1945, Cox Papers; Cox to Clayton, March 29, 1945, Box 860, RG 169; Crowley to Morgenthau, March 30, 1945, Box 860, RG 169.

72. Crowley to Burdick, August 30, 1944, Box 1169, RG 169.

73. Crowley to Mills, June 13, 1944, Box 1170, RG 160; Crowley to Marion T. Bennett, October 24, 1944, Box 808, RG 169; Crowley to Vandenberg, October 24, 1944, Box 808, RG 169. These are replies to criticisms of excess supplies being shipped to North Africa at a time when the American farmer had extreme difficulty procuring parts and equipment.

74. Leighton and Coakley, *Global Logistics and Strategy 1943-1945*, 759; McVey to Leroy-Beaulieu, August 2, 1945, and Beaulieu to McVey, August 10, 1945, both in Box 808, RG 169.

75. OLLA History: "France and the French Empire," 283; *New York Times*, January 6, 1945, 6. The NAEB produced two outstanding guides for future supply programs. They included detailed specifications of articles considered essential for all liberated areas. See Cutler, "Manual of Operations" and "Catalogue for Liberated Areas," n.d., Boxes 173 and and 3220, RG 169. Strong recommendations for the dissolution of the NAJEM are in Smith to Crowley, September 6, 1944, Box 464, RG 169, and Ferguson to Crowley, October 5, 1944, Box 975, RG 169.

76. OLLA History: "France and the French Empire," 83.

77. Camden McVey, "An American's View of France," *State Department Bulletin* 13 (October 7, 1945), 524-25.

78. Ibid.

7.

Arab Nationalism
and the United States

From the very beginning of the economic aid program the United States
encountered a most serious, unforeseen and unresolvable difficulty; and
its consequences for the United States were pervasive and enduring. By
providing material goods the United States unintentionally undermined
the already weakened French hold on North Africa. The natives, who
chafed under French rule, witnessed American generosity and power,
and as the Arab nationalist movement developed, they looked to their
American benefactors for support in lifting the yoke of French colonialism. Once the Allies had driven out the Nazis, the situation became more
complex. The French returned, and determined to gain control, launched
a series of reprisals that appalled many American and British observers.
Since the war took precedence, the American policy was to continue
economic aid, appease the French, and leave internal political matters
in French hands. Those Americans in French North Africa who sympa-
thized with the Arab Cause strongly believed that the Atlantic Charter
and the Four Freedoms should include the Arabs of Morocco, Algeria,
and Tunisia. Despite persuasive arguments that the United States had a
moral responsibility for the future status of the natives, American policymakers warned their representatives against involvement with the nationalists. Unfortunately, the ramifications of the movement eluded most Washington officials, and by the end of the war, as Allied troops departed, the
United States had lost much of the prestige it had acquired from 1941
to 1943.

The Arabs no longer considered the Americans their liberators but
rather the saviors of the French empire who were responsible for the

restoration of French power. For the United States the experience represented one of a number of lost opportunities to retain and expand its influence in an important part of the third world. By refusing to take the initiative in North African political matters, the United States became identified with the anachronistic colonial system. More importantly, by failing to understand the nationalist movement, the United States easily confused it in postwar years with the communist force and opposed it. Thus for over thirty years American policies in this and other colonial areas remained confused and ineffective.

As early as 1941 there were strong indications that by providing economic assistance to the Arabs while trying to prevent the dissolution of the French empire, the United States faced a vexatious problem. As the American consuls circulated through North Africa, they learned that the Arabs' inveterate dislike of the French had increased as the wartime conditions created acute shortages of food, clothing, and other necessities. Three American consuls, Harry Woodruff and Hooker Doolittle in Tunisia, and Kenneth Pendar in Marrakech, developed extensive contacts with the natives and became aware of their intense dissatisfaction with French rule. Moulay Larbi, the judicial khalifa of the pasha of Marrakech and a cousin of the sultan, told Pendar that under French control the Arabs had suffered greatly and had made little progress. A few days later Ahmed Bennani, secretary to the grand vizier of the sultan, hinted that at some time the sultan would request American protection. Both Larbi and Bennani implied that Morrocans would welcome the establishment of an American protectorate.[1]

In Tunisia Doolittle encountered similar sentiments. The Tunisian nationalists derived satisfaction from the French collapse and viewed it as the first step in the liberation of North Africa. Woodruff, who spent eighteen months in Tunis before the invasion, reported that the overwhelming majority of his contacts had no sympathy for the French. Moreover, the Arabs expressed their admiration for American ideals, valued the economic aid, and looked forward to future collaboration in diplomatic and political matters.[2]

The French, keenly aware of their awkward—if not untenable—position, could hardly overlook the effects of American influence on the Arabs. And although the economic assistance furnished through the Murphy-Weygand Agreement fell far short of its anticipated goal, it nevertheless revealed to the natives American generosity, wealth, and more importantly, power. The French, of course, felt threatened from both sides. The Nazis had destroyed their power and prestige on the continent and were undermining their North African empire while the United States was providing goods that the French were unable to supply, thereby exposing more French weaknesses. Appearing in the worse light possible, the French reaction was intense and bitter. A number of ranking officials went so far as to condemn the Murphy-Weygand Agreement as a mistake that had eroded French influence; they feared that the United States would use it to turn the natives against them.[3]

French trepidations and complaints filled pages of state-department documents, and the consuls, especially Doolittle, were constantly forced to defend themselves against French charges. In May 1942 J. Rives Childs informed Hull that the general unrest among the Arabs had caused the French to become "increasingly sensitive to foreign intermixtion with the Arabs," and that the situation is such at present that any foreign contact with the native population other than the most casual is believed impossible without political repercussions."[4] Thus, by November 1942 the Americans in North Africa were in an unusual, if not ludicrous, situation; they had aroused the suspicions of the French and Nazis, and agents of both countries closely followed them.[5]

From the outset the Allies realized that a successful campaign depended to a large extent on native cooperation. The consuls' groundwork, despite French interference, and the economic aid that reached the areas had a considerable influence on the natives. They made common cause with the Americans, and a large number of Moroccan troops joined Allied units. The members of the Permanent Council of War Economy, which represented Algerians, Moroccans, and West Africans, pledged their loyalty to the Allied cause, and Arab leaders requrested more Anglo-American aid to ensure the natives' economic well-being. Such assistance, they argued, could be carried out "within the framework of the Atlantic Charter."[6] However, in Morocco, which for years had been a center of Arab nationalism, the American arrival elevated the hopes of Sultan Mohammed V, and his expectations reflected a literal interpretation of the Atlantic Charter rather than mere promises of economic aid. Unfortunately Roosevelt was almost totally ignorant of the significance of the nationalist movement and further upset the precarious French-Arab balance.

While waiting for de Gaulle to arrive in Casablanca, the president gave a dinner party on January 22, 1943, for the sultan; it became one of the most famous and long-remembered dinners of World War II. Roosevelt and the sultan engaged in a lengthy conversation during which, according to American sources, they discussed Morocco's wealth and resources. FDR suggested training Moroccans in the United States and also the possibility of American contributions to the economic development of Morocco. When the conversation ended, the sultan announced: "A new future for my country."[7]

Both sides, however, interpreted the conversation differently. The Arabs claimed that Roosevelt had guaranteed American support for Moroccan independence after the war, and this interpretation remained with Arab leaders for years. As late as 1961 King Hassan stated "If he [Roosevelt] had not died, the United States would not have failed to accelerate the process of liberation in Morocco."[8] What specific promises, if any, Roosevelt made may never be known, but it is clear that by 1943 Moroccan leaders considered independence a distinct possibility and viewed the United States as a means to that end. As Lloyd Cutler pointed out, about this time a high-ranking Arab told him to inform Roosevelt that Morocco desired to become the forty-ninth state.[9]

Allied troops were not in North Africa very long when the Arabs made specific overtures. In May 1943 Hull informed H. Earle Russell, the American consul general in Casablanca, that the sultan was insisting that since the French were no longer able to ensure Morocco's protection, as stipulated in the Protectorate Treaty of 1912 and recognized by the United States, the protectorate was no longer valid. But because Morocco was, as yet, unable to handle complete independence, the sultan recommended that the United States, England, France, and possibly Spain administer the protectorate. However, according to Hull the United States would not take any steps to alter the political status of Morocco; after consulting with the British both agreed that such a move would increase French resentment and destroy whatever French prestige was left in Morocco.[10]

The North African dilemma became increasingly difficult to resolve. In a letter to Hull, Murphy clearly summarized it: "There is no doubt in my mind that, as a result of the friendly treatment given by the American military authorities to the Moroccan Arabs, we may count on their friendship. At the same time there is also little doubt of their growing hope that the United States may intervene in their behalf to relieve them from the French protectorate." Although he did not foresee such a demand until the cessation of hostilities, it was clear to Murphy that Arab plans included American assistance in future political adjustments. For the most part Moroccan leaders' conversations followed a similar theme; they complained bitterly of French treatment and urged the Americans to adhere to the principles of the Atlantic Charter.[11]

The situation worsened once Allied military control was complete. The French returned and did nothing to regain native support. Throughout the area, first in Morocco and Algeria and later in Tunisia, the French responded with vicious reprisals. Despite the sultan's cooperation, the French acted on the supposition that only harsh measures would discourage the Moroccans from seeking outside support to gain their political objectives. But such tactics only hardened the resistance and increased the attractiveness of the Nationalist Party, which had discarded its program of gradual reform and instead sought rapid and unequivocal independence. Moreover, the French measures were an affront to British and American representatives who had already observed the sordid Arab living conditions.[12]

The question of how to handle the explosive issue of French control and Arab nationalism led to such a division within the state department that the matter eventually reached the president. At the center of the controversy was Hooker Doolittle, whose reports had infuriated the French and prompted their demands for his dismissal. On the other hand his comments forced the United States to reconsider its policy. From the outset it was evident that Doolittle and his supporters held views diametrically opposed to those of Murphy. Doolittle, whose tour of duty in North Africa began in 1933, was more disposed to sympathize with the native cause than Murphy, who endeavored to maintain a rigid objective policy that avoided, as much as possible, native ambitions and left these matters in French hands.[13] Doolittle's reports were devastating and could not be ignored by the state department. Shortly after the liberation of Tunisia he wrote to Hull: "The French military administration in which few changes in mentality or efficiency are to be observed came into Tunisia in a spirit of revenge for their three years of humiliation." According to Doolittle the French colonial administration chose the "Arabs of Tunisia, their Bey and childish attempts at nationalism," as the scapegoat for their incompetence. Furthermore, as he pointed out, the Arabs were not responsible for the German occupation of Tunisia. Indeed, it was two French administrators, Admiral Esteva and General Barre, who permitted the German entry, and it was the French, Doolittle argued, not the bey's government, that had requisitioned food, animals, and conscripted Tunisian labor. Through residential orders Admiral Esteva had effectively established the Germans. Doolittle feared the loss of the prestige the United States had acquired, due to associations with the French. The actions of the French, Doolittle pointed out, "have made the Tunisians more unanimous than formerly in detesting them."[14]

In replying to Doolittle's charges Murphy expressed the official American policy. The United States would not deliberately upset the political status quo nor interfere with the war effort. As Murphy explained the situation, it was not a matter of choosing between the French and the Arabs; the United States, he informed Doolittle, desired "the complete cooperation of the French in all fields and that, you will agree, is more important than the position of the Bey as long as the Protectorate is maintained."[15]

It was not long until Doolittle became one of the most talked about figures in North Africa. Murphy described him as an active partisan and reported that Doolittle's main contacts were with the Tunisian Destour Party, which advocated increased Arab autonomy, better treatment of the population, and eventual independence. Doolittle, however, held similar views for all the North African Arabs. His convictions rested on the firm belief that American statements concerning the Four Freedoms and the Atlantic Charter should include the Arabs, and he believed, as Murphy explained, that "it is our duty to compel the French to act accordingly."[16] To Murphy, however, the Arab question was for the French to resolve, but Doolittle insisted that the United States could not avoid the responsibility for French policy and, more importantly, that since the Arab problem had serious postwar consequences, the solutions should not be based solely on wartime expediency.[17] In the end Doolittle's fate revealed the extent to which the United States went to placate the French. General Charles Mast, the French resident general in Tunis, officially protested Doolittle's behavior, and in conversations with Murphy, Eisenhower, and his Chief of Staff, Major General Walter Bedell Smith, Mast described Doolittle as a threat to French interests and security. Both Eisenhower and Smith agreed that Doolittle had sufficiently upset the French to warrant his removal, and Eisenhower requested that Doolittle's successor be "well balanced and intelligent."[18]

However, Doolittle was not alone in his appraisal of French policy. In October 1943 Wallace Murray brought to the attention of Stettinius a lengthy report prepared by Gordon Browne, a former control officer and OSS operative. Browne's conclusions disturbed Murray enough for him to write: "I think you [Stettinius] will agree with me that when the views held by such persons as Gordon Browne and Hooker Doolittle become current in this country we shall be subjected to rather severe criticism if it is found that we have ignored altogether the principles of the Atlantic Charter and the four freedoms in dealing with these areas."[19]

Browne's report supported Doolittle's arguments and, in some respects, went beyond them. In his opinion French actions had jeopardized American credibility. Prior to the invasion the Arabs had respected the United States, and following it they had become in Browne's words, "violently pro-American." But once the French were reestablished, Arab doubts about the Americans arose. The French sought out and imprisoned Moroccans who had American contacts, and American goods were distributed only through the French. "The suspicion that they are the victims of a gigantic hoax by the American government," Browne wrote, "is beginning to form in the minds of the more educated Moroccans." Browne recognized the consequences of American identification with the sadistic French policies and recommended some positive action by the United States that would ensure a pro-American attitude for generations. He warned, moreover, that "if we choose to ignore their plight, to omit them from the Four Freedoms and the Atlantic Charter, they will be anti-American and will look to Russia for political relief."[20]

Among the ranking American officials Stettinius appeared most sensitive to the reports on French reprisals. In a memorandum to Roosevelt he described French abuse of the Arabs as harsh and repressive, and he argued, "Our assumption of military power in North Africa makes us seem at least morally responsible for present conditions." He also noted that the French refused to permit the printing of a single Arab newspaper and had recently prevented the *Readers Digest* from introducing a new Arabic edition into the area. Stettinius feared, as did Browne and Doolittle, the loss of American influence, and he urged Roosevelt to meet with Doolittle, whom the state department had recalled from Tunis.[21]

The cordial meeting between Roosevelt and Doolittle afforded the president an insight into North African affairs that he had not previously had. The president mentioned Archie Roosevelt who, like Doolittle, had been transferred from North Africa because of his pro-Arab tendencies. Doolittle explained that their pro-Arab inclinations stemmed from the

simple desire to see the Arabs treated decently. The meeting evidently
satisfied Doolittle. He believed that FDR had received sufficient information concerning North Africa, and he was pleased that the president had
made a careful distinction between Algeria, where the French were so
entrenched, and the two protectorates, for which the idea of an international trusteeship interested him.[22] The meeting also had special importance. The president had received a first-hand account of the French
colonial system from one of the most experienced diplomats in North
African matters. Certainly by 1944 Roosevelt and his advisers possessed
a wealth of information from which to determine future policy. Unfortunately American diplomats, chained to anachronistic concepts of world
power, failed to grasp the significance of most of it.

The state department showed increasing concern as descriptions of
French abuses continued to arrive. American officials in North Africa
attributed the native unrest and minor disturbances to French policies,
and Stettinius, acting for Hull, informed the French that the political,
social, and economic conditions of North Africa were of great importance
to the United States. Although he told American diplomats to refrain
from public criticism, he nevertheless instructed them to make it clear
to the French that American interest in the natives would continue.
Stettinius also deplored Doolittle's removal, which Murphy had arranged
under intense pressure. Meanwhile the French, wedded to previous colonial policies, constantly sought scapegoats for their own ineptitude. In January 1944 the search reached familiar ground. In discussing recent disturbances in Fez, General Pruax, the resident general of Morocco, asked
Childs, the American chargé, if Doolittle had any part in it. The stunned
Childs replied that he did not see how it was possible because Doolittle
was in Cairo.[23]

Throughout 1944 the strength of the nationalist movement showed
no signs of diminishing, and the Americans became painfully aware of
Arab intentions to deeply involve both the United States and England.
At the same time American policy revealed little flexibility. The war,
of course, took precedence, and the Allies were determined not to alienate
the French over the native issue. Thus the policy that Murphy had recommended and that the United States had followed from 1942 to 1943
was not drastically altered from 1944 to 1945. On occasion the Americans protested French abuses, attempted to pacify the recalcitrant Arabs,
and insisted that at a later date only the French should determine the

political settlements. But the growing French-Arab conflict forced the United States and Great Britain to make public statements on the matter. The British pointed out that, like the Americans, they had made commitments relative to maintaining French sovereignty in North Africa. They referred to a 1943 statement made by the Lord Privy Seal in the House of Commons: "North Africa is French Territory; the relationship is not that of an occupying power toward a local authority of an occupied region." In citing past statements both countries selected those that emphasized that they had no intention of annexing French territory and, by implication, no desire to dismantle the French colonial structure.[24]

During 1944 the Arabs lobbied extensively to explain their cause and gain support. In Morocco the sultan was furious over a proposal in the Algiers Consultative Assembly that called for the unification of Morocco with Algeria and Tunisia. To the Moroccans such a union was unthinkable. But at the time the American consul general in Casablanca saw little hope for the Moroccan nationalists unless they received support from the United States and Great Britain. He concluded, however, that Arab hopes remained alive because they simply believed that after spending so much money the United States would use this as an "excuse" to either annex the territory or to play an influential role in its administration. His report to Washington did little for the Arabs; he recommended discouraging them so that they would be less demanding at a time when the prosecution of the war was the foremost concern.[25]

In Tunisia the situation was similar. The bey of Tunis wrote King Ibn Saud of Saudi Arabia of his interest in the Pan-Arab Movement and expressed a desire to see the North Africans united in a federation that would become part of the "Union of the Arab World." He further stated that the Allies had the entire support of the Arabs, and he looked forward to Allied aid that "will be precious to us in rapidly realizing great progress as regards our autonomy."[26]

By July 1944 there was little change. In Morocco the relations between the French and natives remained confused and strained. The Black Market, the forced requisition of Arab farm products, the rampant discrimination in the distribution of American aid, and the constant nationalist agitation all contributed to the instability. In Tunisia and Algeria the conditions were no better. More importantly, no solution appeared in sight. Too many of the ramifications of the nationalist movement remained a mystery to the state department, and reports to and from North Africa revealed a willingness to accept the continued French explanations that outside forces—at first the Nazis and later the communists—were responsible for the turmoil among the natives.[27]

In addition the United States faced continued French animosity and distrust. A 1944 OSS report accused the French government's higher echelon of preventing the natives from identifying the United States and England as the sources of economic assistance. To counteract the anti-American propaganda the Office of War Information published in local North African newspapers statistical evidence on the supply of foodstuffs and other commodities. But the effort was far from successful, and C. Burke Elbrick, a state department officer at Tangier, urged a more extensive campaign to identify the nature and scope of American aid.[28]

By the final year of the war the Allies had not settled any of the important questions raised by the Arab nationalists. Although during the war the movement appeared strongest in Morocco, its most violent expression occurred in Algeria. In early 1945 there was no evidence that Arab unrest in Algeria differed considerably, either in form or intensity, from that in Morocco or Tunisia, but as the war in Europe came to a halt, the Algerians grew more restless, more political, and finally engaged in bloody rioting in which thousands lost their lives. In March 1945 the Algerians sent to the American Legation two documents summarizing French-Algerian relations and calling for specific reforms. Most importantly, they demanded the "cessation of all attempts of incorporating Algerian Arabs in the French nation" and urged other democratic nations to support Algerian liberation and sovereignty.[29] There was nothing unusual in these proposals and, in fact, they were similar to Moroccan and Tunisian demands. Nevertheless, on May 8, 1945, as Truman announced the German surrender, rioting erupted in Algeria. The most serious took place in Setif, where the mayor, other officials, and scores of Europeans perished. The French retaliated swiftly, but for several weeks the disturbances spread throughout the county. On May 22 the British reported that six thousand natives had lost their lives and another fourteen thousand were wounded. Although the rioting ceased by the end of May, French reprisals and the controversy over the casualty reports did little to solve the explosive situation.[30] The intensity of the native uprising and the ferocity of French suppression demonstrated the determination of both sides. Furthermore, it revealed to all concerned that France had no intention of radically altering her North African empire and, at best, would sanction only minor reforms.

However, armed with the Atlantic Charter the Arabs looked to the postwar conferences for relief. But their cause suffered a setback when the Allies refused to recognize Morocco as an independent nation. Moreover, the United Nations turned down Morocco's request for admission, and Moselm confidence in the United States began to disappear. An observer pointed out that they were angered by the departure of American troops and no longer viewed the Americans as their liberators.[31]

Despite these reversals there were some encouraging developments for the nationalists. During 1945 the Arab League became stronger, and its secretary demanded for Algeria and Tunisia "the right to attach themselves to the Arab League" and "the freedom to express their own views on their future status."[32] The league also shared the North African natives' assumption that in some way the United States had a moral responsibility for their fate. Abdul Rahman Azzam Bey, the secretary general of the league, voiced his concern over the oppression in Algeria. Like others, Bey interpreted the American triumph as a victory for France, since it saved her North African possessions and reestablished French domination.[33] Bey's charges that the French were responsible for the imprisonment and death of thousands of Arabs troubled Joseph Grew, who informed the French that the situation in Algiers "is a source of anxiety not only to this government but to American public opinion which is deeply conscious of the sacrifices in American lives and material expended in the liberation of North Africa and of subsequent economic aid given to and planned for that area."[34]

Evidently the French paid little attention to American protests. An article in the Rouen daily newspaper, *Normandie,* implied that the United States had contributed to the Algerian uprising. In September 1945 Paul Alling learned from Moulay Larbi that French jealousies and suspicions of the United States had increased. He cited the hostile French reaction to a visit the sultan made to the United States airfield at Marrakech. The resident general had become furious with the sultan for failing to notify him and for going without a French escort. Finally in the fall of 1945 French paranoia reached a ludicrous level. The counselor of the French embassy charged that Doolittle was still encouraging the Tunisian nationalists. This time the French also included his wife and accused both of assisting nationalist leaders. After an investigation the state department described the accusation as absurd.[35] The French, still in search of scapegoats, had fallen back on an old reliable.

It remains difficut to determine whether the United States could have helped prevent the bitter struggle for independence that marked the postwar history of these countries. The preoccupation with the war and the decision not to become involved in North African internal political affairs ruled against American influence at a time when it could have been most effective. The ideal sought in North Africa was security and tranquility while the Allies moved into Europe. And certainly Roosevelt, though he vacillated on the restoration of the French in Indochina, gave no indication that he would support an effort to alter the French North African empire.[36]

The shortcoming of American policymakers, however, was their failure to perceive the impact of the war in broader terms. The Americans did not recognize that the war was having as great an impact on many colonial areas as it was on Europe. Specifically, too few carefully analyzed the nationalistic movement, its long-term implications, and America's relation to it. The United States failed to gauge the deeply rooted native dislike of the French and the irreparable harm done to French prestige. Moreover, neither the military nor the state department clearly thought through the ramifications of liberating North Africa. The plans were all too simple; once the Nazis were defeated, the French would restore political order. The real unforeseen threats, as it turned out, were not only the nationalists but the oppressive tactics employed by the French to curb them. For the state department a situation developed similar to that in China and later Indochina. Those who best knew the countries and recommended far-reaching policies, which included more native self-determination, lost the argument and had to stand aside as the French meted out their vengeance. Once the French realized their inability to cope with the problems, they searched for excuses, and none was more convenient than communism.[37] For Americans this explanation distorted the entire North African picture. As long as the French blamed native unrest on communist influences and those Americans who understood the nationalist movement were virtually ignored, the United States, facing what was viewed as a choice between the communists and a friendly power, supported the latter. Thus a policy hastily and poorly conceived during the war and not drastically altered in the immediate postwar years was responsible for American failures in much of the third world for almost three decades.

NOTES

1. Leon Borden Blair, "Amateurs in Diplomacy: The American Vice Consuls in North Africa 1941-1943," *Historian* 35 (August 1973), 615. Blair's article is one of the best objective treatments of the Americans, especially those under Murphy. For a general history of Morocco *see* Blair, *Western Window in the Arab World* (Austin, Tex., University of Texas Press, 1970).

2. Ibid., 616. *See also* Doolittle to Alling, May 9, 1942, State Department Document 851S.00/209 PS/ET and attached letter to Murphy dated March 17, 1942. Both offer details on the Arabs' dislike of the French and the reasons for it. Also Doolittle points out that neither he nor the other Americans encouraged Arab hatred for the French; it existed long before the Americans arrived. For general coverage of Arab nationalism *see:* Nevill Barbour (ed.), *A Survey of North West Africa* (New York: Oxford University Press, 1962): Lorna Hahn, *North Africa: Nationalism to Nationhood* (Washington, D. C.: Washington Public Affairs Press, 1960); Douglas Ashford, *Political Change in Morocco* (Princeton, N. J.: Princeton University Press, 1961); Richard M. Brace, *Morocco—Algeria—Tunisia* (Englewood Cliffs, N. J.: Prentice Hall, 1964); John P. Halstead, *Rebirth of a Nation: The Origins and Rise of Moroccan Nationalism, 1912-1944* (Cambridge, Mass.: Harvard University Press, 1967); Dwight Ling, *Tunisia: From Protectorate to Republic* (Bloomington, Ind.: Indiana University Press, 1967); Jacques Berque, *French North Africa: The Maghrib between Two World Wars,* trans. Jean Stewart (New York: Praeger, 1967); Allal al-Fasi, *The Independence Movements in North Africa,* trans. Hazem Zaki Nuseibeth (New York: Octagon Books, 1970); Fenner Brockway, *The Colonial Revolution* (New York: St. Martin's Press, 1973); and Philip C. Jessup, *The Birth of Nations* (New York: Columbia University Press, 1974).

3. Blair, "Amateurs in Democracy," 612.

4. Childs to Hull, May 11, 1942, State Department Document 881.00/2150, DNA. *See also* State Department Document 851S.00/ 209 PS/ET, DNA.

5. Luella Hall, *The United States and Morocco, 1776-1956* (Metuchen, N. J.: Scarecrow Press, 1971), 899; *see also* Murphy, *Diplomat among Warriors* (New York: Doubleday, 1964).

6. Hall, *United States and Morocco,* 931.

7. Ibid., 943.

8. Blair, "Amateurs in Diplomacy," 615; Blair rejects the idea that Roosevelt would have worked for Moroccan independence. However, he offers no concrete evidence for this position. Blair simply states that Roosevelt had no more than a "casual concern for Moroccan independence" and that he had not studied the background of Moroccan nationalism. This is hardly convincing. In fact one could argue that out of ignorance the glib president, conversing in French, promised more than he could or would be able to deliver. The situation is even more perplexing when one considers the Anfa Accords signed by Roosevelt and Giraud at Casablanca in 1943. The accords ratified the Clark-Darlan and Murphy-Giraud Agreements of November 1942. These agreements committed the United States to French independence and the recognition of French authority in metropolitan and colonial areas.

9. Interview with Lloyd Cutler, May 26, 1972, Washington, D. C.

10. *Foreign Relations 1943* 4, 738-39.

11. Ibid., 742; 738-46.

12. Hall, *United States and Morocco,* 1001-06.

13. Murray to Berle, July 27, 1943, State Department Document 851S.00/257, DNA. This is an excellent summary of many communications from Doolittle and Murphy. Murray clearly defines the issues and also adds his conclusion: "My own view is that this question may come home to haunt us and that the unduly prolonged policy now being pursued by Mr. Murphy will not be good enough in the long run."

14. Doolittle to Hull, June 1, 1943, State Department Document 851S.00/259 PS/WVS, DNA. In a follow-up report Doolittle described the present French policy as "disastrous"; Doolittle to Hull, June 5, 1943, State Department Document 851S.00/253.

15. Murphy to Doolittle, April 22, 1943, attachment to State Department Document 851.00/259 PS/WVS, DNA. *See also* Murphy to Alling, July 5, 1943, State Department Document 851S.001/34. Murphy saw no reason for the United States to oppose the French deposition of Moncef Bey.

16. Murphy to Hull, June 16, 1943, State Department Document 851S.00/258, DNA. For a good description of the Destour Party and its leader Habib Bourguiba, *see* State Department Document 851S.00/255, DNA.

17. Murray to Berle, July 27, 1943, State Department Document 851S.00/257, DNA.

18. Murphy to Hull, July 30, 1943, State Department Document 851S.00/268 PS/ATB, DNA; Murphy to Hull, July 29, 1943, State Department Document, 851S.00/267 PS/ATB, DNA.

19. Murray to Berle, October 11, 1943, State Department Document 881.00/2678 PS/MO, DNA, and Document 881.00/2752.

20. Ibid.

21. Stettinius to Roosevelt, November 1, 1943, State Department Document 881.00/2680 PS/CF, DNA.

22. Doolittle Memorandum, "Interview with the President," November 9, 1943, State Department Document 851S.00/282 1/2, DNA. The memo is also attached to State Department Document FW 851S.00/257, DNA.

23. *Foreign Relations 1943* 4, 745-46; *Foreign Relations 1944* 5, 537.

24. *Foreign Relations 1944* 3, 773; for similar American statements *see* pages 770-72. *Also See* Chapter 3 for Roosevelt's assurances to Darlan.

25. Hall, *United States and Morocco,* 1007-09; Russell to Hull, January 15, 1944, State Department Document 881.00/2766, DNA. For more detail on Arab nationalism during this time *see* the following State Department Documents: 881.00/2787; 881.00/2772; 881.00/2775. In his article Blair points out that the consul's contacts were with the educated urban Arabs. This is true, but the movement from 1944 to 1945 spread rapidly, although two reports reveal the absence of it in southern Morocco and southern Algeria. The reports are: an unnumbered memorandum from Russell Brooks, March 22, 1944, and State Department Document 851R.00/4-1445, April 14, 1945. For more information on the necessity of United States and British support for the nationalist cause to succeed *see* Robert Dumont, January 11, 1944, memorandum, enclosure number one to Dispatch 91, 800 Native Affairs file.

26. Cole to Hull, January 18, 1944, State Department Document 851S.00/298, DNA. For details *see* the translation of the letter attached to the document.

27. Russell to Hull, July 11, 1944, State Department Document 881.00/7-1144, DNA; Cole to Hull, July 4, 1944, State Department Document 881.00/7-444, DNA; the Arab youth movement is noted in Russell to Hull, State Department Document 881.00/9-2844. The extent of communist and remnants of Nazi influence within the nationalist movement is almost impossible to determine. The former admittedly did support the nationalist cause. The point is that these groups served the French as useful scapegoats to obscure the shortcomings of French policy.

28. Elbrick to Hull, October 30, 1944, State Department Document 881.00/10-3044, DNA; Russell to Hull, July 11, 1944, State Department Document 881.00/7-1144, DNA.

29. Tuck to Stettinius, March 1, 1945, State Department Document 851R.00/3-145, DNA. The Algerian memo from the High Committee for the Defense of Algeria is attached to this document. *See* Lawton to

Stettinius, March 15, 1945, State Department Document 851R.00/3-1545, DNA for a brief description of the political groups and their activity in Algeria. *See also* Lawton to Stettinius, February 9, 1945, State Department Document 851R.00/2-945, DNA. For useful recent works on the Algerian revolution *see*: David Gordon, *The Passing of French Algeria* (New York: Oxford University Press, 1966); William B. Quandt, *Revolution and Leadership: Algeria, 1954-1968* (Cambridge, Mass.: M.I.T. Press, 1969); David and Marina Ottaway, *Algeria: The Politics of a Socialist Revolution* (Berkeley, Calif.: University of California Press, 1970); Alf A. Heggoy, *Insurgency and Counterinsurgency in Algeria* (Bloomington, Ind.: Indiana University Press, 1972); and "The Origins of Algerian Nationalism in the Colony and in France," *The Muslim World* 58 (April 1968), 128-40.

30. Throughout the summer numerous reports arrived at the state department describing the riots and responsibility for them and listing casualty figures. No exact casualty figure will ever be known, but there are interesting discrepancies among the American, British, French, and Arab reports. Some of the reports touch on the communist influence and the communist position on responsibility. The following state department documents are good samples of these reports: 851R.00/5-1045; 851 R.00/5-1145; 851R.00/5-1245; 851R.00/5-1545; 851R.00/5-2245; 851R.00/5-2345; 851R.00/5-2445; 851R.00/6-2846; 851R.00/7-2045; 851R.00/7-2745.

31. Caffrey to Stettinius, April 5, 1945, State Department Document 851R.00/4-545, DNA. This includes a memo from Harry Woodruff on political agitation in North Africa, and Woodruff predicted that in the future "Arab nationalism will express itself more positively still." [Hall, *United States and Morocco,* 1012-13.]

32. Hall, *United States and Morocco,* 1013.

33. Tuck to Grew, June 21, 1945, State Department Document 851R.00/6-2145 CS/D, DNA. This is a summary of Tuck's conversation with Abdul Rahman Azzam Bey. The letter of Bey dated June 20, 1945, is in State Department Document 851R.00/6-2145 CS/MAU, DNA.

34. Grew to American Embassy in Paris, July 30, 1945, State Department Document 851R.00/7-3045, DNA.

35. Fullerton to Grew, July 7, 1945, State Department Document 851R.00/7-745, DNA. (This includes a summary of the article in *Normandie* and also a copy of the original article in French.); Alling to Grew, September 11, 1945, State Department Document 851R.00/9-1145, DNA; memorandum of conversation between L. W. Henderson and Mr. Lacoste, Counselor of the French Embassy, September 24, 1945, State Department Document 851S.00/9-2445, DNA; memorandum of conversation between

Mr. Lacoste and Mr. Merriam, November 1, 1945, State Department Document 851S.00/11-145, DNA.

36. For a careful analysis of Roosevelt's positions on Indochina *see* Walter LaFeber, "Roosevelt, Churchill, and Indochina: 1942-45," *American Historical Review* 80 (December 1975): 1277-95.

37. The role and influence of communism in North Africa remains to be studied. A recent article offers some important insights; *see* Roger Kanet, "The Soviet Union, the French Communist Party and Africa, 1945-1950," *Survey* 22 (Winter 1976): 74-92.

8.

Private Traders Oppose Lend-Lease

The lend-lease administration's method of providing civilian goods to lend-lease countries had a devastating impact on sectors of the American business community. Lend-lease civilian assistance operated on a government-to-government basis, thereby circumventing normal commercial channels and stifling overseas commercial activity. Consequently, throughout the war a serious controversy developed between the commercial community and government officials over the nature and timing of the termination of civilian lend-lease and the resumption of private trade. This was most clearly evident in the struggle over private trade with French North and West Africa.

These areas offered an enormous attraction. French Northwest Africa constituted a vast colonial territory in dire need of goods that the mother country could no longer furnish. Evidently unembarrassed by their voracious appetite for profit, commercial leaders relentlessly pressured the lend-lease administration to restore private trade to these territories. In late 1942 and early 1943 the traders were chiefly concerned with regaining access to their former markets. But as the Allied armies swept through North Africa, the traders, came to recognize, if they had not already done so, that never before had such an opportunity existed for expansion into markets previously monopolized by the French. When the government failed to reopen these territories, the traders' frustration and hostility increased.

Although conflict revealed differences within the administration over the feasibility of such action, the French presented the most formidable obstacle. France's leaders, acutely aware of the situation, struggled to prevent the loss of economic supremacy in the most lucrative part of their empire. They bitterly opposed American efforts and succeeded in delaying the resumption of normal trade relations in North and West Africa until July 1, 1945. Finally at the end of 1945 the French agreed to a limited and conditional American trade program for Continental France.

The Office of the Lend Lease Administration (OLLA) recognized the effect upon private trade of supplying civilian goods through government agencies. It was keenly aware that such a procedure bypassed American import and export houses, freight forwarders, established channels of foreign trade financing, and American distribution services abroad. Furthermore, direct government procurement also threatened the trade position of United States' brands overseas.[1]

After only six months of lend-lease the reactions from these segments of the commercial community were evident. In September 1941 the Foreign Traders Association of Philadelphia expressed grave concern over losses to private trade as lend-lease expanded. In response to an appeal from the association General J. H. Burns, an executive officer in the Office for Emergency Management, Division of Defense Aid Reports, replied that the OLLA was giving serious consideration to private trade and that it would attempt to avoid as much injury as possible to commercial firms. But as Burns pointed out, with the world conditions so unsettled, "many legitimate business interests must give way to considerations to national defense and national aid to nations whose defense is vital to our own." Burns further noted that only in exceptional cases would the government permit lend-lease goods to proceed through commercial channels. In extending such a concession the administration required evidence that it did not discriminate against other commercial interests. Official approval for such an arrangement would occur provided it was absolutely essential for the war effort.[2]

With the shipment of large quantities of civilian goods to North and West Africa the concern of commercial exporters increased. On December 3, 1942, the Leaf Tobacco Company, a large supplier for North Africa, accused the OLLA of functioning as its competitor and feared the loss of business that it had taken the company over twenty years to establish. The firm noted that recent tobacco shipments to North Africa had originated with the Commodity Credit Corporation and asserted, "If such is the case our own Government is now becoming our competitor and our life's work will be lost." Furthermore, the company criticized the distribution of any grade of tobacco that did not conform to previous standards as potentially damaging to postwar business.[3]

The response of the OLLA to such a reaction followed a similar pattern. The agency emphasized that it had no intention of becoming a permanent substitute for normal commercial relations. In the tobacco company's case the OLLA referred its letter to the agricultural administration and advised the firm to remain in close contact with that agency in order to share in the future tobacco business.[4]

The persistent inquiries and criticism from private enterprise plagued the OLLA. A New York export corporation with extensive contacts in North Africa queried the agency as to whether it should maintain its established contacts with North African chambers of commerce. "Is it possible," the company asked "to foresee in the near future a resumption of free trade or should all exchanges be made in a Lend-Lease system?" The firm extended its "services" by offering to handle all the materials the agency sent to North Africa. "We are willing to send our representatives to North Africa," the firm explained, "so as to complete the liaison with our company, and arrange the prompt distribution of these shipments under control of the American authorities."[5] Such a generous offer was typical of the attempts by private traders to take advantage of the disruptions in normal trade relations.

The administration, however, remained determined to retain control of civilian supply. In February 1943 it terminated cable service between the United States and North Africa. The move further angered American traders, because it left many inquiries from North African dealers unanswered and thereby definitely signaled the curtailment of private trade.[6] The government's action reinforced the policy that the OLLA had previously explained to private enterprise: "At the present time, all procurement for this area must be effected through government procurement agencies and all shipping must be in the hands of the War Shipping Administration and the Army."[7] Together with lend-lease functioning as the sole handler of trade with North Africa, the Board of Economic Warfare assumed the responsibility for all purchases made in North Africa.[8]

To placate the business community the OLLA announced that to keep private trade interests viable, the agency would permit the use of trade names on requisitions. Officials urged cooperation between the government and business and assured the latter that the lend-lease administration did not advocate the abolition of commercial trade. On the contrary, the agency insisted, "Lend-Lease is attempting to adjust its operations so as to cause as little harm to the export machinery of the United States as is possible, consonant with our number one job of helping to win the war." The agency further contended that during the first nine months of 1942 lend-lease exports of civilian goods amounted to only 50 percent of the total trade.[9]

The OLLA pointed out that the $3.2 million worth of commercial exports in 1942 compared favorably with the pre lend-lease period. However, on closer scrutiny the figures of the OLLA revealed the growing dominance of lend-lease over private trade. During the last quarter of 1942 the amount of nonmilitary trade handled through lend-lease rose from 47 to 58 percent and for the first time surpassed commercial exportation. As a result, the agency promised to modify its procurement as much as possible in accordance with normal trade routines and to permit greater recognition of trade names and closer contact with exporters. To minimize its effect on private trade the OLLA advised the procurement agencies to respect preferences expressed by foreign governments for goods of certain American suppliers whenever feasible. On reviewing the world trade situation, the agency observed that the closer an area was to military activity the more lend-lease dominated its supply program. Thus, in the Western Hemisphere private trade remained virtually unaffected.[10]

Commercial traders derived little satisfaction from the agency's explanations. American businessmen, eager to exploit the dislocated French Empire, inundated the administration with requests for trade privileges. Prior to the war the United States' share of imports to these areas amounted to only 3 percent. By April 1943 the United States Export Office had received over one hundred applications for licenses to trade with French North and West Africa. American officials, however, revealed less optimism than the commercial interests. They believed that once the war ended most of the trade would return to France, although they felt that in Morocco, where Japan had supplied over 10 percent of the textile imports, the Americans would replace the Japanese.[11]

The exporters and importers within the United States continued to grow impatient over government control of trade. With the collapse of the Nazis in Tunisia in May 1943 they pointed out that the area no longer represented a theater of military operations and that the Allies now controlled the Mediterranean. Furthermore private interests cited the numerous trade inquiries they had received from North and West African firms. A chemical importer protested the existing conditions and insisted that "North African traders of course prefer to deal with established houses here, but so far we haven't been able to bring in anything. The way things are now it's entirely a political matter and under the present regulations we can't even approach our former suppliers." The commercial firms deplored the practice of censuring communications and seriously questioned the government's promises to restore private trade. A restoration of private trade must come shortly, they insisted, if the government was sincere in its assurances to promote normal trade relations. Businessmen considered Northwest Africa an essential area that could provide a large market sorely needed by American exporters due to restrictions placed on world trade. By the end of June 1943, however, the commerce department offered little encouragement. It announced that "no decision has been made as to the time or manner of future resumptions of private trade."[12]

Private trade interests relentlessly pursued the issue, and their criticism of government policy mounted. One firm bitterly complained, "We have been represented in North Africa for fifty years and we are getting smaller tonnage now than we did under the Germans and our whole price structure is being disrupted by Lend-Lease operations." Businessmen argued that private enterprise was a better judge of the market and could operate more efficiently. Lend-lease, they stressed, proved costly, complex, and produced many errors in procurement. The traders pointed out that the lend-lease administration had sent passenger cars to West Africa instead of the much-needed trucks, and in North Africa the agency had imported tires with the wrong wheel base. Furthermore the exporters castigated the OLLA for basing its program on what it thought the area required rather than what it actually needed. This, they claimed, produced excess storage and waste. The business community advocated a restoration of private trade to whatever extent possible in liberated areas, the formation of committees for each geographic area, and assurances that the United Kingdom would receive no advantages.[13]

In October 1943 commercial traders completed a poll that indicated a large majority was not only willing but prepared to resume normal trade relations. Of the more than five hundred exporters who responded, 92 percent believed that a return to normal commercial relations was possible. Of this group, 96 percent required no further preparations for such a resumption, while 62 percent needed more time. Since 72 percent of the merchants who responded had established commercial contacts in

Northwest Africa prior to 1940, the traders presented this as "proof that this desire for direct business with the area is not a war development nor an opening in new trade areas."[14]

Within the administration officials considered proposals to restore private trade. On July 7, 1943, Hector Lazo, the assistant director of the Board of Economic Warfare, announced that private trade would begin soon. BEW, he maintained, had constantly attempted to achieve normal commercial relations but for military reasons had to abandon its efforts. Livingston Short, the lend-lease administrator who served as chairman of the Import Division of the North African Economic Board, also favored the resumption of normal commercial relations. Although the army controlled the docks and unloading areas, Short saw no reason why the government could not adopt a plan whereby private trade would replace the government-to-government procedure. However, he emphasized that with shipping space so limited, the traders would have to coordinate their quantities so as not to exceed the total shipping capacity.[15]

Stettinius reacted favorably to Short's suggestions and expressed a desire to see commercial trade resumed "in the not too distant future."[16] Short also reported that "some French officials have expressed themselves to me as being in favor of a return to private trade and I do not believe we would meet any opposition on that score."[17] Evidently Short had either spoken to the wrong officials or they deliberately deceived him. Adverse French reaction to a restoration of private trade was mainly responsible for preventing its implementation until the war in Europe had ended.

During late 1943 the administration increased its efforts to resolve the difficulties involved in restoring private trade. Unfortunately negotiations with the French proved protracted. In September commercial executives informed the OLLA that their conversations with the French Supply Mission in Washington were inconclusive, unsatisfactory, and had accomplished little. The executives contended that the longer the government extended lend-lease, the longer it controlled trade. The traders feared that even after the withdrawal of lend-lease, the foreign missions would attempt to handle the bulk of purchasing and thereby continue to circumvent normal trade channels.[18]

In October the state department reported on discussions of private trade with the French. The United States had proposed an arrangement whereby American businessmen could enter into purchase agreements with individual exporters in Northwest Africa. But with the French evidently unimpressed by its proposals, the state department concluded that "existing conditions make it impossible at this time to know how soon unrestricted private trade can be resumed."[19]

The outlook for the restoration of trade was not favorable. Aside from the difficulties with the French there were other reasons for the delays: inflation had pushed the prices of African goods above the OPA ceiling and therefore out of the reach of American importers; if private trade resumed it would more than likely move only one way—to North Africa; Furthermore, there was little chance of allotting shipping space to exporters for goods not essential to the war effort; and since the United States had committed itself to supply goods on a government-to-government basis, a general fear prevailed among the French and some American officials that private trade would operate too slowly for the emergency needs of the area.[20]

From North Africa, however, came protests over the procrastination in Washington on the trade issue. The United States Director of Economic Operations of the North African Economic Board, Alexander Royce, stressed the necessity for an immediate resumption of private trade. Royce insisted that "Government agencies in D. C. and BEW in particular, should direct their activities towards the immediate resumption of private trade with French North and West Africa." Failure to do so, he warned, would produce serious consequences since "British traders are, and have been all along doing business with North Africa through the operations of the U.K.C.C. The Americans have missed the boat." The United States, Royce contended, had adopted the line of lease resistance, and "we permitted the issue of private trade to become entangled in the huge Washington inter-agency cob-web. Thus we have lost a great portion of the ground floor in the possible flow of trade which could have been ours." Specifically he urged a return to private trade of a number of specified commodities to West Africa and Morocco by November 15, 1943, and to Algeria and Tunisia by January 1, 1944.[21]

The Foreign Economic Administration denied that there was any "pussy-footing" on the matter. FEA officials believed that a lack of coordination between it and the state department had prevented working out a satisfactory program. Specifically they had failed to reach an agreement with the British and French on policy and a schedule of actual operations.[22]

Leo Crowley, the head of the FEA, placed the highest priority on private trade. On December 9, 1943, he informed Hull that in considering an agenda for the forthcoming negotiations with the French National

Committee of Liberation, the FEA believed "that the subject of perhaps primary importance will be that concerned with the restoration of private trade between this country and French North and West Africa."[23] To Crowley the furnishing of supplies to these areas on a government-to-government basis was no longer necessary. He told Hull that the lend-lease administration intended to discontinue such an arrangement except for supplies ordered prior to January 1, 1944, and in those cases where no other procedures were feasible. The acceptance of a return to private trade, Crowley realized, involved important political considerations by the French. But he was optimistic that the French would agree—at least in principle—and that they would substantially reduce the number of commodities they had received exclusively through lend-lease. He also looked forward to exportation through private channels of noncritical goods from North and West Africa.[24]

Crowley also drafted a letter to Monnet. "We are of the opinion," Crowley wrote, "that the use of the lend-lease procedure for the procurement and export of civilian goods to French North and West Africa is no longer generally required." He insisted on the resumption of commercial relations at the earliest practicable date and trusted that during the forthcoming negotiations "procedure arrangements can be agreed upon to bring about an early restoration of such trade under such regulations as may be required to insure that the available shipping space is utilized in the most effective manner."[25]

Crowley's emphasis on the trade issue and his proposed alterations encountered opposition from the state department. Although the department expressed some agreement with Crowley, Hull informed him, "I do not, however, believe that it would be to this Government's best interests for the Foreign Economic Administration to communicate directly with Monnet its desires in this matter as you suggest in your letter."[26] It was the state department's policy, Hull pointed out, to forebear direct pressure on the French until representatives in Algiers and Washington agreed on the practical arrangements for facilitating a return to private trade. Hull cited suggestions similar to Crowley's and noted that not only had the French rejected them, but that British and American economic experts in North Africa also doubted their worth. The Allied agents in the field had opposed such recommendations on the basis that neither the personnel nor the required distribution machinery were available.[27]

Under these circumstances the state department refused to press the French for an immediate resumption of trade. As Hull put it, "I do not

believe that we should express to the French any views on private trade
other than a general statement of this government's policy, and a request
for full collaboration on the part of the French authorities in implementing that policy as promptly as practical considerations permit."[28]
Crowley had little choice and accepted Hull's position. But as he explained to the secretary of state, his proposals stemmed from the fact
that "the Foreign Economic Administration is under intense pressure
from private business interests in this country which seek resumption
of private trade."[29]

The French immediately expressed an adverse opinion of Crowley's
proposals. On December 15 Judson Hannigan, a lend-lease administrator,
reported that Leroy Beaulieu of the French Supply Council had informed
him of the French government's opposition to the restoration of private
trade in North Africa. Hannigan received the impression that the French
would remain adamant and that their decision appeared irrevocable.[30]

Monnet reinforced the French position by insisting that for some time,
perhaps even a year, the French government would have to control trade.
Moreover, the government, Monnet emphasized, could not permit those
French traders not greatly affected by the war to operate in North Africa
until others, mostly in France, who had formerly dominated North African
trade but were no longer in a position to do so, were able to resume business. As a result of the close ties between North Africa and Metropolitan
France, the French regarded the economies of both as virtually the same.
Thus, they considered it impossible to commence private trade until perhaps one year after the liberation of France.[31]

Specifically the French told Arthur Burns, of the Office of Economic
Progress, that "North Africa should not have private trade until Conti-
nental France is prepared to have private trade."[32] Monnet, however,
promised to investigate the possibility of purchasing agencies of the
French government buying from American exporters. The French also
pointed out that their position on private trade applied only to French
North and West Africa. In other colonial areas such as French Oceania,
New Hebrides, New Caledonia, St. Pierre and Miquelon, the French
West Indies, Madagascar, and Le Reunion private trade could begin immediately.[33]

American officials considered the procedures for carrying on trade
with these areas as a "peculiar form" of private trade. The French government closely regulated imports from the United States based on an established program for each colony. The Ministry of the Colonies determined

the quantity of exports allocated to each foreign country and the price
and conditions of sale for each product. In the opinion of some United
States officials the French employed the term "private trade" merely to
alleviate American apprehensions, since "the procedures outlined might
as well be called a modified form of State Trading." Despite this criticism
the FEA felt that even with the stringent regulations the system provided
for a considerable amount of trade through private channels. But it cautioned: "The importance of this step will depend on whether the French
will stop there or proceed further with the relaxation of controls."[34]

The issue became more controversial when the British and French
agreed to resume private trade in West Africa. Still sensitive to the pressure of private interests, the FEA immediately objected to the French
concessions and insisted that the United States should not permit the
United Kingdom to begin private trade before American firms had an opportunity to do so. The opening of West Africa to British trade, the FEA
asserted, would further anger American business interests. But once again
the state department disagreed. Spokesmen for the department pointed
out that there were two important obstacles that American traders faced
but which the British did not. The first was a lack of dollar resources in
West Africa, where the British had an adequate supply of sterling. Secondly, over a period of many years the British had established extensive trade
connections with West Africa which the United States had not. Moreover,
the reopening of trade between the United Kingdom and French West
Africa, the state department maintained, would assist rather than undermine United States' efforts in the same direction.[35]

The British success infuriated American commercial interests. They
cited the monopolistic practices of the British and French companies
that had excluded American traders from West Africa. As a result of their
domination the United States had existed in the West African economy
only as a producer from which British and French agents purchased goods;
American businessmen were unable to expand their markets and had merely sold their goods to the companies as they did to other countries. With
the situations within the British and French imperial systems greatly altered by the war, business leaders saw an opportunity to eliminate the
inveterate inequities. They emphasized that the United States now held
the superior position as the only supplier of consumer goods and therefore possessed an advantage that had never existed under normal conditions.[36]

Pressure from the commercial groups continued unabated. At an Exec-

utive Policy Committee meeting the FEA representatives cited the criticism emanating from the trade centers over the inability of the exporters
to carry on trade with liberated areas. The denouncements from business
stung the FEA, which felt that these groups were resentful because they
failed to realize that it was the French who prevented the resumption of
trade relations. At the same time, the FEA exhibited a reluctance to accept recommendations from business to send a government-sponsored
fact-finding mission to Northwest Africa.[37]

But the persistence of business prompted government action. In July
1944 under the sponsorship of the FEA and state department, the Special
Economic Mission was created to investigate the prospects of the restoration of United States commercial trade with areas under wartime restrictions. Originally the mission consisted solely of businessmen, but government officials expanded it to include representatives from state, commerce,
and the FEA. The administration desired "to emphasize the unanimity
of public and private United States interest in the problem under consideration by the Mission."[38]

Colonel William Culbertson served as chairman of the mission. He had
previously held senior diplomatic positions in Chile and Rumania, and as
a former Vice Chairman of the Tariff Commission he had acquired extensive knowledge of United States' trade policy. The mission's businessmen
emerged from the ranks of the foreign traders. Three of the four had
close associations with the Foreign Trade Council and held prominent
posts with established import and export houses. They represented the
drug and chemical industries and the producers of automotive equipment
and accessories.[39]

The administration instructed the mission to provide the business representatives with complete access to all sources of information. In issuing
such instructions the administration's purpose was twofold: First, officials
wanted the work of the mission to represent a cross section of opinion
from public servants and private interests. Secondly, and perhaps most
important, was the government's determination to insure extensive circu-
lation of accurate information to businessmen, "who have been previously
urging a program of removal of restrictions—a removal which seems im-
practical to most Government representatives who have actually faced
the problems in the field."[40]

From August 18 until August 28, 1944, in accordance with its instructions "to review the problems involved in returning private trade to normal channels as rapidly as war time conditions permit," the mission ex-

changed views with the French. However, the French refused to discuss
the possibility of an early resumption of private trade. "It was evident,"
Culbertson wrote, "that the traditional closed door policy of the French
was assumed if not expressed." The French contended that the status of
Algeria prevented any alteration in the present trade arrangements in
North Africa until the French Committee of National Liberation (FCNL)
determined and settled the needs of Metropolitan France. Although Culbertson discerned some differences of opinion among the French commissioners, he nevertheless concluded that the majority of them advocated government control and monopoly of trade and industry. Whether
Culbertson's appraisal was totally accurate mattered little, since it had
become clear to him "that the premises on which the Mission was created
and instructed are not acceptable to the majority of the French rulers
who now have been transported to France." Along with their obduracy
the French exhibited an almost total lack of interest in the subject and
proved to be insufferable hosts. Much to the chagrin of the mission "they
were always looking out the window while we were talking." Moreover,
the French commissioners abruptly terminated the discussions by de-
parting for liberated France before the mission had completed its scheduled negotiations.[41]

The mission's report in many ways reflected its reaction to the French
attitude. It advocated a "firm, realistic, non-benevolent policy toward
the French in Paris in order to achieve the economic policy which gave
rise to the Mission." The mission recommended the removal of government controls on trade in Northwest Africa since the area no longer represented a primary military theater. Culbertson's report stressed that wartime restrictions and monopolies were becoming permanent policy and
urged direct action on the part of the government to insure American
enterprise a fair share of world trade in the postwar world. The report
further maintained that lend-lease was only necessary under wartime
conditions and proposed an extensive reduction of such assistance and
complete termination of it by June 1945. It cited the current French
negotiations with the United States for assistance to Metropolitan France
and exhorted officials to seize the opportunity to pressure the FCNL for
a more liberal economic arrangement in North Africa. The mission looked
forward to resumption of a small amount of private trade in early 1945
but felt that the second half of the year offered better possibilities for
substantial increases.[42]

Before Culbertson completed work on the mission's findings, the

French publicly reiterated their views on private trade. On September 6, 1944, Robert Valeur, director of the information committee of the FCNL, asserted that private trade would not resume until the French elected a new government, which he estimated might take six months to one year. The announcement shocked and upset American commercial leaders, who viewed the liberation of France as a means of opening private trade. They expressed concern and fear that such a policy represented a harbinger for all future liberated areas. Some traders reported that from information they had received, French trade would remain on a government-to-government basis for at least two or three years. Valeur denied this, but insisted that "during the period preceding the election, I am pretty certain that the government type trade will be necessary, and possibly the Government that is elected will have to exercise control over the country's resources which may involve close regulation over its trade."[43]

Again the commercial interests assailed the FEA and state department for their lack of progress on the restoration of private trade. The National Association of Manufacturers (NAM) charged that government secrecy concerning lend-lease clouded the trade issue and forced traders to rely on rumor and conjecture in mapping out postwar programs. The association also accused the agencies of failing to undertake an effort to design programs based on proposals from private enterprise. It also contended that within the administration were two conflicting groups: one that worked for the restoration of private trade and another that would cancel all lend-lease debts and continue it after the war under another title.[44]

The United States Chamber of Commerce supported the NAM. The chamber's Foreign Commerce Committee urged the government to confine lend-lease for the rest of the war to military goods including foodstuffs. The committee also insisted on a return of all commercial commodities to private trade and an immediate cessation of lend-lease once the war ended.[45]

As late as December 1944, however, a number of government officials still argued against resuming private trade. Those within the FEA and state who opposed elimination of the government-to-government procedure criticized the application of pressure on the French. They also expressed opposition to those who demanded immediate cash payment for civilian supplies delivered to Northwest Africa. Such proposals, they contended, were unrealistic in light of the chaotic conditions within France. They noted the general disorganization, the almost total lack of non-military transportation, the presence of thousands of Germans in the south, and the battle areas in Northeast France. Thus they urged the immediate restoration of some semblance of normal conditions and deplored the "present heckling by United States representatives for the immediate resumption of private trade with North Africa and France."[46] Together with the uncertain factors in France and the problems of restoring peace in Europe, this group felt that "such subjects as the restoration of private trade in North Africa (in face of the shortages in shipping, difficulties in transportation, etc.) are pretty unimportant."[47]

Amid the pressure from business and the conflicting views within the agencies the state department adopted a definitive policy on private trade. On December 12, 1944, the United States presented its views to the French Ministry of Foreign Affairs through the American embassy in Paris. It informed the French that it based its position on certain recommendations expressed in the report of the Special Economic Mission. In an aide-mémoire the state department reviewed the traditional American policy to foster private trade through commercial channels. It pointed out that the 1945 import programs for North and West Africa were in the process of completion. In light of this and due to the availability of dollar exchange to the French Provisional Government, the United States felt justified in terminating lend-lease to French North and West Africa as of June 30, 1945.[48]

During the intervening period and thereafter the United States hoped that the French "will wish to join the American Government in accomplishing the resumption of normal commercial trade. . . and that bulk procurement through the French Supply Council for French North and West Africa will be limited to those few exceptional cases wherein it is mutually agreed that such bulk purchases are demonstrably more effective." The American representatives in Algiers were to assist French authorities in expediting the flow of private trade. The United States also requested the French Provisional Government and the local governments to send commercial agents to the United States to promote direct contact between American and French firms and thus hasten the resumption of private trade.[49]

On December 27, 1944, the French conditionally accepted the American terms. They generally agreed on the appropriateness of restoring private trade and expressed satisfaction with the steps taken by the United States to facilitate exportation from French Northwest Africa. French authorities promised to issue export licenses to speed the flow of goods from the colonies once they had provided for local, metropolitan, and war needs. The French, however, did not feel that they could immediately apply the system of private purchases in all cases. Since France imported a large number of products for state organizations such as the General Supply Services and the Cereals Office, the French maintained that they could only place such orders through government channels, which the French Purchasing Mission handled. "Consequently, in spite of the positive desire of the French government, the purchases in the United States of supplies for the North African territories can only progressively become private purchases," the French replied. Moreover, "the French Mission will be obliged to continue its activities, it will maintain its necessary contacts for this purpose with competent American Government Agencies."[50]

During a series of follow-up meetings the French informed Culbertson that the French mission would continue to procure bulk items such as coal, wheat, sugar, and oil. When Culbertson pressed for information on specific items that private trade would handle immediately, the French suggested trucks, autos, and farm equipment. The French believed that exportation from Northwest Africa could begin immediately, but they expressed concern over their ability to do so at prices conforming to American ceiling prices. In contrast to his previous experience Culbertson reported that the French exhibited a sincere desire to restore trade in North and West Africa. "The important result," he wrote, "is that a trend was established by the American and French Governments, and that the negotiations in Paris constitute a significant development in the pattern of United Nations post-war commercial relations."[51] Government officials realized that with lend-lease to French North and West Africa scheduled to terminate June 30, 1945, private traders required preparation time before resuming commerce. As a result of American pressure, in early 1945 as a first step the French permitted representatives of American manufacturers to distribute trucks in North Africa, thereby reestablishing the lines of trade before private trade itself commenced. It was for West Africa, however, that officials first reached an agreement on trade resumption. With the 1945 supply program completed and procurement underway, the FEA Mission at Dakar closed its doors. In March the French agreed to a restoration of trade, and American authorities advised commercial interests to forward price lists, catalogs, and other necessary information to the American Consulate at Dakar. Within a few days the consulate received over a thousand letters from United States firms desiring to establish business relations with the French colony.[52]

The agreement stemmed from West Africa's willingness to increase its volume of prewar trade with the United States. Throughout the war the United States exported to West Africa approximately ten times as much material as before the war; thus, a familiarity with and preference for American goods had developed. Moreover, West Africa unlike North Africa had no "Algerian situation," and generally its ties with France were not as binding. Along with this the American government and business executives recognized that from 1945 to 1946 France would of necessity draw heavily on West African products with little to offer in return. Consequently American exporters clamored to fill the vacuum. They believed that the production of West Africa's major items—oilseeds (peanut and palm), cocoa, cotton, kola nuts, rubber, wood, kapok, and sisal—would increase substantially through the application of American management and technology. The bureaucrats and private enterprise agreed that West Africa offered unlimited potential for future economic development and exploitation. The department of state and the FEA warned that the agreement on West African trade led to over-optimism on the part of American traders. Prior to the commencement of private trade the French and Americans had to resolve a number of difficulties. First, the United States had to provide West Africa with dollars and arrange a method of payment. Secondly, it was necessary for the French to devise and distribute commercial licenses. Third, an arrangement for inland transportation by air for commercial travelers was essential, since the railway network in most areas was undependable. Lastly, the French had to provide a list of items for private trade in accordance with existing supply problems. The caution expressed by officials proved accurate. The French proceeded slowly, procrastinated, and remained wary of private trade. During discussions on finding a means to provide West Africa with adequate dollar balances, the French expressed concern over whether private trade could handle the requirements as expeditiously as the government-to-government procedure.[53]

In the meantime American impatience with the French increased. On March 22, 1945, Donald Gilpatric of the state department informed the American minister in Paris, Henry Labouisse, that since the presentation of the aide-mémoire almost half the transition period had elapsed, and they had made little progress with the French. The United States authorities anxiously awaited the French publication of a tentative list of items available for commercial trade. But it was not until March 10, 1945, that representatives of state, commerce, and the FEA could schedule a meeting with Christian Valensi, chairman of the French Supply Council. Valensi arrived late and then refused to resolve the issue. Valensi claimed that there was no discussion of private trade in Paris, nor had he received any instruction on the matter. "The various French representatives at tne meeting," Gilpatric wrote, "raised all sorts of objections to the resumption of private trade, such as delays in commercial communication, questions of shipping priorities, and the need in their opinion, for bulk procurement of practically all the programmed items."[54]

Despite the agreement on private trade in Washington and Dakar, Valensi explained that he could do nothing to implement it without instructions from Paris. American officials became skeptical that such instructions would ever arrive. "In the meantime," Gilpatric informed Labouisse, "pressure from private sources is mounting here. I think we will be forced to make a public explanation if we do not get sufficient cooperation from the French in re-establishing private trade for the Empire by the end of the semester." Gilpatric also noted that the United States lacked any assurance that the French had established a system of licensing or exchange availability, "and the French Supply Council here, while not responsible for those delays seems determined to keep everything in French Government channels."[55]

As a result of French obstructions it was not until the end of April— only two months before the termination date of the North and West African programs—that the United States and France agreed on a list of commodities eligible for private trade. In conjunction with the French Supply Council the state department published on April 29, 1945, an initial list of the articles returned to private trade. This information and other supply data became available to interested commercial concerns in the United States and French Northwest Africa. The announcement also included the required procedures for French and American commercial interests to follow. After selecting a supplier the French importers were to apply to their local authorities for an import license. The issuance of the license included an authorization for the foreign exchange required to complete the transaction. The importer was then free to complete the financial arrangements as in normal commerce. But for the American exporters "the continuing uncertainty and security control of shipping availability, and the resulting changes in the priority of French civilian needs" necessitated the coordination of their efforts with the French Supply Council. Both governments assured private interests that efforts were underway to improve both communications and travel facilities for traders.[56]

During May 1945 the FEA provided further impetus for a return to private trade by arranging a series of meetings between prominent French officials and American importers and exporters. The French delegation consisted of Pierre Pelieu, chief of the French Colonial Supply Mission; Maurice Andlauer, head of the French Colonial Agency in the United States; and Georges Peter, director of Economic and Financial Services, French Ministry of Colonies. Peter announced the creation of the French Colonial Agency in the United States to replace the French Colonial Supply Mission. Peter pointed out that the new agency "was organized to promote relationships between American and French colonial merchants, to serve as a center of information on export and import problems, and to encourage private trade under the best conditions and in the interest of American as well as French merchants."[57]

Inquiries from the business community continued to arrive at the FEA. In response the agency informed traders that the United States had concluded arrangements for private trade to begin with the French colonies as of July 1, 1945. This included trade through private channels at both ends, but only with the empire. For Continental France and Corsica the lend-lease mechanism remained in effect.[58] The FEA recognized that French industrialists and American producers appeared eager to resume commercial supplying, but as Crowley pointed out, "the French Government insists that owing to the shortage of dollar availabilities it must do all the buying of raw materials for France—at least for the next several months." Neither French nor American officials indicated when private trade would return to France. Both sides anticipated an upward trend in the French economy, but they were also aware of the unpredictable nature of it. Moreover, the redeployment of forces from Europe further unbalanced an already unsteady economic situation.[59]

In September 1945, one month after Truman had terminated lend-lease operations for all countries, the French agreed to the resumption of commercial trade for Metropolitan France. Despite the imposed limitations on such transactions the French considered it a first step toward the restoration of normal commercial relations with the United States. However, the French insisted that for the time being the French mission would continue to purchase the bulk of French imports from the

United States. The French emphasized that due to the upheaval and
general deficiencies in Europe "the French Provisional Government feels
that the execution of its extensive reconstruction program requires supervision by governmental authority and an impetus which only these authorities can give."[60]

The French exercised such stringent control over trade that their description of it as a "first step" was somewhat of an overstatement. In
order for private transactions to receive approval the French required
American exporters to justify—to the satisfaction of French authorities—
the contribution of the goods to France's reconstruction program. The
French also limited the commodities for which they would issue licenses.
Those approved were: manufactured products (excluding machine tools,
industrial equipment, agricultural machinery, and trucks) weighing less
than five metric tons and valued at less than $20 thousand per shipment;
spare parts for machinery; certain raw materials, in particular items capable of producing commodities for exportation from France; and seeds
and animals for breeding. Once the French importer met these conditions,
officials assured him that the goods would enter France, that he could
obtain the foreign exchange to pay the American exporter, and that the
French Supply Council would cooperate with the FEA to guarantee shipping space.[61]

By the end of 1945 pressure applied by the United States produced
significant results. American officials had succeeded in restoring to commercial channels approximately 90 percent of the goods destined for
French West Africa. The remainder consisted primarily of bulk food not
easily procurable through private firms. In North Africa roughly 60 percent of the trade returned to private interests, and authorities anticipated
a significant increase in the near future. The furnishing of over $290 mil-
lion worth of civilian goods to the areas during the war did not in itself
guarantee the United States a substantial new market.[62] The postwar
volume of trade depended heavily on the manner in which France restored
and restructured her Northwest African empire. However, by the war's
end there were strong indications that France would never again dominate
these territories as completely as she once had. The general weakness of
France and the growing strength of the native independence movements
prevented a return to prewar colonial conditions. For commercial interests
the outcome of these events would determine the extent of American expansion in North and West Africa.

The intense controversy over private trade discredited both countries. The French, although somewhat hapless, had struggled tenaciously to maintain their economic domination over French Northwest Africa. Their determination succeeded in thwarting American attempts to restore private trade to the area for over two years. The Americans reacted hostilely to the French because they thought the French were callous and ungrateful for American assistance. On the other hand the United States exhibited an aggressive and opportunistic approach that frightened the French. It became quite evident that commercial interests and many government officials sought to exploit the weakened French and to expand in North and West Africa at French expense. Thus the intense struggle over private trade revealed that among the Allies even the spirit of cooperation for the war effort had failed to eradicate inveterate economic competition. In the end the issue served only to embitter relations between the United States and France and to foster distrust and suspicion among the Allies.

NOTES

1. FEA, "Protection of Private Trade Channels," April 1942, Box 229, RG 169.

2. Burns to Thomas Ballagh, September 4, 1942, Box 8, RG 169.

3. Ledreux to Bureau of Foreign and Domestic Commerce, December 3, 1942, Box 59, RG 169.

4. Williams to Ledreux, December 10, 1942, January 4, 1943, and Williams to Myers, December 14, 1942, Box 59, RG 169.

5. J. E. Bernard and Co. to State Department, December 19, 1942, Box 59, RG 169. *See also* State Department Document 851R.24/20, DNA.

6. Williams to Giest, February 1, 1943, Box 59, RG 169; *New York Times,* February 4, 1943, 32.

7. Sturm to Bernard, December 2, 1942, Box 59, RG 169.

8. Ibid.; "State Department Bulletin," January 9, 1943, State Department Document 851R.50/37, DNA; *New York Times,* February 5, 1943, 4.

9. *New York Times,* February 5, 1943, 4.

10. FEA, "Cash Reimbursement Policy," March 26, 1943, Box 211, RG 169; FEA, "Impact on Foreign Trade of Lend-Lease," April 12, 1943, Box 211, RG 169.

11. Rosebery to Beecroft, May 3, 1943, Box 275, RG 169.

12. *New York Times,* June 27, 1943, 6, 11.

13. Latrielle to Alderson, September 29, 1943, Box 1275, RG 169.

14. Miley to Stettinius, "Private Trade Poll," October 18, 1943, Box 59, RG 169.

15. Short to Young, July 29, 1943, Box 59, RG 169; Short to Stettinius, August 11, 1943, Box 59, RG 169.

16. Stettinius to Short, August 13, 1943, Box 59, RG 169.

17. Short to Young, July 29, 1943, Box 59, RG 169.

18. Latrielle to Alderson, "Report on Meeting with Trade to Discuss North Africa, September 24, 1943," September 29, 1943, Box 1275, RG 169.

19. *New York Times,* October 13, 1943, 34.

20. William L. Southworth to Hannigan, October 25, 1943, Box 975, RG 169; Lorwin to Lazo, October 18, 1943, Box 1275.

21. Lorwin to Lazo, October 18, 1943, Box 1275, RG 169.

22. Mitchell to Williams, December 6, 1943, Box 273, RG 169; *New York Times,* December 11, 1943, 4.

23. Crowley to Hull, December 8, 1943, Box 263, RG 169.

24. Ibid.; Crowley to Acheson, December 16, 1943, Box 851, RG 169.

25. Crowley to Monnet, December 9, 1943, Box 763, RG 169.

26. Hull to Crowley, December 31, 1943, State Department Document 851R.24/177, DNA.

27. Department of State Memorandum, December 27, 1943, Box 763, RG 169.

28. Hull to Crowley, December 3, 1943, State Department Document 851R.24/177, DNA.

29. Crowley to Hull, January 27, 1944, Box 763, RG 169.

30. Judson Hannigan, FEA Memorandum, December 15, 1943, Box 763, RG 169.

31. Ibid.; Perkins to Currie, "Résumé of Meeting with Monnet," January 27, 1944, Box 763, RG 169; Hannigan to Lebensburger, February 14, 1944, Box 1275, RG 169.

32. Burns to Hannigan, February 23, 1944, Box 978, RG 169.

33. Perkins to Currie, "Résumé of Meeting with Monnet," January 27, 1944, Box 763, RG 169; Hannigan to Lebensburger, February 14, 1944, Box 1275, RG 169; Valensi to Hannigan, February 27, 1944, Box 1275, RG 169.

34. Lorwin to Lowenstein, May 18, 1944, Box 1069, RG 169.

35. Gilpatric to Hannigan, March 21, 1944, Box 970, RG 169; Han-

nigan to Currie, April 20, 1944, Box 763, RG 169; Merchant to Hannigan, April 21, 1944, Box 1218, RG 169.

36. Woolston to Smith, April 15, 1944, Box 1303, RG 169.

37. FEA, "Notes on Executive Policy Committee Meeting, May 24, 1944," Box 979, RG 169.

38. Donald S. Gilpatric, "Resumption of Private Trade in Liberated Areas: A Progress Report on the Work of the Special Economic Mission," *Department of State Bulletin* 11 (December 10, 1944), 720.

39. Ibid., 720-22. *See also* Hull to Roosevelt, July 20, 1944, PSF, Roosevelt Papers. The president approved the mission after reviewing the nature ot it. Hull's letter also contains a list of the men appointed to the mission.

40. Ibid. For a detailed analysis of the mission's work elsewhere, see John A. DeNovo, "The Culbertson Economic Mission and Anglo-American Tensions in the Middle East, 1944-1945," *Journal of American History* 63 (No. 4, 1977), 913-36.

41. William S. Culbertson, "Report of the Special Economic Mission to North Africa, September 11, 1944," Boxes 970, 975, RG 169; Lowenstein to Scheurer, "Comments on the Report of the Special Economic Mission to North Africa," September 27, 1944, Box 1218, RG 169.

42. Culbertson, "Report of the Special Economic Mission to North Africa."

43. *New York Times,* September 6, 1944, 27.

44. Ibid., October 23, 1944, 5.

45. Ibid., November 20, 1944, 13.

46. Hannigan to Currie, December 4, 1944, Box 1218, RG 169.

47. Denby to Currie, December 8, 1944, Box 1218, RG 169.

48. Charles I. Bevans, ed., *Denmark-France,* Vol. 7: *Treaties and Other International Agreements of the United States of America, 1776-1949* (Washington, D. C.: Department of State, 1971), 1070-72; OLLA History: "Ships and Shipping," 58-59; Department of State Aide-Mémoire, December 12, 1944, Box 464, RG 169. *See also* Stettinius to the American Embassy in Paris, December 1, 1944, Box 464, RG 169. Stettinius's cable contains instructions that were almost identical to the official aide-mémoire of December 12.

49. Ibid.

50. Bevans, ed., *Denmark-France,* 1070-72; "Reply to the United States Aide-Mémoire," December 27, 1944, Box 464, RG 169. The American Aide-Mémoire and the French reply constituted a general agreement between the two countries. A copy of each is also in: United States

Department of State, *Foreign Relations of the United States, 1944,* Vol. 3 (Washington, D. C.: United States Government Printing Office, 1965), 764-69 (hereafter referred to as *Foreign Relations 1944* 3). The passage is quoted from Bevans, ed., *Denmark-France,* 1072-74; it differs slightly, though not substantially, from a similar paragraph in *Foreign Relations 1944* 3, 768-69.

51. Culbertson to State Department, January 2, 1945, Box 464, RG 169; *see also* Culbertson, "Principles of Economic Policy," *Department of State Bulletin* 12 (February 25, 1945), 299.

52. OLLA History: "Ships and Shipping," 60; FEA Bulletin, "Trade Relations Supplement," March 5, 1945, Box 3189, RG 169.

53. FEA Bulletin, "Trade Relations Supplement," March 5, 1945, Box 3189, RG 169.

54. Gilpatric to Labouisse, March 22, 1945, Box 3189, RG 169.

55. Ibid.

56. "Resumption of Private Trade to French North and French West Africa," *Department of State Bulletin* 12 (April 29, 1945), 832-34. This includes the total list of goods eligible for Northwest African trade.

57. OLLA History: "Ships and Shipping," 60. *See also* President of the French Supply Council, "The Organization of Private Trade between the United States and the French Colonies," n.d., Box 3189, RG 169.

58. Davidson to Sanders, May 14, 1945, Box 1170, RG 169.

59. Crowley to Rizon, July 26, 1945, Box 813, RG 169. *See also* Rizon to Crowley, July 16, 1945, and Crowley to Rizon, August 31, 1945, Box 813, RG 169.

60. "Restoration to Private Channels of Certain United States Exports to France," *Department of State Bulletin* 13 (September 9, 1945), 358.

61. Ibid.

62. OLLA History: "Ships and Shipping," 61.

9.

The Scene Shifts to France, and a Master Agreement Is Negotiated

Following the Normandy invasion the army assumed the responsibility for civilian supplies and provided the minimum requirements based on its "disease and unrest formula." French and American civilian officials protested the limited aid and designed programs to supplement the army's assistance. At the same time they demanded a termination of military responsibility, and in early 1944 American and French representatives attempted to complete arrangements for a definitive civilian lend-lease agreement to cover Metropolitan France. The task proved exceptionally difficult. The United States procrastinated, hoping for an early termination of the European war, which would eliminate the need for such an understanding. Furthermore, in August and September 1944 plans formulated by the FEA, the state department, and the French included provisions for large quantities of reconstruction material for postwar use. Morgenthau spearheaded the opposition to such proposals. He succeeded in postponing an understanding until the FEA and state agreed to include specific payment arrangements for nonmilitary goods as an integral part of the master agreement. More importantly, however, the controversy within the administration, which was precipitated by considerations of lend-lease proposals for France, served to focus attention on the broader and more volatile issue of the role of lend-lease in the post-war world.

In late 1943 American authorities commenced studies of conditions within France in order to establish estimates of supplies required during and immediately following liberation. The French Empire, they concluded, could furnish minimum assistance. Unlike the British the French had only become seriously "Empire export-minded" since World War I. Specifically the experts anticipated that the empire could provide approximately 50 percent of the required foodstuffs. More importantly it could not supply a number of essential foods, such as animal feed, milk, butter, and cheese. Furthermore, the empire did not produce many of the raw materials that France desperately needed. Officials calculated that the empire could provide approximately two million of the seven million tons that France required for one year.[1]

With the limited assistance available from the empire prewar France had also suffered from a chronic and sometimes very large trade deficit. Only twice in forty years had France's exports paid for her imports, and following liberation it would take France considerable time to recover even this trade. Such a situation had a serious impact on France's foreign exchange. For the duration of the war officials eliminated the possibility of France accumulating any appreciable amount of foreign exchange.[2]

Between 1938 and 1943 France's total industrial production had declined approximately 40 percent. Moreover, the Germans had confiscated two-thirds of the production. The occupation had also depleted French stockpiles, and whatever remained the Allies required for war production. The textile industry, France's most noted industry, lacked raw materials and could produce practically nothing for exportation. The empire's exports could provide only a moderate amount of foreign exchange, estimated at approximately $53 million, and most of this the colonies required for their own purposes. The only positive aspect of the French economic situation was the large supply of gold and dollar assets the French possessed in the United States.[3]

The occupation had exacted a severe toll on the French population. In March 1944 the *New York Times* cited a study that indicated that the average Frenchman's daily caloric intake consisted of only 1,100 calories, compared to the recommended 3,100. Rickets, anemia, and high blood pressure were common with the absence of drugs, vitamins, and disinfectants, and the stillborn baby rate had escalated to a record high. In considering the ramifications of such depravity the *New York Times* concluded, "It may take a generation to rebuild human values that the Germans ruthlessly destroyed and that money alone cannot renew."[4]
As of August 1944, an American representative in France reported that over 155,000 Frenchmen had perished in German camps; 850,000 were prisoners of war in Germany, and of these, 300,000 worked as slave labor.

The Germans had deported approximately two million civilians whose condition remained unknown. Over one million children had succumbed from malnutrition, and the death rate among French children was eight times higher than children in Germany.[5]

Despite the estimates and projections few envisioned the devastation, destruction, and ruin that the process of liberation entailed. On June 6, 1944, the Allied landings in Normandy transformed France into a theater of intense and bitter warfare. Two months of fighting cost the lives of 83,000 civilians, including 4,000 children. In areas where the most severe fighting occurred, the destruction was enormous. The three cities of Le Havre, Rouen, and Caen suffered heavy damange. The hostilities had destroyed two-fifths of Le Havre, one-fourth of Rouen, and four-fifths of Caen. In Le Havre and Rouen over ten thousand inhabitants died and fifty thousand were left homeless. Without coal, wood, or gas Rouen halted all industrial production.[6] After less than six months of fighting an American official in France reported that the cost of war to France was incalculable and commented, "France no longer ranks among the Great Powers."[7]

In September 1944 the United States and Britain sent a fact-finding team to France. Known as the Weir-Green Mission the Allies instructed it to ascertain France's potential to manufacture items in short supply necessary for the prosecution of the war. Officials realized that such *ad hoc* missions hardly provided the solution for keeping in touch with economic conditions affecting long-term planning. However, they proved valuable for appraisals of current conditions. The Weir-Green Mission recommended that the Allies furnish raw materials and utilize French sources for the production of military clothing, X-ray tubes, certain chemicals, batteries, cotton cloth, and some auto accessories.[8]

As the Allied army routed the Germans in France, Belgium, and the Netherlands, Roosevelt recognized the need for more comprehensive information on conditions within these countries. Consequently on January 20, 1945, the president commissioned his friend and adviser, Judge Samuel Rosenman, "to examine and report to me the steps to be taken in the joint interests of our country and the fighting Allies in winning the war with respect to the flow of vital supplies other than finished munitions to these countries." Furthermore, Roosevelt instructed Rosenman to determine "what the needs of these countries will be for supplies and services to repair the destruction and devastation of the war and to build some of the economic foundations of peace in terms of possible credits or other financial assistance at hand or through recommendations for appropriate legislation."[9] Rosenman's work produced one of the most complete reports on conditions within these countries.

As in other liberated areas the most urgent needs of France consisted of coal, improvements in the internal transportation network, larger and more balanced diets, and raw materials. Of these necessities coal classified as the most vital prerequisite for the restoration of France's economic health. Prior to the war France consumed seventy-five million tons of coal per year, thirty million of which it imported. By December 1944 France's coal supply had fallen by two-thirds. During the previous winter there was practically no coal for heating private homes. Although no figures were available, authorities attributed the marked increase in deaths of the very young and aged to a lack of coal. Whatever the impact the Allies agreed that the French population could hardly endure another heatless winter. However, during the course of liberation the coal problem became more complex as the plight of the miners worsened. The fighting destroyed mining areas, tools, and equipment, and the cessation of work prompted insubordination among the miners. Due to the indispensable nature of their work, the miners had received some preferential treatment by the Germans and complained bitterly that their lot was better under the Axis. The destruction of mining facilities also increased the burden on the Allies to import more coal into France than in the prewar period.[10]

The food situation in France offered little encouragement and in many respects represented the most critical deficiency. Prior to the war France was approximately 80 percent self-sufficient in food supply. But the occupation radically altered the agricultural balance. The Germans extracted huge quantities of food, and in November 1942 the Allies eliminated North Africa as a source of supply. Along with this, actual production declined significantly due to the lack of labor, fertilizers, and reduced feed imports. Although destruction to food production and processing facilities remained slight, this was offset by the disruption of internal transportation, which prevented producers from moving goods to large consumption areas. At times Paris existed for a week or more without meat, while its daily milk supply declined from its peacetime level of 1,000,000 liters to 350,000. Moreover, due to the shortage of supplies and shipping during the early stages of the invasion, the United States and Great Britain

failed to meet even the minimum military food requirements. The United
States had to furnish the bulk of these supplies since the Russians or Germans controlled the surplus-producing areas in Eastern Europe.[11]

The French transportation network clearly revealed the impact of the
occupation and the subsequent task of liberation. By February 1945 the
French possessed only 7,500 locomotives from a prewar level of 16,500,
and most of these were obsolete and inefficient. In addition 137,500
working trucks remained out of a prewar total of 475,000. Observers
reported very few cargo trucks on the road, and those in operation were
worn and ineffective. The Germans had confiscated vehicles, parts, and
equipment for military purposes, and since June 1940 there were no new
vehicles available in France. Thus experts concluded that a French request
for 100,000 vehicles and 5,000 locomotives was not excessive. Moreover,
the fighting had destroyed over 1,000 bridges, tunnels, and trestles.[12]

The Allies attempted to remedy the decline of industrial production
by restoring manufacturing for immediate military objectives. Although
the program yielded satisfactory results, officials doubted that it could
reach significant proportions and emphasized that it in no way represented
a major effort.[13] As Monnet noted, "In spite of what has been done, the
economic life of France is steadily approaching extinction."[14] The raw
materials for industry contributed little to French needs, as most of it
went into the French rearmament program. "This expansion of the
French Army," Rosenman wrote, "will impinge sharply on the already
serious manpower shortage in certain specialized fields and upon France's
gravely restricted coal and transportation resources." Rosenman's prog-
nosis revealed little evidence of optimism. The destruction or damage
of over 40,000 farms and 1,200,000 private dwellings necessitated the
billeting of over five million civilians with other families and under un-
sanitary conditions. This situation alone, Rosenman stressed, represented
an enormous rehabilitation project. Rosenman concluded that France
required a long-range effort so extensive that it was virtually impossible
to place a dollar value on it.[15]

Amid the destruction and economic dislocation the United States
attempted to furnish civilian assistance to Metropolitan France. Prior
to D day the United States had established basic priorities in liberated
areas. Roosevelt's directive of November 10, 1943, assigned to the military
the responsibility for providing civilian supplies during the initial stages
of military operations. The president designated such goods furnished

by the army as Plan A supplies. On January 29, 1944, Stimson made it quite clear to Hull that the items procured by the war department would rest on the "prevention of disease and unrest formula" and would consist solely of food, medical, and sanitation supplies. The state department and the FEA, Stimson emphasized, shared the responsibility for the planning and procurement of supplies required during the later stages.[16]

In arranging for assistance to France, officials did not anticipate any radical deviation from this procedure. In March 1945 Hull cabled the American embassy in London that the army had no interest in any extensive program for the rehabilitation or reconstruction of industrial life in France. After studying conditions within France, the primary Allied objective was to concentrate on France's ability to feed, clothe, and shelter the population from her own resources. American officials felt that the United States should not attempt to rehabilitate France's industrial system during the course of the war. Rather, the Allies focused on reestablishing limited manufacturing to improve the economy, assist in the war, and reduce importation.[17]

Despite the apparent necessity for the military's role in civilian supply, civilian authorities experienced difficulty adjusting to it. In Italy, where this first went into effect on a large scale, the FEA expressed extreme dissatisfaction. On April 13, 1944, E. E. Hunt, chief of the FEA's Italian division, described the army as lacking concern for their responsibilities in civilian matters. "The root of the problem," Hunt wrote, "is the disproportionate priority given to immediate military needs as compared with civilian necessities." Furthermore, he emphasized, "it is clear that civilians and the civilian point of view must be a recognized and respected part of military operations and must be given an appropriate status."[18]

The French shared the concern of the American civilian administrators over the limits of the military program. Prior to the invasion Monnet had submitted proposals for extensive relief and rehabilitation. General John Hildring, the head of the military's Civilian Affairs Division, informed him that his requirements went far beyond anything the army would provide. Hildring reinforced the army policy of furnishing only the minimum supplies necessary to prevent disease and unrest behind the lines. The FEA, hardly reconciled to the army's role, criticized Plan A as barely related to France's minimum needs. Consequently the agency supported French requests for additional material and with the French pressured the military either to agree to a specific termination date for its responsibility or effectively supplement Plan A in France.[19]

In order to meet their more extensive needs the French submitted two "quick repair" supply programs in August 1944. They requested 150,000 metric tons of repair items for trucks, railroad stock, maintenance facilities, public utilities, and industry. On September 24 American and French civilian authorities drew up a long-range program comprising 8,500,000 metric tons—2,000,000 of which the United States would supply. And in October the French presented the first part of a program for materials most needed immediately following the termination of military responsibility.[20] Subsequently, in November the French submitted three other requests that completed the "emergency program." This list clearly revealed the magnitude of the French requirements and included 9,000 trucks and buses, 475,000 squares of prepared roll roofing, 28,500,000 square feet of wallboard, 89,000 squares of asbestos, cement, or galvanized roofing, 5,950,800 pounds of horseshoes, 1,983,600 pounds of horseshoe nails, and barracks of all types valued at $5,750,000.[21]

The size and nature of the program prompted Leo Crowley, the director of the Foreign Economic Administration, to issue priority instructions for France. He requested the combined boards of all government agencies to render immediate decisions on the French requests. As in the early stages of the North African operation, Crowley directed the agencies to consider end-use justification very generally, since the nature of the program dictated bypassing of close screening. Furthermore, the programs confirmed that France required less relief and more raw materials than anticipated.[26]

French authorities feared that a lack of these materials would increase the country's unemployment and thereby produce serious political repercussions.[22] Of the French officials, Monnet appeared as one of the few who comprehended the supply situation. He worked closely with Supreme Headquarters Allied Expeditionary Force (SHAEF), since the United States expected France to play a major role in presenting priority programs.

In order to facilitate matters in France, the Allies established a Four Power Committee consisting of representatives of the SHAEF Mission, the French Committee on Importations, and economic advisers from the FEA and the United Kingdom. The committee examined and discussed

French programs in light of actual port and inland transportation conditions. At its first meeting on November 20, 1944, the committee reviewed the "Eight Months Program" or "Monnet Program," which would extend until June 30, 1945. This program was based more on what the port and transportation system could handle rather than on actual needs and served as an addition to the earlier emergency programs. Nevertheless, it contained many of the same items: steel products, building materials, industrial equipment, agricultural supplies, food, metals, and minerals. The Four Power Committee considered the program moderate and recommended it for approval.[23]

The Allies also created four other committees to concentrate on the railway system, harbors, inland waterways, and shipping. The lines of communication for the French programs flowed through a somewhat complex bureaucratic structure. After the Four Power Committee studied the program, the SHAEF French Mission, composed of members of the army's Civilian Affairs Division and assisted by American and British economic advisers, reviewed it. The program then went to Washington, where it received consideration from the Combined Civil Affairs Committee (CCAC), headed by Assistant Secretary of War, John McCloy. Although dominated by military personnel, the CCAC also included a representative from the state department and a member of the British Foreign Office. The CCAC passed its recommendations to the Combined Liberated Areas Committee (CLAC), which was under the direction of Acheson. This Committee represented the state department, treasury, FEA, and the British Embassy, treasury, army and Ministry of Supply. In May 1944 the United States had created the Liberated Areas Committee (LAC), also chaired by Acheson. It concentrated on analyzing American contributions to ongoing programs and projected plans for extensive economic rehabilitation. The work of its subcommittee, LACs, completed the process for commending procurement. An administrator from the FEA directed LACs, which consisted of members from state and treasury along with representatives from the procurement agencies—the War Production Board, the War Shipping Administration, and the War Food Administration.[24]

The success of the Allied forces in France had precipitated a rapid German withdrawal, thereby preventing the implementation of a widespread scorched-earth policy. Thus sufficient crops remained so that no immediate outbreak of food riots occurred. However, during 1944 the dearth of civilian imports in Northwestern Europe was responsible for malnutrition and starvation, even if they did not assume dangerous proportions. Due to the inadequacy of damaged harbors SHAEF found it impossible to import large quantities of civilian supplies. During 1944 SHAEF imported into northern France only 21 percent of its minimum program; in southern France the imports reached 75 percent, but the total quantity was small.[25]

The shortcomings of the civilian program left the army extremely vulnerable to criticism from French and American civilian authorities. The army itself, however, was caught in a desperate situation. In the rush across France the advance simply outdistanced the supply lines and sources. The objective, of course, was to defeat Hitler, not rehabilitate France's economy. Under such circumstances it was inevitable that the civilian program would suffer—through no one's fault. Nevertheless French and American civilian supply officials pressured the military to do more and to eventually turn over to them the responsibility for civilian supply. As early as September 1944 General Hildring assured the French and the FEA that the army would seriously consider proposals for a termination of military responsibility. The army also indicated that it was anxious to get out of the civilian-supply business and set January 1, 1945, as a tentative termination date.[26]

Eager to play an expanded role in the war and to begin economic reconstruction, the French emphasized the importance of a national import program. On January 2, 1945, Monnet formally requested shipping space for his program and noted, "This is a firm request for shipping—it is a firm request because of the fact of liberation and of the fact of continued warfare."[27] The war department, however, rapidly withdrew its January 1 termination date when it appeared that the civilian agencies, and especially the War Shipping Administration, desired to include shipping assignments for national import programs under their jurisdiction. Consequently the army insisted upon retaining the civilian-supply programs under military auspices until the shipping shortage eased.[28]

The military's position precipitated a controversy with the civilian agencies and the British, who also supported the concept of national import programs. In January 1945 Great Britain sent Sir Richard Law to the United States to negotiate the issue directly with Harry Hopkins. On January 14, 1945, Hopkins and Law concluded an agreement for the commencement of national import programs on a limited scale. The task of developing the schedules for the first half of 1945 fell to Oscar Cox of the FEA and Britain's Thomas Brand. They worked out the necessary requirements for the lend-lease countries concerned and also designated the sources of supply. At Yalta the Allies discussed the Law-Hopking Agreement and the Cox-Brand schedules. They received a tacit approval, although the British effort to grant priority to European rehabilitation over the Pacific war failed.[29]

By mid-January 1945 the military faced a dilemma in Europe. It was quite evident that the military relief program based on the disease and unrest formula was obsolete. The German army had not yet collapsed, and the war department feared that relinquishing control would produce an adverse effect on operations. The military's previous experiences in Italy and France revealed that the Italian government and the French Provisional Government possessed less effective control than the army had assumed. In France the Provisional Government had assumed control of the railroads but had proved so inept that officials returned the responsibility to the American army.[30]

The civilian agencies, however, anticipated the termination of military responsibility prior to any announcement of a target date. Under the Law-Hopkins arrangement the national import programs for France and Belgium commenced and gradually gained momentum by the end of January. Monnet persuaded American authorities to consolidate the French relief and national import program into one entity under French control. The civilian agencies, and in particular the War Shipping Administration, supported Monnet's efforts.[31] Rosenman recommended that Roosevelt write Stimson outlining a policy for the termination of the military control over civilian supply. As Rosenman accurately portrayed it: "To limit the standard of assistance to the military level of provision any longer than is necessary, is to restrict treatment to first aid long after the patient is in need of a major operation."[32]

Finally on March 6, 1945, SHAEF proposed transferring the civilian supply programs for France to the civilian agencies—effective as of March 30. The war department granted its approval but set the date back until the end of April. Since the military delivered coal and petroleum in bulk for both military and civilian consumption, it established September 1, 1945, as the terminal date for military handling of these supplies.[33] Following the German surrender Truman relieved the army of the responsibility for civilian supply in the liberated European countries. He acknowledged the success of the military programs in having prevented disease and unrest, but asserted, "Once liberation of a country has been accomplished, however, I feel that the best interests of the United States and of the liberated country itself require termination of this military responsibility as soon as the military situation permits."[34]

While the American military and civilian agencies maintained the French supply programs, French and American officials recognized the need for a more definitive and permanent lend-lease agreement. Both sides agreed that the *Modus Vivendi* had serious shortcomings and existed merely as an interim arrangement. On January 7, 1944, Monnet brought to the attention of American authorities Article V of the *Modus*, which required the French to pay cash for civilian goods but also stipulated that "revision of the payment provisions of this *modus vivendi* will be made should the situation require."[35] Monnet also pointed out that during the negotiations that lead to the *Modus*, the French had expressed doubts about the ability of the FCNL to continue such payments. This apprehension assumed greater significance during late 1943 and 1944, when the number of American troops in North Africa decreased while the volume of imports increased. Moreover, Monnet estimated that the total resources of the French committee, excluding funds frozen in the United States, amounted to $50 million. This approximated the French debt for civilian supplies at that point. Therefore, he desired to invoke the revision clause to modify the payment arrangement. He also asserted that the situation clearly illustrated the need for a more satisfactory lend-lease agreement.[36]

In response to Monnet's appeal the state department defined its position. Acheson urged Monnet to investigate closely with the FEA and the treasury department specific courses that the French could pursue to offset their payment deficit. He indicated that the United States would accept a reasonable method of supplying more dollars to the French committee. But until there was further clarification of the French financial status, Acheson rejected any modifications of French obligations under terms of the *Modus.*[37]

Undersecretary of State Stettinius advised Crowley of state's policy and informed him that the frozen French funds were under restrictions for "protection and asylum." He pointed out that the assets remained blocked except for authorized use in special cases of a noncontroversial nature—such as payment for packages sent to French prisoners of war. Stettinius also stressed that the state department had no intention of discussing the use of these funds for payment of lend-lease bills. Rather, he advised Crowley to impress upon the French the necessity of mobilizing their gold and dollar resources under the control of the FCNL.[38]

The French payment question became an integral part of broader negotiations for the conclusion of a lend-lease agreement. The decision to employ the frozen French assets to pay for packages that the United States provided for the French prisoners of war distressed Monnet. The French had proposed that the United States furnish such goods on a straight lend-lease basis, but Acheson informed Monnet that this was out of the question. Monnet pointed out what he considered the inconsistency of the American position—sanctioning the use of French gold while refusing to recognize the FCNL as the government of Metropolitan France. Acheson argued that the United States policy did not involve the question of money or recognition; the state department interpreted the Lend-Lease Act to state that all countries pay for prisoner-of-war supplies. They could not treat the French any differently.[39] Despite Acheson's explanation, the inconsistency in American policy remained apparent.

The French also discussed at length their difficulties in accruing dollar balances. The basic problem, from their point of view, involved selling a large volume of French colonial products to Great Britain but purchasing most of their goods from the United States. Acheson noted that negotiations were in process for the purchase of more gold from the French empire, and officials expressed hope that it would amount to $60 million. At the same time, the state department suggested that the French could meet their financial debt through the sale of newly mined gold and by the utilization of dollar assets in the French treasury in Africa.[40]

Since the United States refused to alter the payment arrangements, the French approached the British on the possibility of converting sterling to dollars to improve their dollar balances. Chiefly because of purchases by British troops, the French in North Africa had accumulated sterling balances amounting to roughly $160 million; but their dollar resources declined to less than $30 million. The French requested: authorization to employ five million pounds to discharge part of its debt to the United States; the conclusion of arrangements for the sale of more goods for dollars, either by diverting present allocations from the United Kingdom to the United States or by having the British make part of their payment in dollars; an increase of imports from sterling areas; and a reduction of imports from dollar areas.[41]

The British who were as destitute, if not more so, than the French, could not offer much assistance to alleviate the French plight. Ben Smith, the British resident Minister in Washington, rejected the request to convert five million pounds to dollars and the proposal for Great Britain to pay a portion of French colonial goods in dollars. The British agreed, however, to forego their interest in the 1944-45 cocoa crop in West Africa and to cease buying gold from French Equatorial Africa. In both cases they recommended that the French sell the products to the United States. Smith also indicated a desire to explore the possibility of selling more goods to the French colonies.[42]

The negotiations with the French, however, concentrated on considerations of basic principles upon which a formal lend-lease agreement would rest. By the end of April 1944 Monnet and Acheson had exchanged aide-mémoires defining lend-lease relations between the United States and territories under the control of the FCNL. The discussions attracted the attention of Roosevelt, and on May 3 he instructed Hull to obtain his personal approval before completing any lend-lease agreement with the French. On June 27 Hull informed the president that the state department contemplated two lend-lease agreements, as well as a program for the production of war necessities within France.[43]

On July 15, 1944, Hull submitted to Roosevelt a memorandum stipulating the basis on which the United States would furnish lend-lease assistance to Metropolitan France. As in the past the United States would provide supplies for the French army on a straight or credit lend-lease basis. Short-life civilian goods and short-life industrial maintenance articles would also be furnished by the United States on a straight lend-lease basis. This assistance would continue "until such time after the end of hostilities in Europe as the president may determine to be necessary in the war effort." Thereafter, such supplies either in inventory or contract, which the United States had agreed to make available, would be received and paid for on credit arrangements under 3(c) of the Lend-Lease Act. The memo also provided for long-life industrial materials necessary for French manufacturing. Hull's memorandum also included provisions for reciprocal aid or reverse lend-lease. The French agreed to provide military equipment, munitions, supplies, services, and facilities to American forces. The French would also export any available raw materials not in short supply and required for use in the American war industry.[44]

On July 18, 1944, Roosevelt approved the conditions of the memorandum, which served as a basis for continued negotiations. On August 25 talks resulted in a joint acceptance of a "Memorandum Relating to Lend-Lease and Reciprocal Aid." Its terms committed both governments to a continuation of discussions with the intention of concluding a lend-lease and reciprocal-aid agreement applicable to Continental France. The terms of such an understanding would take effect as of June 6, 1944.[45]

While both sides expressed satisfaction over the progress of the discussions, they also recognized the critical need for large-scale civilian aid for France. However, no arrangement existed to cover such assistance. Consequently on September 4, 1944, Crowley proposed to Monnet that the French inform the FEA of the supplies required for Metropolitan France. He stipulated that payment for such goods "will be made in dollars, with the understanding, however, that all payments made or to be made for supplies received by the French Committee are to be subject to such arrangements for payment and for the receipt of reciprocal aid as may be finally determined upon in the pending lend-lease agreement.[46] The following day, Monnet accepted the proposal. On September 19 Crowley supplemented the understanding by providing a release for the French should they no longer desire certain supplies procured for them. Under these circumstances the FEA would charge only the net losses to the United States, including cancellation charges.[47] The Crowley-Monnet exchange constituted an interim arrangement for civilian assistance to France until the conclusion of a formal lend-lease agreement.

In considering proposals for the lend-lease understanding American officials encountered serious difficulties not easily reconciled. On September 7 the FEA informed Roosevelt that a question of utmost importance had arisen, which divided American officials and "on which the President may wish to make the decision." The issue was lend-lease credit arrangements for French industrial goods with a postwar utility. The French desired to purchase a large quantity of desperately needed industrial equipment and related materials for economic reconstruction. The aggregate program totaled approximately $2 billion, for which the French proposed to use long-term credit.[48]

The July 15 memorandum, which Roosevelt had approved, provided for the furnishing of long-life materials. Such products the United States had agreed to supply on a credit basis but only where they were "essential to the war in Europe or for the support of Allied armed forces in the 'im-

mediate period' following the end of hostilities in Europe." Since July,
however, the state department had altered its position on long-life goods.
It advocated eliminating the tie between the supplying of these lend-lease
goods and the end of the war in Europe. This modification would have
permitted the furnishing of a larger volume of reconstruction materials
on a lend-lease basis. The treasury opposed such a policy, while the FEA
contended that the decision "depends upon the role which France is to
play in the Pacific war."[49]

The argument in favor of a liberal expansion of lend-lease credit had
considerable merit. Along with the obvious need for reconstruction supplies officials stressed the connection between France's economic situation and her political stability. Furthermore, both the United States and
France realized that no other credit mechanism existed, and neither foresaw the development of any for at least six months.[50] Quite naturally the
French had expressed a strong preference for a liberal lend-lease arrangement. The July 15 memorandum had dissatisfied the French, and they
refused to accept its terms. Instead Monnet had begun work with Acheson
and Cox on a new understanding. Yet every proposal the French presented
went beyond the memorandum approved by Roosevelt.[51]

The opposition denounced the recommendations to utilize lend-lease
for reconstruction purposes. Lend-lease, they insisted, existed solely as
a wartime measure and not for any postwar functions. Numerous congressmen raised objections on this basis unless the French would play an
important role in the Pacific war. The treasury argued that France's gold
and dollar balances eliminated the necessity for extending credit.[52] The
proposals for providing lend-lease credit for French reconstruction raised
the broader issue of the role of lend-lease in postwar rehabilitation and
had a permanent impact on the future of lend-lease to all countries.

In this controversy the FEA sought presidential direction. Thus it became Roosevelt's decision to permit the July 15 memorandum to stand
or to accept modifications of it. The FEA also requested guidance on
whether the agreement should be broad, narrow, or provisional.[53]

On September 11, 1944, the state department informed Roosevelt
of the progress made on considerations for an agreement with the French.
Hull had proposed that the United States provide long-life goods based
on a list attached to the final agreement. Such goods, Hull stipulated,
"which are contracted for or purchased before you determine that aid
under the Act is no longer necessary for the prosecution of the war, we

shall deliver (subject to your right of cancellation in the national interest) and the French shall accept and pay for on credit terms." Hull also recommended that the FEA submit the proposed French programs to Roosevelt for his approval before including them in the list. Stettinius reported that the FEA had approved these recommendations.[54]

The state department and the FEA concluded a draft of a lend-lease agreement for France. The arrangement permitted the supply of long-life industrial goods to France under long-term credits provided for under section 3(c) of the Lend-Lease Act. It allowed the French to submit requisitions until the end of the war with Japan and also stipulated that once the FEA had received French requests, it would furnish the material regardless of the terminal date of the war in the Pacific. This in effect would assist in the large-scale reconstruction of France. The arrangement also extended the period for providing short-life industrial goods until the defeat of Japan.[55]

The state department submitted its proposal for Roosevelt's consideration at the Second Quebec Conference in September 1944. The treasury department, represented at the conference by Morgenthau, immediately voiced its opposition. Morgenthau argued that the new proposals guaranteed reconstruction commitments without congressional approval and presented Congress and the public with a *fait accompli*. Should Congress terminate lend-lease following the cessation of the war in Europe, "any attempt to rely on large requisitions placed under a previously existing agreement with the French (having no relation to the war in Europe) as permitting the reconstruction of France would be politically impossible and highly undesirable," Morgenthau asserted. Such a program, the secretary feared, would lead the French to presume that Roosevelt had sanctioned a reconstruction operation for France. "The door will be wide open for reconstructing France under the Lend-Lease Act," Morgenthau insisted, "without understandings as to the role of France in the future of Europe and of the world, particularly of French participation in the war against Japan." He cited testimony of Assistant Secretary of War John McCloy and General Hildring that indicated that France's production would have little impact on the war in Europe; and France's assistance in the war against Japan "can be put in your right eye."[56]

Morgenthau's opposition represented an extension of his previous objections to a liberal program for the French. He had clashed with the state department over the use of frozen French assets and vociferously argued against supplying even military assistance to France on a credit lend-lease basis. Therefore he insisted that the French would construe the acceptance of this new arrangement as a "major political victory arising from the strategy of playing one department of the United States Government against another on financial questions."[57]

Amid conflicting departmental opinions Roosevelt acted. On September 15 he approved a memorandum recommending an indefinite postponement of the French negotiations.[58] On September 20 Morgenthau informed Stimson that at Quebec "Churchill was violently opposed to the United States making any lend-lease arrangement with the French."[59] As Morgenthau later explained, "The British felt very, very strongly. The French have come out of this thing with a lot of money and they are coming out of it with none."[60] Morgenthau also reported that when he spoke to Roosevelt, he agreed with the British position and that "the President didn't really want to give them any Lend-Lease."[61]

The issue of French lend-lease also fell under the close scrutiny of the war department. Stimson, a veteran at testifying before Congress for lend-lease extensions and appropriations, described it as a "throny question" but emphasized the function of lend-lease as a war measure. Like Morgenthau he appeared very sensitive to congressional reaction. "To give it to the French would turn it into a relief fund and might arouse strong congressional opposition," Stimson wrote.[62]

A meeting on September 20 in Hull's office revealed some disagreement within the war department. McCloy defended the steps taken to conclude an agreement. He pointed out that Roosevelt was cognizant of the discussions with the French and had in fact approved the continuation of the negotiations. McCloy disagreed with the treasury representative, who insisted that this meant very little. McCloy argued that the decision at Quebec was contrary to the language and spirit of the earlier documents. He contended: "We had pressed the French heavily in order to get them committed on gold and on their willingness to pay for Plan A supplies in cash, the French certainly understanding that they would be able to proceed forth with discussions as to the manner in which 3(c) credits could be given them for their more extended program." The meeting accomplished little and adjourned with a decision to investigate the matter more thoroughly. McCloy's description of the entire situation as a "very confused state of affairs" aptly summarized it.[63]

Stimson's position, however, remained unaltered and applied to all lend-lease countries. He approved of postwar lend-lease to England but stressed that any attempt to implement it without congressional approval was a grave mistake. At a cabinet meeting in October 1944 he urged that Congress be consulted "if we are going to go into making use of lend-lease appropriations in the post-war period or when there was no longer any connection between them and the actual fighting of the recipient. In a later conversation with Hopkins, Stimson told him he had warned Roosevelt that lend-lease "was not intended for the rehabilitation of other countries."[64]

While the debate over French lend-lease progressed, the United States significantly altered its policy toward de Gaulle's government. On October 23, 1944, Stettinius, as Acting Secretary of State, announced the recognition of the French Provisional Government as the de facto government of France. The United States qualified its recognition by including reservations "insuring both the institution of a democratic regime in France and the ultimate endorsement of that regime by popular expression."[65]

Official recognition represented a triumph for de Gaulle's diplomacy and strengthened his administration's efforts to restore order and unity within the country. Washington officials felt that recognition entitled the French to preferential treatment to facilitate "the commercial and financial relations of the government with the United States and especially with its situation in regard to lend-lease."[66]

The new status accorded de Gaulle's government increased the pressure on the state department to finalize a lend-lease agreement. Roosevelt, however, had turned the matter over to Morgenthau without rescinding his instructions on postponement. On October 24, eager to clarify the situation, Stettinius conversed with Morgenthau. In reply to Stettinius's inquiry the secretary of the treasury informed him that the matter was not in his lap, but "just under where I sit." The state department, however, could not assume the blasé attitude of Morgenthau. As Stettinius pointed out, the French and American representatives had agreed with Morgenthau's approval to the August 25 memorandum providing for a continuation of negotiations leading to a formal agreement. "Now we're getting toward November," Stettinius declared, "we've got a full Ambassador now and the French are needling the hell out of our fellows. . . and we've got to say something to them."[67]

Although Morgenthau had frustrated Stettinius, it had become quite evident that the admistration could not "sit on it" indefinitely. Initially it had hoped for an early cessation of the European war, thereby eliminating the necessity for any further lend-lease arrangements. However, as the winter of 1944 approached, the war in Europe continued to rage, and France required enormous amounts of civilian aid. The pressure on the state department and the FEA mounted as the French presented a civilian lend-lease program valued at $2,575,000,000 and covering an eighteen-month period.[68]

During December the FEA and the state department devised another lend-lease arrangement for the French. The terms approximated those submitted to Roosevelt at Quebec. At a cabinet meeting on January 19, 1945, the agencies presented the proposals. Once again Morgenthau denounced their liberal nature. However, he recognized that some understanding with the French was essential. He felt it had become increasingly more difficult to refute the French argument that the United States treated the French differently than the other Allies.[69] Although Morgenthau rejected the proposals submitted by state and the FEA, he nevertheless supported Crowley's recommendations to work out some agreement with the French. Morgenthau later maintained that without his backing "the President would never have given the green light on the French lend-lease matter."[70]

Consequently, in late January the administration resumed considerations of various proposals. Morgenthau and Assistant Secretary of State Joseph Grew agreed that the munitions and nonmunitions program should rest on the same principles as the British understanding. However, Morgenthau informed Stettinius that for the nonmunitions program the United States should first determine France's gold and dollar resources, both actual and prospective. The Treasury believed that the United States should determine the extent to which the French would use their financial resources to pay for their nonmunitions requirements and then assign lend-lease aid accordingly. This process, Morgenthau argued, should occur prior to the signing of any lend-lease agreement. But the state department desired to sign a general agreement and later determine the French financial position and payment arrangements.[71]

Morgenthau remained obdurate. On January 25 at a meeting with FEA and state department representatives he insisted on a clear-cut definition of what the agreement intended. "It is important," he asserted, "that if the French are going to be requested to cut down their dollar balances that they understand this from the beginning. It is important that they have some idea of the nature and amount of the supplies that they can expect under the agreement." Furthermore, he maintained, "From a purely business standpoint, the United States should make every effort to get what we want before giving away most of our chips."[72] Despite some confusion within the department, State acquiesced and agreed that the final arrangement should include definitive financial conditions. Consequently the terms for French compensation for civilian goods "were more severe than the State Department had recommended, though Monnet considered them 'entirely fair.'"[73]

In the meantime Monnet met with Morgenthau and informed him of his plans to return to Paris shortly. Monnet also indicated that he intended to discuss lend-lease with French leaders. In the absence of any agreement Monnet inferred that his people would have a difficult time comprehending why the United States should treat them differently than the Russians or British in lend-lease matters. Morgenthau expressed regret over the failure to complete negotiations but suggested that Monnet delay his departure, since the secretary had high hopes of presenting him with a formal agreement, which he could take to Paris.[74]

The acceptance of Morgenthau's position prompted an extensive examination of the French gold and dollar position. This covered the possible accrual rate of the assets as well as the payments required of the French for civilian supply. At the same time American officials broke down the $2,575,000,000 French eighteen-month program (January 1, 1945 to June 30, 1946) into two general categories. The first comprised food, raw materials, and short-life equipment valued at $1,675,000,000; the other consisted of long-life industrial goods with postwar utility worth $900,000,000.[75] Analysis of the French economic situation revealed that as of June 1946, French assets would total approximately $2,500,000,000. During this eighteen-month period officials estimated that French expenditures would approach $900,000,000. With these projections representatives from FEA, state, war, and treasury considered various formulae to determine the percentage of the lend-lease program for which the French should pay. They desired to reduce French gold and dollar assets without undermining France's economic future.[76]

With these considerations in mind American officials hammered out an arrangement during the first week of February.[77] On February 10, 1945, they presented to Monnet a set of documents that comprised the proposed master agreement. Monnet expressed a general satisfaction with the terms. He raised objections to the inclusion of Plan A supplies under cash payment, but his subordinates informed him that since August, they had committed France to pay for such items. Therefore, Monnet once again insisted on the establishment of a terminal date for furnishing Plan A supplies.[78]

Monnet returned to France with the agreement. Reports from American representatives there noted, "French officials seemed very well pleased with the lend-lease proposals."[79] On February 24, 1945, the French approved the agreement. The *New York Times* reported that the understanding impressed both de Gaulle and his cabinet.[80]

NOTES

1. Office of Economic Warfare (hereafter referred to as OEW), "Report of the French Empire's Resources: Relative to the Needs of a Liberated France during the First Year, and Possible Foreign Exchange Resources," September 8, 1943, Box 312, RG 169. Other reports covered numeours aspects of France's wartime conditions. See OEW, "Northern France: Emergency Civilian Requirements of Food, Textiles, and Coal," October 1943; OEW, "Northern France: The Manpower Situation with Respect to Transportation and Goods Handling," October 1943; FEA, "French Mediterranean Ports and Their Hinterlands," November 1943, all in Box 171, RG 169.

2. Ibid. *See also* unsigned letter from Paris to Morgenthau's assistant Harold White, November 21, 1944, Morgenthau Diary.

3. Ibid.

4. *New York Times,* March 13, 1944, p. 14. Less than a year later in a letter to Stettinius (January 2, 1945, Hopkins Papers), Monnet reviewed the situation in 1944 and cited similar conditions and figures.

5. Millner to FEA, "Current Conditions in France," October 9, 1944, Box 813, RG 169. Although dated in October, the report refers to conditions in August.

6. Ibid.; Judson Hannigan, "Report on Trip to Paris and London, September 1 to September 27, 1944," Box 160, RG 169.

7. Millner to FEA, "Current Conditions in France," October 9, 1944, Box 813, RG 169.

8. Wigder to Lorwin, "Memo on the Weir-Green Mission," December 27, 1944, Box 1229, RG 169.

9. Roosevelt to Rosenman, January 20, 1945, PSF, Roosevelt Papers.

10. Samuel I Rosenman, Report to the President of the United States, "Civilian Supplies for the Liberated Areas of Northwest Europe," April 26, 1945, Box 3218, RG 169. The FEA files are replete with reports on

the French coal situation and efforts to improve it. The most enlightening are: Cox to Hopkins, June 19, 1945, Hopkins Papers; Cox to McCloy, June 30, 1945, Hopkins Papers; FEA, "Report of Brunson MacChesney," June 27, 1945, Box 808, RG 169; Monnet to Ickes, July 2, 1945, Box 813, RG 169; Crowley to Patterson, July 24, 1945, Box 813, RG 169; "Coal Program for France, 1945-1946," n.d., Box 3222, RG 169.

11. Rosenman, "Civilian Supplies for the Liberated Areas of Northwest Europe," April 26, 1945, Box 3218, RG 169; Caffery to the State Department, January 18, 1945, Box 813, RG 169.

12. Rosenman, "Civilian Supplies for the Liberated Areas of Northwest Europe," April 26, 1945, Box 3218, RG 169.

13. Ibid.

14. Monnet to Stettinius, January 2, 1945, Hopkins Papers.

15. Rosenman, "Civilian Supplies for the Liberated Areas of Northwest Europe," April 26, 1945, Box 3218, RG 169; Angell to Crowley, June 6, 1945, Box 1134, RG 169; FEA, "Emergency Shelter Procurement for France," June 6, 1945, Box 3222, RG 169; James Stillwell, "Civilian Supply Problems in Europe," *State Department Bulletin* 12 (May 20, 1945), 917-19; Monnet, Press Release, April 23, 1945, Stettinius Papers.

16. Stimson to Hull, January 29, 1945, Box 3218, RG 169. The Army also drew up plans and estimates of needed supplies based on the amount of destruction in the wake of the German retreat. For details of these *see* Coakley and Leighton, *Global Logistics and Supply 1943-1945,* 763-75; and Stillwell, "Civilian Supply Problems in Europe," 917-19.

17. Hull to Embassy in London, March 3, 1945, Box 23, RG 169.

18. Hunt to Currie, April 13, 1944, Box 3218, RG 169.

19. Hildring to Monnet, May 19, 1945, Box 25, RG 169; Monnet to McCloy, August 30, 1944, Box 1464, RG 169; Strauss to MacDuffie, September 1, 1944, Box 25, RG 169; Ferguson to Cleveland, September 7, 1944, Box 464, RG 169; Cleveland to Shubert, "Plan A: Commodities Brought into France," September 7, 1944, Box 464, RG 169.

20. OLLA History: "France and the French Empire," 277-80; "First Emergency Supply Program for France," List 1-A, October 15, 1944, Box 3221, RG 169. *See* Appendix 7 for a complete list.

21. OLLA History: "France and the French Empire," 280; "First Emergency Program for France," List 1-B, November 4, 1944, Box 3221, RG 169. *See also* "First Emergency Program for France," List 1-C, November 15, 1944; "First Emergency Program for France," List 1-D, November 23, 1944, both in Box 3221, RG 169. *See* Appendix 8 for other items.

22. Crowley to Eaton, October 6, 1944, Box 25, RG 169; Gridley to FEA, "On Conversations with Monnet," October 16, 1944, Box 25, RG 169.

23. Gridley to FEA, "On Conversations with Monnet," October 16, 1944, Box 25, RG 169; OLLA History: "France and the French Empire," 285-88, 295-97; *New York Times,* November 26, 1944, 13. The detailed considerations and recommendations of the Four Power Committee are found in "Meeting of the Four Power Committee," November 20, 1944, Box 3222, RG 169.

24. OLLA History: "France and the French Empire," 283; McCollester to FEA, December 1944, Box 915, RG 169; Rosenman, "Civilian Supplies for the Liberated Areas of Northwest Europe," April 26, 1945, Box 3218, RG 169; Coakley and Leighton, *Global Logistics and Strategy 1943-1945,* 748-49, 772-73; FEA, "Civilian Supplies for Metropolitan France: Statement of Procedures for Provision of Civilian Supplies," November 27, 1944, Box 3222, RG 169.

25. Coakley and Leighton, *Global Logistics and Strategy 1943-45,* 779-80; "Meeting of the Four Power Committee," November 20, 1944, Box 3222, RG 169.

26. Coakley and Leighton, *Global Logistics and Strategy 1943-45,* 780-81; Strauss to MacDuffie, September 1, 1944, Box 25, RG 169; Cleveland to Shubert, September 7, 1944, Box 25, RG 169.

27. Monnet to Stettinius, January 2, 1945. Hopkins Papers.

28. Coakley and Leighton, *Global Logistics and Strategy 1943-1945,* 781-82.

29. Ibid., 782-84; OLLA History: "France and the French Empire," 371.

30. Coakley and Leighton, *Global Logistics and Strategy 1943-1945,* 786-87.

31. Ibid. *See also* William Clayton, "Memo on Conversation with Undersecretary of War Patterson," January 30, 1945, Box 25, RG 169; Henry Labouisse, "Progress Report Number Two," February 1945, Box 915, RG 169; Glickman to Lorwin, "Progress Report Number Three," May 1, 1945 (covers the period through March and is a strong recommendation for ending military responsibility), Box 915, RG 169.

32. Rosenman, "Civilian Supplies for the Areas of Northwest Europe," April 26, 1945, Box 3218, RG 169.

33. Coakley and Leighton, *Global Logistics and Strategy 1943-1945,* 787-88; Glickman to Lorwin, "Progress Report Number Three," May 21, 1945, Box 915, RG 169.

34. Coles and Weinberg, *Civil Affairs,* 893-94. Two documents in this

collection reveal that the Dutch and Belgians, unlike the French, did not desire the termination of military responsibility. Evidently they believed that the military would have more success in procuring materials than the civilian agencies.

35. *Modus Vivendi; Foreign Relations 1944* 3, 748.

36. *Foreign Relations 1944* 3, 748-49; Angell to Coe, January 7, 1944, Box 763, RG 169; Rupert to Perkins, January 20, 1944, Box 763, RG 169.

37. Acheson to Monnet, January 27, 1944, Box 763, RG 169; *Foreign Relations 1944* 3, 749-50.

38. Howard to Cox, "French Dollar Payment," February 4, 1944, Boxes 975, 763, RG 169. An even harder line against the French is taken in Currie to Acheson, March 2, 1944, Box 763, RG 169.

39. *Foreign Relations 1944* 3, 751-55; Ferguson to Cox, March 16, 1944, Box 763, RG 169.

40. Ibid., Acheson to McCloy, April 4, 1944, Map Room, Roosevelt Papers.

41. Smith to Monnet, May 19, 1944, Box 808, RG 169; Aide-Memoire, June 6, 1944, Box 808, RG 169.

42. Ibid.

43. *Foreign Relations 1944* 3, 753-55; copies of these are also in Box 975, RG 169. *See also* Hull to Roosevelt, June 27, 1944, PSF, Roosevelt Papers.

44. Memorandum for the President, July 15, 1944, Boxes 977, 1069, RG 169. The same information is in a memorandum dated July 20, 1944; *see Foreign Relations 1944* 3, 757-58.

45. FEA, "Minutes with Respect to the Attached Memorandum Agreed to at the Meeting [with] French Delegations on July 28, 1944," Boxes 977, 1069, RG 169; *Foreign Relations 1944* 3, 758-60; Memorandum Relating to Lend-Lease and Reciprocal Aid, August 25, 1944, Boxes 977, 1069, 3221, RG 169.

46. Crowley to Monnet, September 4, 1944, Box 970, RG 169; also in PSF, Roosevelt Papers.

47. Monnet to Crowley, September 5, 1944, and Crowley to Monnet, September 19, 1944, Box 970, RG 169 and PSF, Roosevelt Papers.

48. FEA, "French Lend-Lease Policy," September 7, 1944, Boxes 977, 1069, RG 169.

49. Ibid.

50. Ibid.

51. Morgenthau Diary, January 31, 1945. This information came to

light in a discussion in Morgenthau's office in answer to a question as to why a lend-lease agreement had not been signed on the basis of the July 15 memorandum.

52. FEA, "French Lend-Lease Policy," September 7, 1944, Boxes 977, 1069, RG 169.

53. Ibid.

54. *Foreign Relations 1944* 3, 760-61; Stettinius to Roosevelt, September 11, 1944, Box 733, RG 169.

55. Morgenthau Diary, "Status of the Lend-Lease Negotiations as of September 14, 1944."

56. Ibid.

57. Ibid.

58. Neither this researcher nor the editors of *Foreign Relations* located this memo of September 15. However, a number of references are made to it. *See Foreign Relations 1944* 3, 762; Stettinius to Roosevelt, October 3, 1944, Stettinius Papers; Morgenthau Diary, September 19, 1944.

59. Stimson Diary, September 20, 1944.

60. Morgenthau Diary, January 29, 1945.

61. Ibid.; Stimson Diary, September 20, 1944.

62. Stimson Diary, September 20, 1944.

63. Ibid.

64. Ibid., October 9, 1944; October 13, 1944; October 19, 1944.

65. *New York Times,* October 24, 1944, 4.

66. Ibid.

67. Morgenthau Diary, October 24, 1944.

68. OLLA History: "France and the French Empire," 258-59; Monnet to Stettinius, January 2, 1945, Hopkins Papers; Cox to Labouisse, February 21, 1945, Cox Papers (This is a useful source where Cox summarized the developments leading to the final agreement.).

69. Acheson to Stettinius, December 21, 1944, Stettinius Papers; State Department, "Summary of the Proposed Lend-Lease Agreement with the French," December 30, 1944, Stettinius Papers; Grew to Morgenthau, January 13, 1945, Morgenthau Diary; Morgenthau Diary, January 25, 1945.

70. Morgenthau Diary, January 25, 1945.

71. Grew to Morgenthau, January 22, 1945, Morgenthau Diary; Morgenthau to Stettinius, January 23, 1945, Morgenthau Diary; Morgenthau Diary, January 25, 1945; Cox to Labouisse, February 21, 1945, Cox Papers.

72. Morgenthau Diary, January 25, 1945.

73. John Morton Blum, *From the Morgenthau Diaries: The Years of War, 1941-1945* (Boston: Houghton Mifflin, 1967), 304. *See also* Morgenthau Diary, January 27, 1945.

74. Morgenthau Diary, January 24, 1945.

75. Ibid., February 6, 1945; Cox to Labouisse, February 21, 1945, Cox Papers.

76. Cox to Labouisse, February 21, 1945, Cox Papers.

77. Details of these discussions are in the Morgenthau Diaries. Morgenthau kept a careful record of the conversations. The most informative were those of January 29 and 30, 1945, and February 1 and 5, 1945. The final meeting on the subject took place on February 6, 1945.

78. Morgenthau Diary, February 13, 1945, "Description of Meeting with Monnet on February 10."

79. State Department Daily Summary, February 19, 1945, Stettinius Papers.

80. State Department Daily Summary, February 24, 1945, Stettinius Papers; *New York Times,* February 24, 1945, 6.

10.

The Impact of the Master Agreement, Termination, and the Final Lend-Lease Settlement

Publication of the French agreement had a significant impact on lend-lease. Unlike other agreements the French accord specifically provided for furnishing civilian materials with a postwar utility. Congressional reaction from Republicans and conservative Democrats was immediate and hostile. In the House it resulted in the passage of an amendment to the Lend-Lease Act that prohibited the employment of lend-lease for any similar postwar commitments. In the Senate an amendment sponsored by Robert Taft and requiring the termination of shipments of lend-lease supplies as of VJ day failed by one vote. Thus, Congress clearly expressed its determination to employ lend-lease solely as a wartime measure. Truman, cognizant of and sensitive to congressional opinion, abruptly terminated lend-lease at the end of the war in the Pacific. However, neither Truman nor Roosevelt had organized any significant programs for the immediate postwar period. Lend-lease functioned as the major source of civilian supply to European countries, and its termination threatened to produce economic chaos in France. Consequently, the administration extended lend-lease shipping arrangements until mid-1946 but did little else. At the same time Truman instructed officials to work quickly in concluding liberal settlements with lend-lease countries. Despite its "generous" nature the French settlement left the struggling, economically deprived nation with a substantial lend-lease debt. In 1958, plagued with political and economic turmoil, France defaulted on her debt, and the United States agreed to postpone the 1958 and 1959 payments until 1981.

On February 28, 1945, the administration announced the signing of a formal lend-lease agreement with France. The understanding consisted of three parts: a Master Agreement, or statement of principles, identical to those concluded with Russia, China, and Great Britain; a Reciprocal Aid Agreement; and a 3(c) Agreement, which represented the first understanding of its type with any ally. The 3(c) arrangement, the *New York Times* commented, for the first time provided "the furnishing of civilian goods and equipment useful not only for the prosecution of the war but for reconstruction following the cessation of hostilities."[1]

The administration derived authorization for such an agreement from the Lend-Lease Act itself. In fact 3(c) referred to the specific section of the act that originally permitted the government to fulfill contracts or understandings with foreign countries until July 1, 1946. When Congress extended the act, it also granted power to the president to complete contracts until July 1, 1949.[2] The French agreement, concluded late in the war, took advantage of the 3(c) provisions, and in so doing, raised the issue of the utilization of lend-lease in the postwar world.

In publicizing the agreement the authorities stressed that all the supplies and services to the French had a direct connection with the war. "The basic purpose of the whole program," the administration declared, "is to enable all the French resources and the whole French nation, soldier, workers, producers, and farmers to be mobilized and used for the war against the common enemy." Officials also clarified the program's limitations. The agreements excluded services and supplies solely for reconstruction. "Supplies required by the French solely for post-war purposes will have to be handled by other means since the Lend-Lease Act is, and is being administered as a war supply measure," they asserted.[3]

In regard to military equipment the French arrangement did not deviate significantly from other lend-lease agreements. The Combined Chiefs continued to allocate war materials to the French through the Munitions Assignment Board. At the time of the signing of the agreement the United States had already fully equipped 300 support units and 225,000 French soldiers in eight divisions. The United States had also furnished supplies and material for a French Air Force of 15,000 men.[4] In the European campaign the impact of this assistance was evident. The French had performed an "indispensable" function in the landings in southern France, Stimson pointed out. The French action culminated in the capture of Marseilles and Toulon, a march up the Rhone Valley through Lyon, and a successful junction with Eisenhower on the German frontier. As Stimson emphasized, "it is proper to say 'indispensable' because without those French divisions, the American forces could not have carried through that campaign without any comparable saving of losses on our side. As it was, these losses were at a minimum."[5]

The civilian program, however, differed considerably from previous arrangements. During meetings in Morgenthau's office officials determined the maximum civilian assistance the United States would furnish to France. Authorities determined that the previously submitted "eighteen-month program" should serve as the basis for the French program. The administration broke down the program into two large categories. Designated as Schedule I and Schedule II, they became annexes to the Master Agreement and specified the materials that the French would receive.[6]

Schedule I consisted of consumable and short-life goods and services:

	Value
Raw Materials for War Use and Essential Civilian Supply (Cotton, Metals, Steel, Chemicals, Synthetic Rubber, Drugs, Medical Supplies, etc.)	$ 840,000,000
Food	185,000,000
Petroleum Supplies	132,000,000
French Prisoner-of-War Supplies	40,000,000
Short-Life Manufacturing Equipment for War Production	250,000,000
Freight Charges (Rental and Charter of Vessels)	220,000,000
	$1,675,000,000[7]

The United States agreed to furnish the Schedule I items on a straight lend-lease basis, but under the 3(c) arrangement the French could continue to receive these goods after the war terminated by paying for them in thirty equal installments beginning July 1, 1946, at an interest rate of 2 3/8 percent.[8]

Long-life capital goods comprised Schedule II. Such materials were to enable France to produce and transport military equipment and other items essential to the Allied forces. Ideally this would relieve the pressure on American production facilities as well as conserve valuable shipping space. Under Schedule II the United States provided:

	Value
Locomotives	$200,000,000
Railway Cars	120,000,000
Harbor Watercraft	32,000,000
Fishing Fleet	8,000,000
Inland Water Craft (Barges)	50,000,000
Metal Work Machinery	100,000,000
Industrial Equipment	150,000,000
Machinery for Mines, Arsenals, etc.	100,000,000
	$900,000,000[9]

The long-life goods played a major role in the war effort, but obviously a large part of their utility served postwar purposes. Consequently the United States required payment for the items regardless of when they arrived in France. The French agreed to pay 20 percent down, and the United States arranged credit terms identical to those for short-life supplies. The United States agreed to furnish these materials and other vital war goods until the president determined that they were no longer necessary for the prosecution of the war.[10] Commenting on the program Monnet asserted, "Our general intention is to request and receive the articles and services in Schedule I and Schedule II up to the full amount of the goods provided therein."[11]

The timing of the French agreement was most unfortunate. Even in 1943, when lend-lease had reached its pinnacle of popularity, opposition was clearly evident. Much of it was an extension of anti-New Dealism, which interpreted lend-lease as a huge Works Progress Administration (WPA) spending project on an international level. Shortages and rationing at home also contributed to dissatisfaction with lend-lease. Ubiquitous rumors attributed to lend-lease the responsibility for shortages of meat, butter, food, canned goods, and cigarettes. Reports circulated that while Americans experienced a shortage of shoes, lend-lease furnished large quantities of footwear to England. In North Africa the United States supposedly distributed shoes to the natives who never wore them, and tons of diaper cloth supplied to North Africa reportedly went to native chieftains, who used them as headdresses, while American infants went diaperless. Other basic concerns also influenced American attitudes toward lend-lease. The expense of financing a global war, a fear of depleting American resources, and the anxieties over political and economic stability in the postwar world all contributed to growing dissatisfaction with lend-lease.[12]

During 1944 distrust of lend-lease became more apparent. The Roosevelt administration countered by pouring out press releases magnifying the indispensable function that lend-lease performed in the war effort. Stettinius published a comprehensive, popular, and well-received account of lend-lease. The administration also expended considerable time emphasizing reverse lend-lease in order to placate those who continually protested that the United States received little in return for its generous contributions.[13]

Despite these efforts the hearings and debates in Congress over the extension of lend-lease revealed a mounting concern over the future of the program. Although in 1944 the measure to extend the act for another year had passed by a vote of 63 to 1 and 334 to 21, these large margins were deceptive. The House and Senate probed every aspect of lend-lease. In general both houses expressed a willingness to extend lend-lease as a war measure. The politicians, however, feared that the president might utilize the broad power that the act had conferred on him and employ lend-lease for postwar purposes.[14] Consequently when Congress extended the act, it adopted an amendment prohibiting the president from incurring or assuming "any obligations on the part of the United States with respect to post-war economic policy, post-war military policy or any post-war policy involving international relations except in accordance with Constitutional procedures."[15]

As the war progressed and the momentum swung to the Allies, the American people appeared to pay less attention to lend-lease. Despite the administration's campaign, public interest and knowledge of lend-lease declined. In December 1944 pollster Hadley Cantril reported a 10 percent reduction in those familiar with lend-lease. Another poll revealed that only 22 percent of those questioned thought that Russia had supplied most of its own weapons; the remainder either knew nothing about the subject or believed that the United States had supplied most of Russia's weapons.[16]

Suspicion in Congress of America's allies also increased. The attitude prevailed that Britain's effort in the war fell considerably short of her potential. Many viewed Great Britain as attempting to supplement her resources and wealth and desirous of getting as much out of the war as possible. The feeling toward Russia, which was never overwhelmingly sympathetic, turned to hostility as the Red Army overran Eastern Europe. The Catholic Church in particular denounced the communist incursions in Poland.[17] And in August 1944 Senator Kenneth McKellar of Tennessee introduced a resolution to permit the United States to confiscate the island possessions of the Allies as well as those of the Axis. He advocated seizing French Caribbean islands since "France owes us an enormous sum for the last World War and has not paid us, and in this war has deserted us."[18]

Throughout late 1944 and early 1945 Stimson, Cox, Acheson, and Crowley vigorously defended lend-lease. They consistently affirmed that lend-lease operated as a war measure and that the Administration had no intention of employing it for postwar rehabilitation. But the publication of the French agreement shattered whatever confidence the House and the Senate had placed in such assurances. For despite the administration's position and Crowley's statement that "lend-lease will not be used for the purpose of post-war rehabilitation and reconstruction,"[19] the French agreement clearly provided for the furnishing of certain capital goods with a postwar utility.

A survey by the administration, however, prompted the conclusion that the French agreement "was well received." Administration analysts cited favorable commentary in the New York *Herald Tribune,* the *St. Louis Post-Dispatch,* the *Minneapolis Tribune,* the *Spokane Spokesman Review,* and the *Philadelphia Bulletin.* The Patterson Press, however, cynically described the agreement as requiring the American taxpayers to assess themselves of $2.5 billion and present it to France in the form of goods.[20] But the New York *Herald Tribune* countered that "the French understanding was hardly sufficient, and did not begin to remedy a grave economic situation in France."[21] An unpublished Princeton Poll taken at the time of the French Agreement revealed that 84 percent favored aid to France and 66 percent felt that the United States contributed as much as it could. In March 1945, Sydney Hillman of the CIO, the *San Francisco Chronicle,* the *Springfield* (Massachusetts) *Chronicle,* and the *St. Louis Post Dispatch* all urged the United States to send more aid to France.[22]

Analysis of the French reaction revealed enthusiastic acceptance tempered by a realistic emphasis on the agreement as a war measure only. On March 1, 1945, *La Liberation* reported that "supplies and services which would benefit only reconstruction of the country are excluded. France's needs in that sphere will have to be met through other means." On March 2 *La Dépeche Paris* published a front-page story on the value of Franco-American accords and concluded, "Thanks to them, our industry will resume activity; our food supply will improve and our transports will receive material." Furthermore, the article noted "that although the intention of the assistance had been to increase French collaboration in the war effort, it will also facilitate the transition from war to peace. On March 20 *Les Nouvelles du Matin* ran a series of articles titled "Lend-Lease, or the Machine for Winning the War." "The first three articles were more than enthusiastic in giving unstinted credit to America for the tremendous achievements in production, transportation, and organization which have made the system work," the report noted. "The ensemble could hardly have been more impressive if an American publicity agent had composed the tribute."[23]

Despite the endorsements more poignant commentaries raised serious questions. The *New York Times* asked whether the form of French lend-lease assistance did not cross and duplicate the Bretton Woods Plan. The *Washington Post* supported congressional misgivings over the enlargement of the Export-Import Bank if lend-lease provided goods for postwar use under long-term payment provisions.[24]

The French Master Agreement struck Congress like a bombshell, and the controversy it produced had far-reaching ramifications. At the time of its publication the House was in the process of holding hearings to extend the Lend-Lease Act for another year. A number of congressmen immediately denounced the French accord as a devious tactic designed to circumvent the Johnson Act. Five influential Republicans, John Vorys, Robert Chiperfield, Karl Mundt, Lawrence H. Smith, and Bartel Jonkman, voiced their dissatisfaction with the agreement to the chairman of the House Foreign Affairs Committee, Sol Bloom. They informed him in no uncertain terms that the Lend-Lease Act as it stood conferred broad enough powers on the president to permit him to employ it for postwar rehabilitation and reconstruction. They expressed a determination to prohibit Roosevelt from using lend-lease in Europe in any way beyond the length of hostilities. The Republicans demanded more extensive hearings and subjected lend-lease to the closest scrutiny in its four-year history.[25]

The administration, as usual, paraded spokesmen Crowley, Acheson, Stimson, and Cox before the House Committee. They clarified and defended the French agreement. Crowley explained that "war supplies having a long life may also have a residual peacetime use to the countries to which they are sent. Accordingly, the French agreement provides for such lend-lease supplies." The French understanding with its provision for postwar deliveries benefited the United States: "Our financial liabilities in liquidating the lend-lease program will be minimized and our surplus problem after the war reduced," Crowley contended. The basic difference between the French arrangement and other lend-lease agreements, as Crowley viewed it, was that the French consented "to pay for long life articles and articles produced too late to be of use in the war, in place of leaving the question open and negotiating it later."[26]

Acheson testified that the FEA had designed far-reaching plans, since it could not merely guess at the war's termination date. Consequently, Acheson maintained, it took every precaution to assure that the French taxpayer, and not the American, bore the burden. Specifically he informed the committee that the administration possessed two alternatives: "You can say, we will go ahead with this plan, but the moment the fighting has stopped we will end it, leaving us 'holding the bag.'" Or, as Acheson further explained, "You can say what we have said in this agreement, which is that these items for the civilian population you get on lend-lease up to a point where the President says they are not necessary for the prosecution of the war, and from then on the French must take them. . . . And they must pay for them!"[27] Cox emphasized that France differed considerably from North Africa. "The North African situation was handled as a special ad hoc case," he pointed out. "It was not of the same nature or scope as Metropolitan France either in size or its potentiality at that time as a base of military operations."[28] Since D day France had increasingly become the Allies' European war base.

As expected, the Democratic majority accepted the administration's position. "The French agreement," it reported, "concluded at a late stage of the war in Europe, protects United States interests by determining some of the obligations of France in advance of the war's conclusion." Moreover, the majority supported the French accord as "in keeping with the administration of the Lend-Lease Act as a war supply measure," and asserted that postwar reconstruction and rehabilitation required separate consideration by Congress.[29]

Despite the wealth of favorable testimony and the administration's enormous effort, the Republican minority remained unconvinced. Representative Chiperfield described the French arrangement as existing in a "twilight zone which seems to provide a way for lend-lease to go into post-war reconstruction for many years to come."[30] The Minority Report of March 8 specifically attacked the French understanding: "The French agreement of February 28, 1945, is by its very terms a post-war agreement." For this group the French accord clearly revealed the potential postwar implications of the extensive power that the Lend-Lease Act conferred on the president. "The broad definition of defense articles," the Republicans argued, "gives the President power to carry out the collective security formula by supporting the post-war economy of any country whose defense he deems vital to our defense."[31] The question simply involved the desire of Congress to extend lend-lease power and practice into the postwar world. The minority report warned against such a policy and with a tinge of isolationism showing concluded that "Lend-Lease failed as a means to keep us out of the war. If it is projected into the post-war period it may again fail to keep us out of war."[32]

In light of these objections the Republicans sponsored an amendment to prohibit the conclusion of any agreements under the Lend-Lease Act designed for postwar reconstruction. The amendment received considerable support from Republicans and conservative Democrats in both houses. The administration and the Democrats on the House Foreign Affairs Committee feared that a prolonged floor fight would delay the extension of lend-lease and reluctantly accepted the amendment to section 3(c). The amendment prohibited the president from employing lend-lease for postwar rehabilitation, but it exempted the French Master Agreement and the outstanding contracts arranged through it. Arthur Krock, who closely followed lend-lease matters, pointed out that interest in the imposition of such a limitation rose tremendously following the announcement of the French accord. A *New York Times* editorial referred to the amendment as a "perfectly proper one," and emphasized that the administration must manage reconstruction independent of lend-lease and under the auspices of other agencies.[33]

In the Senate lend-lease and the French understanding encountered even more determined opposition. Senator Robert Taft vociferously argued that the exemption of the French agreement from the House Amendment rendered it virtually meaningless. He denounced the $2.5 billion French arrangement and declared that "more than one half of this appears to be for permanent use, and hardly any of it will get to

France before the end of the German war. . . in effect the act is being used to make a post-war loan to France."[34] The 3(c) agreement, Taft asserted, took advantage of a "loophole" in the original act. Consequently, the Ohio senator proposed an amendment that would terminate all lend-lease transfers without exception once the war ended.[35]

The conservative Republican was not without considerable support. Robert La Follette, Jr., the Wisconsin Progressive, backed Taft and insisted on the right of Congress to determine the role of the United States in the postwar world. The Taft Amendment, La Follette declared, "will force the executive to come back to Congress and to permit the policy making arm of government, under our Constitution, to discharge its responsibility." Millard Tydings agreed with Taft, and although he advocated a generous policy during the postwar period, the Maryland senator emphatically warned, "I do not want to sign a blank check for use after the war is over. The blank check era ought to end with the cessation of hostilities."[36] And Senator Arthur Vandenberg disliked the implications of the French deal. "It indicated," he maintained, "that it is intended to carry over into the post-war period." Vandenberg demanded proposals from the administration for postwar rehabilitation and stressed that reconstruction assistance must exist apart from lend-lease and fall under the supervision of Congress.[37]

The strong support for Taft's position barely failed to achieve legislative success. The Senate rejected the amendment when Vice-President Harry S. Truman cast the tie-breaking vote. The voting closely followed party lines with thirty-seven Democrats and two Republicans rejecting it, while thirty-four Republicans, four Democrats, and the Progressive La Follette voting in favor of it. On April 10, 1945, the Senate extended the Lend-Lease Act for one year and provided for a three-year "clean up" period in order to dispose of surplus stocks and arrange final settlements.[38]

Truman's vote marked his first important action as vice-president. The vote evidently had a significant meaning for him. Reflecting on it, he noted, "I was not given many other tasks. Two days after I became Vice-President, Roosevelt left Washington for the Yalta conference, and during the short period I served as Vice-President he was not actually in the capitol more than thirty days."[39] Two days after the Senate vote fate thrust the vice-president into the nation's highest office, ill-prepared and uninformed of his predecessor's designs.

The closeness of the Senate vote had a marked impact on the new president. As an active and experienced senator he understood "that if we were to use lend-lease funds for rehabilitation purposes we would open ourselves to a lot of trouble with the Senate."[40]

A month after VE day Truman clarified his position on lend-lease in a reply to representatives Chiperfield, Vorys, Mundt, Jonkman, and Smith. "Our recent lend-lease agreements with France, Belgium and the Netherlands," he wrote, "will be carried out by Lend-Lease funds to the fullest extent consistent with changed war conditions and the basic purposes of Lend-Lease aid."[41] On the matter of postwar reconstruction, the president informed the five Republicans: "I am of course in full agreement with you. . . that the Lend-Lease Act does not authorize aid for purposes of postwar relief, postwar rehabilitation, or postwar reconstruction."[42]

With respect to the French attitude toward lend-lease, the administration expressed more dissatisfaction than previously. On April 17, 1945, Judson Hannigan, chief of the FEA's French Division, cabled the American embassy in Paris that the French erroneously thought that the lend-lease agreement was similar to a "bank deposit against which they are free to draw at their own discretion." He also pointed out that it had become increasingly more difficult to distinguish between war supply and postwar assistance. The feeling in Washington, Hannigan stressed, was that relations between the two countries required improvement, and he urged a more extensive publicity campaign in France detailing lend-lease contributions.[43] Two months later a poll by the Office of War Information (OWI) indicated that only a small percentage of the French public was aware of the significance, extent, and effectiveness of lend-lease. The OWI also reported that there was a tendency on the part of the French to emphasize reciprocal aid much more than American assistance. Consequently administration officials urged a tougher policy toward France, especially so she would not expect the United States and Britain to assume the entire burden of rehabilitation.[44]

Two incidents arose in the military theater that eventually had an enormous impact on the French military lend-lease program. In April contrary to orders from the Combined Chiefs of Staff, French forces refused to withdraw from the city of Stuttgart. Consequently, on April 28, 1945, Eisenhower announced the suspension of all issuances of military equipment for the newly organized French Metropolitan Program units. Without mentioning the Stuttgart incident Eisenhower maintained that with the war rapidly concluding, no reason existed for equipping additional French forces.[45] While French authorities in Washington negotiated for a revision of Eisenhower's order, another controversy erupted that eventually shattered French hopes for completion of its rearmament program. The incident, more serious than any in the past, almost terminated Franco-American cooperation.[46]

By May 1945 French forces had successfully driven the Germans out of Northwest Italy, and the victorious French seized an area known as Val d'Aosta. As in the case of Stuttgart the French refused to comply with an order from the Combined Chiefs to evacuate the territory. This time, however, the French remained adamant. They desired to annex the area and refused to withdraw on grounds that it would appear as a retreat. The distasteful affair was even more regrettable since, on May 11, the French in Washington had given assurances that no incidents similar to Stuttgart would recur.[47]

On June 6 Truman cabled de Gaulle of his deep concern over the refusal of the French leader to follow orders. The president referred to a letter from the French General Paul Doyen, which inferred that the French would physically resist American orders. Such an "unbelievable threat," Truman declared, would shock the American public, and he exhorted de Gaulle to reconsider his position. At the same time, the president informed de Gaulle of his directive to terminate the issuance of all lend-lease military supplies.[48]

Truman's message produced the desired results. De Gaulle agreed to evacuate Val d'Aosta, but Truman never completely lifted the embargo on the issuance of military equipment to the French. On July 29 he informed the Joint Chiefs of Staff that military lend-lease would continue but only in cases where the joint chiefs determined that such aid supported the Allies' redeployment operation. Truman's decision reflected the new post-VE day lend-lease policy. There was great division within the administration over the continuation of lend-lease in general once the war in Europe ended. Truman, beset by conflicting opinions, waited for weeks before establishing a policy. The new approach considerably reduced lend-lease to all nations.[49]

Thus a military incident, prolonged and heated from an overabundance of pride and determination, had an enormous impact on the future of lend-lease. The military controversies, the termination of hostilities in Europe, the undetermined role of the French in the Far East campaign, and above all Truman's sensitivity to congressional opposition to any lend-lease after the war all influenced Truman to toughen his policy and move toward a termination of the French rearmament program.

Despite difficulties with the French the civilian program continued to operate and expand. During the spring and summer of 1945 the amount of goods imported increased significantly. Despite the hopes of the military its aid program fell far short of anticipated results. From D day until May 31, 1945, the military imported only four hundred thousand tons of civilian supplies. Coal and petroleum amounted to another one billion tons, but the military consumed more than it had imported. During 1944 imports amounted to a "mere trickle" and averaged only about thirty-five thousand tons per month. This was less than North Africa received, "and a minute fraction of what France normally imported before the war."[50]

In January 1945 shipments organized by the FEA of purely civilian supplies supplemented the military program. The civilian output commenced on a modest basis with five ships in January and increased to forty by June. This raised the tonnage to France to approximately one hundred fifty thousand tons per month or a total of approximately one million tons during the first six months of 1945. Lend-lease provided most of this tonnage valued at $150 million.[51]

The civilian supply program to France had expanded enormously by the time the two atomic bombs cruelly and abruptly terminated the war against Japan. When Japan capitulated, the administration began drawing up plans for the cessation of lend-lease. On August 17 Crowley, Leahy, and two Truman appointees, Secretary of State James Byrnes and Secretary of the Treasury Fred Vinson, discussed with the president the necessary steps for its conclusion. Vinson argued for the retention of lend-lease to prevent economic chaos in Europe and to function as a bulwark against communism. The others, however, agreed that the administration could not possibly extend lend-lease beyond the conclusion of the war.[52]

Truman wasted little time in terminating lend-lease. On August 20, 1945, the president directed Crowley to cancel lend-lease contracts to all countries unless they agreed to place them on a cash payment basis. Thus, after four and a half years and an expenditure of $42 billion, this experiment in foreign aid ceased.[53] The *New York Times* reported that in Washington there was "neither fanfare over its accomplishments nor official regret at its passing."[54]

The administration carefully explained its action. Crowley pointed out that its discontinuance was not at the discretion of him or Truman. "The question of discontinuing Lend-Lease is one that was settled by Congress . . . when the Act was extended and appropriations granted, Congress made very clear that it intended Lend-Lease expenditures to end with the war. President Truman and myself were impressed forcibly with this intention and we both made promises at that time which were kept."[55] The *Washington Post* supported Truman's action and noted that the Senate had also approved of it. A Roper Poll revealed that 49 percent of those questioned favored Truman's decision; only 19 percent felt he should have extended it for a year to assist the deprived nations.[56] The president's initiative, however, jolted and stung the largest lend-lease recipient. On August 24 the British Prime Minister Clement Attlee told a shocked and hushed House of Commons that the termination of lend-lease "without consultation and proper discussion has placed Britain in a very serious financial position."[57]

The French reaction hardly resembled that of the British. On August 18 Crowley had informed Monnet that the United States would not accept any further requisitions for services or supplies under terms of the Master Agreement. Furthermore, he stipulated that the articles in Schedule I—those on a straight lend-lease basis—were no longer necessary for the prosecution of the war. Thus, Crowley directed that any supplies not acquired as of August 18 "shall be transferred to your Government only against payment upon the terms and conditions set forth in the Agreement."[58]

On August 21 de Gaulle arrived in Washington for discussions with Truman. The French declared that the president's announcement had not surprised them. They showed little interest in biting the hand of the Allies' rich uncle and thereby precipitating needless antagonisms over the termination of lend-lease. Rather, they concentrated on immediate and conclusive discussions to arrange for a smooth transition period. Specifically they desired clarification of the economic assistance they could expect and the financing that the United States would proffer.[59]

France's economic position was extremely precarious. The French lend-lease program was based on the continuation of the war into 1946 and provided for approximately $2.5 billion worth of imports. At the time of the administration's termination of lend-lease, the United States had shipped only $150 million on a credit basis and another $250 million under the terms of the 3(c) understanding. Thus the French faced the difficult problem of securing emergency financing in order to maintain the supply of essential materials.[60]

To make matters worse, following the defeat of Germany the FEA set a time limit for supplying lend-lease goods to France. With only the military occupation and redeployment process in operation, the FEA had established December 31, 1945, as the final date for the shipment of lend-lease supplies. At the time the agency thought that the Allies could fulfill France's requirements prior to 1946.[61]

From August to December 1945 the random adjustments the administration made in the French program clearly revealed the consequences of a lack of planning for the immediate postwar period. On August 27 Crowley informed Monnet that the United States would continue to provide under lend-lease terms ocean transportation for supplies already contracted for under terms of his letter of August 18. The shipments would operate under this arrangement until thirty days after the official announcement of VJ day, when the French would pay the costs of transportation.[62]

Three days following the announcement of VJ day Truman clarified military lend-lease policy. On September 5 he issued instructions for the termination of such assistance. The order became effective as of VJ day and ended virtually all lend-lease by the war and navy departments. The directive provided for continued aid to Allied troops of medical supplies, rations, and shelter that foreign countries could not supply. The United States considered such assistance a liquidating measure that would terminate in March 1946. Much to the dismay of the French, Truman's order ended France's rearmament program.[63]

By December conditions within France exhibited little improvement and in some ways had worsened. As winter approached an acute shortage of coal plagued the country, and strikes and internal transportation difficulties threatened to generate complete chaos. The Truman administration hurriedly reviewed its supply policy and concluded that the enforcement of the December 31 deadline for shipping lend-lease goods would lead to severe hardship in France. Consequently, on December 6 the United States extended its delivery date to June 30, 1946, for goods contracted for through the procurement agencies. Interestingly the Department of Agriculture had earlier extended its date for furnishing essential food to France.[64]

As the United States struggled with improvised arrangements to maintain the French economy, it set in motion negotiations to conclude final lend-lease settlements. Having assumed office under trying circumstances, Truman's task in arranging settlements appeared difficult. As in other cases Roosevelt had left no definitive guidelines for concluding agreements. The British, on the other hand, had clarified their position in at least one way. In April 1944 Churchill had informed Stettinius, "I must make it clear to you, as I have to the President, that we aren't going to pay the Lend-Lease debts. That will have to be adjusted some place else along the lines of utilizing bases, Empire preferences, tariffs, etc."[65]

Although Truman stumbled through lend-lease policy from April until December, his handling of the settlements demonstrated decisiveness, wisdom, and courage.[66] Both he and the state department desired liberal and speedy conclusions; yet serious obstructions threatened such a policy and course of action. Public opinion during the last nine months of 1945 revealed that only 25 to 30 percent of those polled felt that the defeat of the Axis was sufficient payment for lend-lease. Other polls indicated that 50 to 83 percent of the American people thought the United States should receive payment for its aid. The percentage of those who favored partial repayment or full reimbursement had increased between April and VJ day.[67]

Congress exhibited a similar attitude. A number of congressmen, including the two powerful Democrats Richard Russell and Walter George, believed that the United States should receive concessions in the form of raw materials, bases, and airfields in return for lend-lease. In 1943 the Truman committee had presented similar recommendations, and in 1945 Representative William Colmer's special committee on postwar economic policy reinforced these proposals. Yet there were exceptions, most notably the conservative senator from Ohio. "It would be most unfortunate," Taft argued, "if the huge sum of approximately $30,000,000,000, less approximately $3,000,000,000 in reverse lend-lease, should hang as a debt over the world for years to come, as did the debts of the First World War." Furthermore he asserted that "after it became apparent that those debts could not be repaid and would not be repaid, I thought that they should be canceled. I have the same feeling with respect to present lend-lease obligation."[68]

Despite the opposition and only scattered support, Truman pressed for liberal terms. In his *Twentieth Report to Congress on Lend-Lease Operations* the president emphasized the contributions of lend-lease to concluding the war with the least loss of American life. He indicated that this alone was justification and payment for lend-lease. Above all, he warned, the United States must not repeat the errors following World War I. As he accurately pointed out, the Allies had consumed most of the $42 billion worth of lend-lease provided by the United States. In his postwar message to Congress Truman noted that the Allies could not pay the United States in dollars for the "overwhelming portion" of lend-lease advanced to them. "But this does not mean that all lend-lease obligations are to be canceled," he carefully stated. Rather, Truman stressed the goal of achieving "settlements of our wartime lend-lease relations which will permit generally a sound world-wide economy and will contribute to international peace and our own national security."[69]

A poignant comment came from the *New York Times*. In supporting Truman's policy it concluded, "The truth of lend-lease is that it was never lend and never lease; it was weapons in the hands of brave young men from other countries who took the place of our own soldiers."[70]

To expedite the settlements the administration established committees to deal with the postwar understandings. On November 16, 1945, Assistant Secretary of State for Economic Affairs William Clayton created the Lend-Lease War Claims and Surplus Settlement Committee. The committee defined the principles on which the United States would seek to conclude settlements, including pipeline and inventory agreements; it acted as the primary committee with the aid of a subcommittee in negotiating final accords; and it recommended specific understandings for approval. The Department of State's Foreign Liquidation Commissioner Thomas B. McCabe served as the committee's chairman. The members consisted of representatives from the treasury department, the Office of War Mobilization and Reconversion, and officials from various divisions of the state department. In December 1945 the administration established a subcommittee or working group comprised of officials from state, war, treasury, and the navy under the direction of Henry R. Labouisse, Special Assistant to Clayton. The working group prepared the basic studies and material for negotiations with the French. The subcommittee presented its recommendations for a final settlement to the National Advisory Council on Internal Monetary and Financial Problems. On January 18, 1945, the working group held its first meeting and two months later commenced negotiations with the French delegation led by Leon Blum and Jean Monnet.[71]

The French Master Agreement provided a basis for the ends sought in a final understanding. Article VII directed that the benefits that the United States would receive from the French "shall be such as not to burden commerce between the two countries, but to promote mutually advantageous economic relations between them and the betterment of worldwide economic relations."[72] The administration felt that France in particular should receive as liberal terms as feasible. In early 1946 reports from France revealed the serious economic shortcomings the nation faced. Moreover Ambassador Jefferson Caffery wrote that the 1946 import program would substantially reduce France's gold and dollar resources. Fearing possible political repercussions from the deteriorating economic situation, Caffery urged a benevolent attitude toward any French requests for a large loan. "To refuse it or to chop it down to an unimportant sum, in my considered opinion, will pull out one of the last props of substance and of hope from those in France who want to see France remain an independent and democratic country."[73]

In light of these considerations and the desire of the United States to restore France, the administration negotiated a final settlement. The discussions proved extensive, since they included most of the outstanding wartime economic questions and not merely lend-lease. However, much of the emphasis did focus on lend-lease issues. As a guideline for all settlements the National Advisory Council on Internal Monetary and Financial Problems established the interest rate for war debts at 2 percent over thirty-five years. The council directive provided a five-year grace period for principal payments but with no waiver of the interest. Clayton informed the council that the French Master Agreement included a provision for the postponement of installments upon mutual agreement by both nations. The council accepted the stipulation and approved of its inclusion in the final settlement.[74]

The French placed special emphasis on specific lend-lease arrangements. Of particular interest to them were the charges for goods received under

the Crowley-Monnet exchange and Plan A. The French also submitted
a valuation of reverse lend-lease, and they desired adjustments on the unpaid balance of the North and West African debt. Under the Crowley-
Monnet understanding the United States had transferred approximately
$23 million in civilian supplies. The French argued that the United States
should consider these transfers as straight lend-lease, since most of these
goods were similar to those furnished on a straight lend-lease basis under
the Master Agreement. They also pointed out that failure to arrive at an
early agreement necessitated the Crowley-Monnet arrangement and that
these goods supplemented Plan A. The United States countered that the
Crowley-Monnet understanding specifically required cash payment—much
of which the French had already provided. Aside from this a memorandum
annexed to the February 28, 1945, agreement and widely publicized stated
that the United States expected payment. Under these circumstances the
administration rejected the French modifications.[75]

Since its inception, plan A was an irksome issue. The nature of the
goods and the time of their arrival, the French contended, made them
eligible for classification as straight lend-lease. The American working
group endorsed the French position. However, since the war department
anticipated payment for the $130 million program, the subcommittee
submitted the question to the National Advisory Council, which ruled
in favor of the French.[76]

The French requested modifications in the outstanding debt for goods
shipped to North and West Africa. As in 1944 the French delegates once
again invoked Article V of the *Modus Vivendi,* which provided for revisions of payment arrangements. The French maintained that they had
received only $80 million from American troop pay, and therefore the
United States should not hold them liable for any debt beyond this. Consequently they insisted that the United States consider all transfers to VJ
day above this amount, less inventories, as straight lend-lease. The administration accepted the French proposals and waived $176 million formerly
subject to repayment.[77]

Both sides considered reciprocal aid an intrinsic part of lend-lease. Aside
from the economic advantages, reverse lend-lease provided for the administration a means of avoiding the political accusations of "paying rent for
the trenches," which emerged following World War I. The basis for reciprocal aid came from Section 3(b) of the Lend-Lease Act, which stated

that benefits to the United States "may be payment or repayment in kind or property, or any other direct or indirect benefit which the President deems satisfactory."[78]

During the early stages of lend-lease, the administration established a policy for the evaluation of such assistance. It insisted on an accurate evaluation. Therefore, in August 1942 Acheson instructed Stettinius that the OLLA should maintain a record of quantities "in all cases of articles received as reciprocal aid and the record should also, where practicable, be expressed in monetary terms."[79] Hull reinforced the position that the state department was unwilling to accept ambiguous guidelines and directed that any agencies receiving such assistance transmit sufficient quantitative descriptions to the OLLA to serve as a basis for evaluation estimates.[80]

Following the North African invasion the French and natives furnished significant assistance to the American forces. The aid assumed many forms and consisted of the use of harbor and transportation facilities, the employment of local labor, the providing of raw materials, including shipments of phosphates to the United States, and the acquisition of available buildings for use as warehouses, depots, and barracks. But the overwhelming bulk of reverse lend-lease was obtained in Metropolitan France. There the United States forces confiscated over forty thousand pieces of real estate ranging from small dwellings to magnificent hotels. The military employed thousands of French workers whose salaries the French government paid. The army assumed control of the entire transportation system and all the necessary equipment it could salvage. Unfortunately the extent of the military's demands reduced the economy of many areas to a lower level than during the Nazi occupation.[81] Reports indicated that in the Paris area alone over one thousand French nurses served in American hospitals. Over two hundred factories in Paris turned out essential spare parts for the indispensable repair areas servicing military equipment. The entire operation contributed enormously to the speed of the Allied advance. By early 1945 over one hundred thousand French laborers assisted in the war effort. The most significant achievements were the production of tires from American raw materials, the manufacture of steel girders used to bridge the Rhine, and the furnishing of approximately two million American combat uniforms.[82]

Despite American efforts to obtain accurate evaluations, obviously much of the assistance was hardly conducive to precise record keeping.

To simplify matters officials organized the assistance into the following categories: miscellaneous military equipment; facilities and equipment; agricultural, industrial, and other commodities; and testing, reconditioning, etc., of defense articles, services, and expenses. When questions arose with the French, American officials tended to accept a higher rather than lower figure. Both sides finally settled on $800 million as the approximate value of French reciprocal aid; of this, about $100 million came from North and West Africa.[83]

Despite the temper of public opinion on lend-lease repayment, officials concluded a "generous and liberal settlement" with the French. The total lend-lease aid to France amounted to approximately $3.5 billion; it consisted of $2,252,000,000 in military aid, $1,043,000,000 in civilian assistance, and $130,000,000 under Plan A. The United States wrote off all military aid and did not require payment for goods lost, destroyed, or consumed during the war; this the administration considered the price of victory. The United States made no payment for reverse lend-lease, and there was no adjustment for such goods in American hands on VJ day since both sides considered these items as necessary for current consumption with no substantial postwar value. French and American officials considered the settlement a final one, arrived at from available figures, and not subject to future accounting.[84]

The United States reserved the right to recapture military lend-lease property in French possession. But officials indicated that it would not exercise the right except in the case of American naval vessels and lend-lease merchant ships, which the French were to return. The agreement also prohibited the French from retransferring lend-lease military or civilian items to any country outside the French empire without presidential consent.[85]

The accord, however, did require payment for certain supplies. The French agreed to pay $300 million for surplus civilian supplies and to provide payment of $420 million for civilian goods in the "pipeline" since VJ day. Thus the total French lend-lease debt stood at $720 million. The United States did not insist on immediate payment but arranged credit terms with an interest rate of 2 percent. The interest was due on July 1 of every year through 1950. Beginning in July 1951 the French were to start interest and principal payments in equal installments over a thirty-year period. The agreement also included a loan of $650 million from the Export-Import Bank, which supplemented the $1 billion in credit

France had already received since VE day; $550 million of this had also come from the Export-Import Bank. Officials pointed out that the credit was small compared to France's trade deficit, but they emphasized that France could apply for additional assistance to the International Bank for Reconstruction and Development once it began operating.[86]

The French also granted significant concessions. Of utmost importance for American commercial interests, the French agreed to pursue a policy that would fully restore private trade. France agreed to limit government procurement to a few specified items and equipment for public corporations and agencies. The Supply Council continued to function in the United States but at a reduced level; it concentrated chiefly on liquidating outstanding contracts and made arrangements for limited purchases. The French also promised to employ normal trade channels and to terminate the operations of the Supply Council as soon as possible.[87]

Signed on May 28, 1946, the settlement appealed to French and American authorities. Truman and French President Felix Gouin (who had replaced de Gaulle in January) issued a joint statement describing it as "a substantial step toward the achievement of the international economic cooperation which is the prerequisite of a peaceful and prosperous world." In France the agreement had political overtones; coming on the eve of an important election, analysts interpreted it as a victory for the western-oriented Socialist party and a setback for the communists. Although VE day was only one year in the past, in commenting on the French settlement the *New York Times* emphasized the emerging struggle between the free world and the communist nations. Described as a "generous settlement" and "an investment in Democracy," the editorial stressed that France "at the moment of her greatest weakness holds the key to the fate of Democracy in Europe." The writer urged the United States to employ its resources "to encourage moderate and liberal forces in France and save, if we can, the order on which our future depends as much as hers." As in the case of lend-lease, the editorial concluded, "Loans to Britain and France are likewise an investment in a system of government and a way of life."[88]

There was very little difference in general principle between the final French and British agreements. However, England had accumulated a lend-lease debt of over $20 billion, which the United States wiped off the books. As with the French the United States required payment for stocks of civilian supplies held by the British as of VJ day and also for goods in the "pipeline." The total British debt came to $650 million, or approximately $70 million less than that of the French. The agreement with Great Britain also included provisions for an additional credit of $3.75 billion and payment terms identical to those of the French.[89]

Clearly, from considerations of debt and credit the British had received a much more favorable settlement than the French. However, the general impression remained that of the lend-lease recipients, "England had the least capacity to pay."[90] Yet in relationship to France, this represented a faulty conclusion. Though England had fought longer and contributed more extensively to the war, her resources were greater; the British trade position and empire holdings were far superior to those of France. Aside from this, the German air blitz, as devastating as it was, in no way inflicted as extensive and irreparable damage on England as the occupation and liberation had on France. Furthermore, the French had provided periodic payments of millions of dollars for civilian lend-lease supplies, which England had received on a credit basis. The inequities were obvious, even to the French at that time. And the argument continually presented by the administration (especially by Morgenthau) that the French should pay cash due to their large gold and dollar balances was specious at best, as it completely overlooked the incalculable cost of French reconstruction.

With this in mind, the question later arose as to how generous the French settlement really was or if any description of it in such terms was relative. Such a question once again raised the issue of the basic shortcomings in American economic planning for the postwar period. Despite the numerous reports from overseas on the weakness of the disrupted French economy, the Roosevelt administration had refused to act in a manner that would convince the public of the necessity of restoring a strong France, nor had it prepared any substitute programs once lend-lease ended. In the face of congressional and public opposition to lend-lease as a postwar measure, Truman terminated it and then attempted to alleviate the economic plight by concluding "reasonable" agreements. Fortunately a few years later, with the support of the American people, Truman found a solution to the economic problems of France and other countries through the Marshall Plan and subsequent foreign-aid programs.

Few would argue that the $720 million lend-lease debt did not represent a significant improvement over the $4 billion French debt from World War I. Yet even this amount, in light of France's economic shortcomings, became an incubus. In 1958 the French settlement reached its denouement. France, reeling from economic turmoil and political instability, appealed to American officials for an adjustment of the French payment terms. The French agreement had provided for a "postponement" of payments should both governments determine that due to "extraordinary and adverse economic conditions" payment was not in the best interests of either country.[91] The United States agreed to the French proposals, and on January 30, 1958, Jean Monnet and Douglas Dillon, undersecretary of state for Economic Affairs, initialed an agreement that deferred French installments for 1958 and 1959 until July 1, 1981.[92]

NOTES

1. *New York Times*, March 1, 1945, 1.

2. Public Law 11, 77th Congress, 1st Session, H. R. 1776, "An Act to Promote the Defense of the United States," passed March 11, 1941, extended and amended 1943, 1944, 1945.

3. Crowley, Morgenthau, and Grew, Press Release, February 28, 1945, Stettinius Papers and Box 972, RG 169.

4. Ibid.; Monnet, Press Release, April 23, 1945, Stettinius Papers. For details of the French military program *see* Vigneras, *Rearming the French*.

5. State Department Press Release, February 28, 1945, Box 972, RG 169.

6. Ibid. The *New York Times* published the French Agreement on March 1, 1945, 1. *See also* Bevans, ed., *Denmark-France,* 1075-92, and OLLA History: "France and the French Empire," 261-68.

7. Ibid.

8. Ibid.

9. Ibid.

10. Ibid.

11. Monnet, Press Release, April 23, 1945, Stettinius Papers.

12. George C. Herring, "An Experiment in Foreign Aid: Lend-Lease, 1941-1945" (Ph. D. thesis, University of Virginia, 1965), 401-02; George C. Herring, "Lend-Lease to Russia and the Origin of the Cold War, 1944-1945," *Journal of American History* 56 (June, 1969), 102-03.

13. Ibid., 406; Stettinius, *Lend-Lease Weapon for Victory* (New York: Macmillan, 1944).

14. Ibid., 406-08; Herring, "Lend-Lease to Russia," 103-04.

15. "An Act to Promote the Defense of the United States," as amended, 1944.

16. Herring, "An Experiment in Foreign Aid," 420.

17. Ibid.

18. *New York Times,* August 19, 1944, 14.

19. FEA, "Statement of Crowley before the House Foreign Affairs Committee," Press Release, March 5, 1945, Stettinius Papers.

20. State Department, "Attitudes on Foreign Policy, January-August 20, 1945," Relations with France Special Report 71, Stettinius Papers; State Department, "Fortnightly Survey of American Opinion on International Affairs," March 2, 1945, Stettinius Papers; State Department, "Summary of Public Opinion Developments," March 2, 1945, Stettinius Papers.

21. State Department, "Daily Summary of Public Opinion Developments," March 3, 1945, Stettinius Papers.

22. State Department, "Public Attitudes on Foreign Policy, January-August 20, 1945," Relations with France Special Report 71, Stettinius Papers.

23. Office of War Information, "The French Press on Lend-Lease (February to April 1945)," Stettinius Papers.

24. State Department, "Fortnightly Survey of American Opinion on International Affairs," March 20, 1945, Stettinius Papers.

25. *New York Times,* February 28, 1945, 13; March 3, 1945, 4.

26. U. S. Congress, House of Representatives, Committee on Foreign Affairs, *Hearings on H. R. 2013. A Bill to Extend for One Year the Provisions of an Act to Promote the Defense of the United States,* 79th Congress, 1st Session (Washington, D. C., 1945), 140, 142. Copies of the testimony for the extension of the lend-lease act are in Box 3141, RG 169.

27. Ibid., 153.

28. Ibid., 28.

29. Ibid., Majority Report, 3.

30. *New York Times,* March 3, 1945, 4.

31. U. S. Congress, House of Representatives, Committee on Foreign Affairs, *Hearings on H. R. 2013. A Bill to Extend for One Year the Provisions of an Act to Promote the Defense of the United States,* 79th Congress, 1st Session (Washington, D. C., 1945), Minority Report, 4.

32. Ibid., 6.

33. Herring, "An Experiment in Foreign Aid," 417-18; *New York Times,* March 13, 1945, 1; March 14, 1945, 7; March 15, 1945, 22.

34. *Congressional Record,* 79th Congress, 1st Session, 3222.

35. Ibid., 3218; *New York Times,* April 10, 1945, 1.

36. *Congressional Record,* 79th Congress, 1st Session, 3233.

37. *New York Times,* April 11, 1945, 1; April 10, 1945, 1.

38. Ibid.; Herring, "An Experiment in Foreign Aid," 418-19; Herring, "Lend-Lease to Russia," 104.

39. Harry S Truman, *Memoirs.* Volume 1, *Year of Decisions* (New York: Doubleday, 1955), 195.

40. Ibid., 98.

41. Ibid., 231.

42. Ibid., 232; Herring, "Lend-Lease to Russia," 110-11. He points out that Truman, beset by division over lend-lease, delayed for weeks any firm policy for post-VE day lend-lease. Once he decided, he reduced lend-lease considerably.

43. Hannigan to Labouisse, April 17, 1945, Box 25, RG 169.

44. Bailen to MacChesney, June 6, 1945, Box 840, RG 169; Lebensburger to Crowley, July 10, 1945, Box 1229, RG 169.

45. Vigneras, *Rearming the French,* 361.

46. Ibid., 367.

47. Ibid.

48. Ibid., 368; Herring, "Lend-Lease to Russia," 110.

49. Ibid. For Truman's account of the entire affair, *see* Truman, *Year of Decisions,* 239-42. An extensive analysis of the British reaction to Truman's July 29 directive is in Herring, "An Experiment in Foreign Aid," 448-53, and "Lend-Lease to Russia," 111.

50. Camden McVey, "An American's View of France," *State Department Bulletin* 13 (October 20, 1945), 525.

51. Ibid.

52. Herring, "An Experiment in Foreign Aid," 453.

53. Ibid., 454; *New York Times,* August 22, 1945, 1.

54. *New York Times,* August 23, 1945, in Herring, "An Experiment in Foreign Aid," 454.

55. FEA, Statement of Leo Crowley, August 25, 1945, Box 3191, RG 169.

56. *Washington Post,* August 24, 1945, 14; Hadley Cantril, ed., *Public Opinion, 1935-1946* (Princeton: Princeton University Press, 1951), 415. Box 896, RG 169, contains numerous newspaper clippings on the subject of lend-lease termination. The vast majority approved Truman's action, concentrated on descriptions of Britain's bitter reaction, and stressed the availability of American loans.

57. Quoted from *The Times* (London) in the State Department's "News Digest," August 25, 1945, Stettinius Papers.

58. Crowley to Monnet, August 18, 1945, Box 1173, RG 169.

59. *New York Times,* August 23, 1945, 10; August 25, 1945, 4; *Washington Post,* August 25, 1945, 1.

60. McVey, "An American's View of France," 529.

61. OLLA History: "France and the French Empire," 378-79.

62. Crowley to Monnet, August 27, 1945, Box 273, RG 169.

63. Vigneras, *Rearming the French,* 371-72, 399.

64. OLLA History: "France and the French Empire," 378-80; Mac-Duffie to Mack, December 6, 1945, Recent Accessions Box, RG 169.

65. Stettinius, "Diary of London Trip, March 10-May 4, 1944," April 18, 1944, Stettinius Papers. This diary offers excellent insights into the British attitudes toward lend-lease and postwar cooperation.

66. In May 1945 Truman caused a major controversy with the Russians by abruptly halting their lend-lease shipments. Although the inexperienced and ill-advised president rescinded his order, the incident had far-reaching repercussions. For an excellent analysis of the subject *see* Herring, "Lend-Lease to Russia."

67. Herring, "An Experiment in Foreign Aid," 459-60; Cantril, ed., *Public Opinion, 1935-1946,* 413-15; Department of State, "Current Opinion on Lend-Lease Settlement," August 9, 1945, Box 229, RG 169. This report also concluded: "There is outright opposition to its continuation after the war as a relief and rehabilitation measure."

68. *Congressional Record,* 79th Congress, 1st Session, 3222.

69. U. S. President, *Public Papers of the Presidents: Harry S. Truman, 1945* (Washington, D. C.: U. S. Government Printing Office, 1969), 306. A copy of Truman's *Twentieth Report to Congress on Lend-Lease Operations for the Period Ended June 30, 1945* is in Box 896, RG 169.

70. *New York Times,* August 31, 1945, 16.

71. OLLA History: "France and the French Empire," 403-04. The National Advisory Council on Internal and Financial Problems consisted of Fred Vinson, William Clayton, Henry Wallace, Marriner Eccles (chairman of the Federal Reserve Board), and William C. McC. Martin (chairman of the Export-Import Bank).

72. Bevans, ed., *Denmark-France,* 1077.

73. United States Department of State, *Foreign Relations of the United States, 1946,* Vol. 5 (Washington, D. C.: United States Government Printing Office, 1969), 413, 432 (hereafter referred to as *Foreign Relations 1946* 5).

74. Ibid., 456-57.

75. OLLA History: "France and the French Empire," 427-28. The entire settlement is published in Bevans, ed., *Denmark-France,* 1126-65. For records of some of the meetings and correspondence that produced the final settlement *see Foreign Relations 1946* 5, 410-33.

76. OLLA History: "France and the French Empire," 430; Bevans, ed., *Denmark-France,* 1143-44; *Foreign Relations 1946* 5, 410-33.

77. OLLA History: "France and the French Empire," 430-33.

78. "An Act to Promote the Defense of the United States," as amended, 1945.

79. Acheson to Stettinius, August 22, 1942, Stettinius Papers.

80. Hull to the American Embassy in London, November 4, 1942, Box 3159, RG 169. *See also* FEA, "Valuation of Reciprocal Aid," October 29, 1942, Box 3142, RG 169.

81. *New York Times,* November 15, 1944, 6; OLLA History: "France and the French Empire," 398-400; Rosenman, *Report to the President of the United States,* "Civilian Supplies for the Liberated Areas of Northwest Europe," April 26, 1945, Box 3218, RG 169.

82. OLLA History: "France and the French Empire," 398-400; *New York Times,* November 15, 1944, 6; Caffery to Stettinius, May 5, 1945, "Report on Reverse Lend-Lease," Hopkins Papers; FEA Press Release, June 23, 1945, Box 25, RG 169.

83. OLLA History: "France and the French Empire," 398-99; *New York Times,* May 29, 1946, 1, 13.

84. OLLA History: "France and the French Empire," 432-36; *New York Times,* May 29, 1946, 1, 12, 13; Bevans, ed., *Denmark-France,* 1126-29.

85. *New York Times,* May 29, 1946, 1, 12, 13; Bevans, ed., *Denmark-France,* 1129.

86. *New York Times,* May 29, 1946, 1, 12, 13; Bevans, ed., *Denmark-France,* 1165.

87. Press Release, *State Department Bulletin* 13 (May 28, 1946), 996; *New York Times,* May 29, 1946, 1, 12, 13.

88. *New York Times,* May 29, 1946, 7; May 30, 1946, 20.

89. Herring, "An Experiment in Foreign Aid," 463. Truman's *Twenty-First Report to Congress on Lend-Lease Operations for the Period Ended September 30, 1945,* Box 896, RG 169, revealed that the French had paid a total of $222 million for civilian supplies shipped to North Africa.

90. Herring, "An Experiment in Foreign Aid," 462.

91. *New York Times,* May 29, 1946, 12; Bevans, ed., *Denmark-France,* 1127.

92. U. S., *United States Treaties and Other International Agreements* (Washington, D. C.: Department of State, 1958), 9, 68.

Epilog

From the beginning of economic assistance during the German occupation, to the signing of the Master Lend-Lease Agreement, and to the termination of lend-lease, aid to France produced a number of controversies. From early 1941 until the North African invasion the British strongly objected to even token assistance and worked to prevent it. On the other hand the French complained bitterly of promises of aid that were never kept and criticized American sensitivity to political events in Vichy, which from time to time halted the assistance. In North Africa a paradox developed. The French considered American efforts at implementing the Murphy-Weygand agreement to be half hearted, but even before the invasion they gradually came to regard American goods, the presence of Americans, and their influence on the natives as a threat to their empire. And after the invasion American-North African relations were radically altered, never to be the same.

During the war the United States slowly, almost unwittingly, became so entwined with North Africa through economic aid and military affairs that it could not possibly extricate itself without alienating either the Arabs, the French or both. It was simply impossible to continue indefinitely a policy that promised the colonizer that its empire would remain intact and at the same time support the principles of the Atlantic Charter and the Four Freedoms. The choice that the United States made revealed that its commitment to self-determination did not go beyond the rhetoric. As early as 1943 Wallace Murray perceived the weakness of such a position. In reviewing the issue of Arab nationalism, Murray prophetically wrote

in a memo to Berle: "My own view is that this question may come home
to haunt us and that the unduly prolonged policy now being pursued by
Mr. Murphy will not be good enough in the long run."[1]

Despite an American policy that favored the colonial power, French
distrust and suspicions of American motives had increased by the war's
end. In June 1945 John Goodyear, the American chargé in Morocco,
acquired a letter supposedly written by a high French official. Goodyear
reported that the author criticized lend-lease as a "vast Utopia, a snare
and a delusion." The letter also accused the United States of moving into
Morocco's agricultural and phosphate industries and asserted that the
United States desired to turn Morocco into an American colony after the
war.[2] This was not a concern that the French took lightly. American economic activity, the military occupation, the overtures to the United States
from the increasingly militant nationalist leaders, and, above all, the Arab
impressions of Roosevelt's conversation with the sultan combined to in-
still in the French a fear that the United States would replace her in North
Africa.

In the postwar years, however, the United States revealed that it had no
intention whatsoever of destroying French hegemony in the Maghrib. It
took no decisive steps to support the Arab nationalists and in fact lost
much of their respect. Writing in 1952, only four years before Moroccan
and Tunisian independence, an American observer commented, "The
North African Arabs do not feel that we [United States] were their
'liberators' as we tried to convince them that we were. They only know
that we were the 'liberators' of their hated enemies, liberating the French
so that they could continue to misuse the Arab."[3]

Even in the area of private trade, where during the war the French were
so vulnerable, the United States in postwar years did not expand apprecia-
bly its trade at French expense. During the 1960s American exports to
North Africa increased from $79.2 million to $136.1 million, and imports
rose from $12.4 million to $20.5 million. These figures, however, represent only a small percentage of North Africa's total trade, and in the immediate postwar years the percentage was less. For Morocco American
imports amounted to approximately 7.5 percent of its total, and less than
4 percent of Moroccan goods were exported to the United States. Although
France no longer monopolized North African trade as in the prewar years,
during the 1960s approximately one-third of Morocco's trade was with
France.[4] Thus the considerable effort put forth by the commercial groups

during the war did not have a significant impact in the postwar years. In fact American officials in North Africa worked at maintaining guarantees for American trade that were established in commercial treaties long before the war. The events of the immediate postwar years explain the lack of extensive American trade development. The United States concentrated on rebuilding Europe and recognized that in order to rehabilitate the French economy, France's lucrative colonial markets in Northwest Africa would have to play an essential role.

Unfortunately for North African-American relations the United States' reaction to communism prevented her from distinguishing between nationalist movements and international communism. Clearly in the prewar, war, and immediate postwar years, communism was not a major force in North Africa.[5] But during the Cold War the United States failed to make the necessary distinctions, and in North Africa American support went to the French on the erroneous assumption that decolonization was the first step in the eventual establishment of a communist state.

Only over Algerian independence did the United States become somewhat embroiled in a controversy with the French, and this resulted mostly from the efforts of one man, Senator John F. Kennedy. Although Morocco and Tunisia received their independence in 1956, Algeria was a special case. Administered for decades as an integral part of France, the French refused to give it up and until 1962 engaged in a cruel, bloody war with the nationalists. During those years Kennedy spoke often in opposition to past colonial practices and was especially vocal in his criticism of the French in Algeria. The administrations did not share his views, and he repeatedly clashed with Acheson, Dulles, and others. Kennedy's commitment, however, was well-qualified. He was attempting to find a more flexible approach as an alternative to supporting what he considered to be anachronistic colonial policies and nationalist movements that might be communist. As one scholar accurately described it, "Kennedy favored nationalism, but nationalism on America's terms."[6] In short, he preferred a nationalistic movement that also crusaded against communism. Kennedy's positions on Viet Nam and Algeria during the fifties are of great interest. He was not without influence, and his speeches placed a severe strain on French-American relations.

Finally the lend-lease arrangements worked out with France late in the war were extremely significant. Probably more than anything else, the French Master Agreement prompted Congress to make it clear that lend-lease was not to be used for postwar rehabilitation. The heated debate in Congress caused Truman to cut back on lend-lease supplies after VE day and to terminate lend-lease almost immediately after the defeat of Japan. But the importance of civilian lend-lease was not overlooked. The Truman and subsequent administrations recognized the influence of economic aid in world affairs, and when economic and political chaos threatened western Europe, Truman, through the Marshall Plan, once again instituted civilian aid programs.

The French lend-lease debt has caused few problems in the postwar period. In 1946 and 1947 payment plans were established whereby the French agreed to pay a total of $685 million at 2 percent interest in annual installments through 1980. In 1958 a new agreement postponed the scheduled 1958 and 1959 payments until 1981 and 1982. The agreement, signed by Douglas Dillion, under secretary of state for Economic Affairs, and Jean Monnet, was part of a program aimed at stabilizing France's faltering financial position. According to the treasury department the assistance proved to be "highly successful." In 1962 France had evidently recovered and paid the installments due in the 1980s and their annual payment. At present the French owe approximately $116 million. The payments are on schedule, and they expect to make the last one, approximately $30 million, in 1980.[7]

NOTES

1. Murray to Berle, July 27, 1943, State Department Document 851S.00/257.

2. Paul J. Zingg, "The Cold War in North Africa: American Foreign Policy and Postwar Muslim Nationalism, 1945-1962," *Historian* 39 (November 1976): 45.

3. Ibid., 48. In recent years, a number of articles have appeared on the United States and North Africa. *See* Michael Brett, "The Colonial Period in the Maghrib and Its After-Math: The Present State of Historical Writing," *Journal of African History* 17 (no. 2, 1976), 291-305; Carl L. Brown, "The United States and the Maghrib," *The Middle East Journal* 30 (Summer 1976), 273-90; Roger Kanet, "The Soviet Union, the French Communist Party and Africa, 1945-1950," *Survey* 22 (Winter 1976), 74-92; and Ronald J. Nurse, "Critic of Colonialism: JFK and Algerian Independence," *Historian* 39 (February 1977), 307-26.

4. Zingg, "The Cold War in North Africa," 44.

5. Ibid., 40-41. *See also* Roger Kanet, "The Soviet Union, the French Communist Party and Africa, 1945-1950"; and Ronald J. Nurse, "Critic of Colonialism, JFK and Algerian Independence." Zingg concludes: "Fitted with political blinders, the United States essentially saw the Maghrib as an attendant area to East-West conflict. Such perception universalized a condition which never threatened to dominate North Africa—communism—and negated the significance and reality of a true global phenomenon—Third World nationalism." The author's conclusion is one that is shared, and early evidence for this is found during the war years and developed in Chapter 7.

6. Nurse, "Critic of Colonialism: JFK and Algerian Independence," 308. Nurse's article also includes a brief comparison with Kennedy's positions on Viet Nam and is a valuable study.

7. Telephone conversation with Monsieur André Velasco, French Embassy, May 6, 1977: Treasury Department Press release, April 19, 1962, provided by André Velasco.

The Lend-Lease Act

Section 1.

Further to promote the defense of the United States, and for other purposes

Be it enacted by the Senate and House of Representatives of the United States of America in Congress assembled, That this Act may be cited as "An Act to Promote the Defense of the United States."

Section 2.

As used in this Act—

(a) The term "defense article" means—

    (1) Any weapon, munition, aircraft, vessel, or boat;

    (2) Any machinery, facility, tool, material, or supply necessary for the manufacture, production, processing, repair, servicing, or operation of any article described in this subsection;

    (3) Any component material or part of or equipment for any article described in this subsection;

    (4) Any agricultural, industrial or other commodity or article for defense.

Such term "defense article" includes any article described in this subsection manufactured or procured pursuant to section 3, or to which the United States or any foreign government has or hereafter acquires title, possession, or control.

(b) The term "defense information" means any plan, specification, design, prototype, or information pertaining to any defense article.

Section 3.

(a) Notwithstanding the provisions of any other law, the President may, from time to time, when he deems it in the interest of national defense, authorize the Secretary of War, the Secretary of the Navy, or the head of any other department or agency of the Government—

    (1) To manufacture in arsenals, factories, and shipyards under their jurisdiction, or otherwise procure, to the extent to which funds are made available therefor, or contracts are authorized from time to time by the Congress, or both, any defense article for the government of any country whose defense the President deems vital to the defense of the United States.

    (2) To sell, transfer title to, exchange, lease, lend, or otherwise dispose of, to any such government any defense article, but no defense article not manufactured or procured under paragraph (1) shall in any way be disposed of under this paragraph, except after consultation with the Chief of Staff of the Army or the Chief of Naval Operations of the Navy, or both. The value of defense articles disposed of in any way under authority of this paragraph, and procured from funds heretofore appropriated, shall not exceed $1,300,000,000. The value of such defense articles shall be determined by the head of the department or agency concerned or such other department, agency, or officer as shall be designated in the manner provided in the rules and regulations issued hereunder. Defense articles procured from funds hereafter appropriated to any department or agency of the Government, other than from funds authorized to be appropriated under this Act, shall not be disposed of in any way under authority of this paragraph except to the extent hereafter authorized by the Congress in the Acts appropriating such funds or otherwise.

    (3) To test, inspect, prove, repair, outfit, recondition, or otherwise to place in good working order, to the extent to which funds are made available therefor, or contracts are authorized from time to time by the Congress or both, any defense article for any such government, or to procure any or all such services by private contract.

    (4) To communicate to any such government any defense information, pertaining to any defense article furnished to such government under paragraph (2) of this subsection.

    (5) To release for export any defense article disposed of in any way under this subsection to any such government.

(b) The terms and conditions upon which any such foreign government receives any aid authorized under subsection (a) shall be those which the President deems satisfactory, and the benefit to the United States may be payment or repayment in kind or property, or any other direct or indirect benefit which the President deems satisfactory.

(c) After June 30, 1943, or after the passage of a concurrent resolution by the two Houses before June 30, 1943, which declares that the powers conferred by or pursuant to subsection (a) are no longer necessary to promote the defense of the United States, neither the President nor the head of any department or agency shall exercise any of the powers conferred by or pursuant to subsection (a); except that until July 1, 1946, any of such powers may be exercised to the extent necessary to carry out a contract or agreement with such a foreign government made before July 1, 1943, or before the passage of such concurrent resolution, whichever is the earlier.

(d) Nothing in this Act shall be construed to authorize or to permit the authorization of convoying vessels by naval vessels of the United States.

(e) Nothing in this Act shall be construed to authorize or to permit the authorization of the entry of any American vessel into a combat area in violation of section 3 of the Neutrality Act of 1939.

Section 4.

All contracts or agreements made for the disposition of any defense article or defense information pursuant to section 3 shall contain a clause by which the foreign government undertakes that it will not, without the consent of the President, transfer title to or possession of such defense article or defense information by gift, sale, or otherwise, or permit its use by anyone not an officer, employee, or agent of such foreign government.

Section 5.

(a) The Secretary of War, the Secretary of the Navy, or the head of any other department or agency of the Government involved shall, when any such defense article or defense information is exported, immediately inform the department or agency designated by the President to administer section 6 of the Act of July 2, 1940 (54 Stat. 714), of the quantities, character, value, terms of disposition, and destination of the article and information so exported.

(b) The President from time to time, but not less frequently than once every ninety days, shall transmit to the Congress a report of operations under this Act except such information as he deems incompatible with the public interest to disclose. Reports provided for under this subsection shall be transmitted to the Secretary of the Senate or the Clerk of the House of Representatives, as the case may be, if the Senate or the House of Representatives, as the case may be, is not in session.

Section 6.

(a) There is hereby authorized to be appropriated from time to time, out of any money in the Treasury not otherwise appropriated, such amounts as may be necessary to carry out the provisions and accomplish the purposes of this Act.

(b) All money and all property which is converted into money received under section 3 from any government shall, with the approval of the Director of the Budget, revert to the respective appropriation or appropriations out of which funds were expended with respect to the defense article or defense information for which such consideration is received, and shall be available for expenditure for the purpose for which such expended funds were appropriated by law, during the fiscal year in which such funds are received and the ensuing fiscal year; but in no event shall any funds so received be available for expenditure after June 30, 1946.

Section 7.

The Secretary of War, the Secretary of the Navy, and the head of the department or agency shall in all contracts or agreements for the disposition of any defense article or defense information fully protect the rights of all citizens of the United States who have patent rights in and to any such article or information which is hereby authorized to be disposed of and the payments collected for royalties on such patents shall be paid to the owner and holders of such patents.

Section 8.

The Secretaries of War and of the Navy are hereby authorized to purchase or otherwise acquire arms, ammunition, and implements of war produced within the jurisdiction of any country to which section 3 is applicable, whenever the President deems such purchase or acquisition to be necessary in the interests of the defense of the United States.

Section 9.

The President may, from time to time, promulgate such rules and regulations as may be necessary and proper to carry out any of the provisions of this Act; and he may exercise any power or authority conferred on him by this Act through such department, agency, or officer as he shall direct.

Section 10.

Nothing in this Act shall be construed to change existing law relating to the use of the land and naval forces of the United States, except insofar as such use relates to the manufacture, procurement, and repair of defense articles, the communication of information and other noncombatant purposes enumerated in this Act.

Section 11.

If any provision of this Act or the application of such provision to any circumstance shall be held invalid, the validity of the remainder of the Act and the applicability of such provision to other circumstances shall not be affected thereby.

Approved, March 11, 1941.

Note: In 1943, 1944, and 1945, Congress extended the Lend-Lease Act for one-year periods. In 1944 Congress amended the act slightly, and in 1945 the legislative body passed the following significant amendment to the Lend-Lease Act:

"That subsection (c) of section 3 of such Act is further amended by striking out the period after the word 'earlier,' inserting a semicolon, and the following new language: 'Provided however, that nothing in section 3(c) shall be construed to authorize the President to enter into or carry out any contract or agreement with a foreign government for post-war relief, post-war rehabilitation or post-war reconstruction; except that a contract or agreement entered into in accordance with this Act in which the United States undertakes to furnish to a foreign government defense articles, services, or information for use in the prosecution of the present war and which provides for the disposition, on terms and conditions of sale prescribed by the President, of any such defense articles, services, or information after the President determines they are no longer necessary for use by such Government in promoting the defense of the United States shall not be deemed to be for post-war relief, post-war rehabilitation or post-war reconstruction.'"

The French Master Lend-Lease Agreement

Whereas the Government of the United States of America and the Provisional Government of the French Republic declare that they are engaged in a cooperative undertaking, together with every other nation or people of like mind, to the end of laying the bases of a just and enduring world peace securing order under law to themselves and all nations;

And whereas the Government of the United States of America and the Provisional Government of the French Republic, as signatories of the Declaration by United Nations of January 1, 1942, have subscribed to a common program of purposes and principles embodied in the Joint Declaration known as the Atlantic Charter, made on August 14, 1941, by the President of the United States of America and the Prime Minister of the United Kingdom of Great Britain and Northern Ireland;

And whereas the President of the United States of America has determined, pursuant to the Act of Congress of March 11, 1941, that the defense of any French territory not under the control of the Axis is vital to the defense of the United States of America;

And whereas the United States of America has extended and is continuing to extend to the Provisional Government of the French Republic aid in resisting aggression;

And whereas it is expedient that the final determination of the terms and conditions upon which the Provisional Government of the French Republic receives such aid and of the benefits to be received by the United States of America in return therefor should be deferred until the extent of the defense aid is known and until the progress of events makes clearer the final terms and conditions and benefits which will be in the mutual

interests of the United States of America and France and will promote
the establishment and maintenance of world peace;

And whereas the Government of the United States of America and the
Provisional Government of the French Republic are mutually desirous of
concluding now a preliminary agreement in regard to the provisions of
defense aid and in regard to certain considerations which shall be taken
into account in determining such terms and conditions and the making
of such an agreement has been in all respects duly authorized, and all
acts, conditions and formalities which it may have been necessary to
perform, fulfill or execute prior to the making of such an agreement in
conformity with the laws either of the United States of America or of
France have been performed, fulfilled or executed as required;

The undersigned, being duly authorized by their respective Governments for that purpose, have agreed as follows:

ARTICLE I

The Government of the United States of America will continue to supply the Provisional Government of the French Republic with such defense
articles, defense services, and defense information as the President of the
United States of America shall authorize to be transferred or provided.

ARTICLE II

The Provisional Government of the French Republic will continue to
contribute to the defense of the United States of America and the strength-
ening thereof and will provide such articles, services, facilities or information as it may be in a position to supply.

ARTICLE III

The Provisional Government of the French Republic will not without
the consent of the President of the United States of America transfer title
to, or possession of, any defense article or defense information transferred
to it under the Act of March 11, 1941 of the Congress of the United States
of America or permit the use thereof by anyone not an officer, employee,
or agent of the Provisional Government of the French Republic.

ARTICLE IV

If, as a result of the transfer to the Provisional Government of the
French Republic of any defense article or defense information, it becomes

necessary for that Government to take any action or make any payment in order fully to protect any of the rights of a citizen of the United States of America who has patent rights in and to any such defense article or information, the Provisional Government of the French Republic will take such action to make such payment when requested to do so by the President of the United States of America.

ARTICLE V

The Provisional Government of the French Republic will return to the United States of America at the end of the present emergency, as determined by the President of the United States of America, such defense articles transferred under this Agreement as shall not have been destroyed, lost or consumed and shall be determined by the President to be useful in the defense of the United States of America or of the Western Hemisphere or to be otherwise of use to the United States of America.

ARTICLE VI

In the final determination of the benefits to be provided to the United States of America by the Provisional Government of the French Republic full cognizance shall be taken of all property, services, information, facilities, or other benefits or considerations provided by the Provisional Government of the French Republic subsequent to March 11, 1941, and accepted or acknowledged by the President on behalf of the United States of America.

ARTICLE VII

In the final determination of the benefits to be provided to the French Republic in return for aid furnished under the Act of Congress of March 11, 1941, the terms and conditions thereof shall be such as not to burden commerce between the two countries, but to promote mutually advantageous economic relations between them and the betterment of worldwide economic relations. To that end, they shall include provision for agreed action by the United States of America and France, open to participation by all other countries of like mind, directed to the expansion, by appropriate international and domestic measures, of production, employment and the exchange and consumption of goods, which are the material foundations of the liberty and welfare of all peoples; to the elimination of all forms of discriminatory treatment in international commerce, and to the reduction of tariffs and other trade barriers; and, in general, to the attainment of all the economic objectives set forth in the Joint Declaration made on August 14, 1941, by the President of the United States of America and the Prime Minister of the United Kingdom.

At an early convenient date, conversations shall be begun between the two Governments with a view to determining, in the light of governing economic conditions, the best means of attaining the above-stated objectives by their own agreed action and of seeking the agreed action of other like-minded Governments.

ARTICLE VIII

This Agreement shall take effect as from this day's date. It shall continue in force until a date to be agreed upon by the two Governments.

Signed at Washington in duplicate this 28th day of February, 1945.

For the Government of the United States of America:

Joseph C. Grew

For the Provisional Government of the French Republic:

H. Bonnet   Jean Monnet

Execution of Supply Programs for North Africa

I. Petroleum Products

Name	Minimum Needs of North Africa for 9 Months	Exportations Actually Made in 9 Months (March to December 1941)
Gasoline for Automobiles	84,000 tons	10,535 tons
Oil	39,000 ”	11,235 ”
Gas Oil	69,000 ”	12,427 ”
Fuel Oil	45,000 ”	8,491 ”
Lubricating Oils	12,000 ”	813 ”
TOTALS	249,000 tons	43,501 tons

II. Other Goods (cont'd.)

Name	Minimum Needs of North Africa for 6 Months Shown by Quotas Accepted by Dept. of State	Exportations Actually Made in 6 Months (July to December 1941)
Tea	3,150 tons	1,415 tons
Condensed Milk	2,550 "	1,360 "
Pharmaceutical Products	1,000 "	1 "
Cotton Goods	13,000 "	2,445 "
Bags	5,500 "	178 "
Tobacco	2,000 "	984 "
Iron Wire	7,250 "	382 "
Copper Sulphate	6,400 "	200 "
Sugar	91,000 "	14,095 "
Agricultural Mchs & Spare Parts	2,800 "	5.5"
Coal	220,000 "	11,179 "
Coke	1,800 "	896 "
Rosin	4,000 "	1,117 "
Binder twine	2,700 "	1,133 "
Paraffin	4,000 "	702 "
Nails	4,200 "	103 "
Readymade Garments	2,270 "	1 "
Machines other than Agricultural & spare parts	2,000 "	Nil
Cotton Thread	830 "	"
Rayon Thread	70 "	"
Woolen Thread	300 "	"
Woolen Cloth	900 "	"
Rayon Cloth	900 "	"
Used Cloth	870 "	"
Potassic Manure	5,000 "	"
Nitrogenized Manure	3,400 "	"
Insecticides	2,600 "	"
Sulphur	3,367 "	"
Pyrites	3,000 "	"

Name	Minimum Needs of North Africa for 6 Months Shown by Quotas Accepted by Dept. of State	Exportations Actually Made in 6 Months (July to December 1941)
Other Chemical Products	4,000 ”	”
Papers and Cartons	13,000 ”	”
Matches	420 ”	”
Threaded Cotton for Matches	16 ”	”
Bicycles	1,955 units	”
Rubber Articles	300 tons	”
Tin	50 ”	”
Anti-Friction Metal	10 ”	”
Electric Bulbs	500,000 units	”
Electric Apparatus	1,000 tons	”
Tools	650 ”	”
Crude Copra	700 ”	”
Tar	4,000 ”	”
Asphalts and Bitumens	2,400 ”	”
Glassware	1,000 ”	”
Calcium Carbide	4,240 ”	”

Note: Tons are metric tons.

Goods for North Africa Approved by the Board of Economic Warfare, July-August, 1942

Sugar	8,000	Metric Tons	
Powdered Milk	1,100	”	”
Tobacco	400	?”	”
Used Clothing	1,000	”	”
Blue Paper	50	”	”
Cotton Goods[1]	3,230	”	”
Green Tea[2]	525	”	”
Matches[3]	300	”	”
Camel Cigarettes	3,000,000	Units	
Thermometers	25	”	
Milk Pumps	12	”	

1. On the condition that they were for native use only and not textiles with military value.

2. Only the type used by the natives and packaged according to BEW and OWI Specifications.

3. Packaged according to OWI Specifications.

Goods Requisitioned by the British for the Free French as of July 1942

Pharmaceuticals	$ 350,000
Manufactured Tobacco	20,000
Flour and Milk	350,000
Trucks, Tractors, Engines	1,000,000
Machine Tools and Tools	400,000
Ferrous and Non-Ferrous Metals	500,000
Gasoline, Petroleum and Oil	200,000
Speed Boats	200,000
Miscellaneous	400,000

French Holdings in Gold and American Dollars, November 1943

Gold		$2,300,000,000
In French Africa	$935,000,000	
In the British Empire	580,000,000	
In the U. S.	500,000,000	
In Martinique	285,000,000	
Official dollar balances in the U. S.		340,000,000*
Private dollar balances in the U. S.		235,000,000

*Of this the French had deposited $225 million for the account of the Central Bank and Government of Metropolitan France, $85 million for the account of the French Treasury in Africa, and $23 million for the account of French Indo-China.

First Emergency Supply Program for France, List 1-A, October 1944

Food	53,400	metric tons
Products for Agriculture	39,000	,, ,,
Medical Products and X-ray Equipment	31,312	,, ,,
Textiles	41,500	,, ,,
Rubber	19,500	,, ,,
Petroleum and Petroleum Products	8,920	,, ,,
Minerals, Metals and Ores	49,060	,, ,,
Chemical Products	10,657	,, ,,
Paper and Paper Pulp	17,000	,, ,,
Total	270,349	metric tons

First Emergency Supply Program for France, List 1-B, November 4, 1944

Replacement Parts for Vehicles	1,000	metric tons
Batteries	77	,, ,,
Spare Parts	1,685	,, ,,
Milk Cans	200	,, ,,
Gaskets	150	,, ,,
Hose and Tubing	7	,, ,,
Auto Fan Belts	10	,, ,,
Ball and Roller Bearings	75	,, ,,
Brake Parts	50	,, ,,

Bibliography

Due mainly to government restrictions historians have yet to subject all World War II lend-lease programs to close scrutiny. Until the late 1960s state department classification prevented investigation of the two chief sources of lend-lease information—the records of the Foreign Economic Administration and the manuscript collection of Edward R. Stettinius, who was successively lend-lease administrator, undersecretary of state, and secretary of state.

The first scholarly study of lend-lease is Warren Kimball's *The Most Unsordid Act: Lend-Lease, 1939-1941* (Baltimore: Johns Hopkins Press, 1969). In this comprehensive and detailed work Kimball analyzes the background, origin, and political history of lend-lease. The book ends with the passage of the Lend-Lease Act in March 1941 and thus does not cover its implementation. Kimball's bibliography is extensive and valuable.

In 1965 George C. Herring completed "An Experiment in Foreign Aid: Lend-Lease, 1941-1945." Recently declassified, Herring's contribution is a thoroughly researched scholarly presentation, which covers virtually every aspect of lend-lease from its introduction in Congress until its termination. As a Stettinius Fellow at the University of Virginia, Herring had access to and relied chiefly on the Stettinius manuscripts. His dissertation traces lend-lease policy and development and also provides an invaluable insight into the elaborate mechanism of lend-lease operations. Herring reviews most of the area programs but concentrates on and emphasizes the two largest recipients, England and Russia. His cursory treatment of the French program leaves considerable latitude for additional work on this important subject. The bibliography is exhaustive and basic for future studies. Herring's published work, *Aid to Russia,*

1941-1946 (New York: Columbia University Press, 1973), is an excellent study of the implementation of lend-lease.

Not surprisingly, the records of the Foreign Economic Administration (National Archives Washington Records Center, Suitland, Maryland) provided the most extensive and essential material for this study. Designated as Record Group 169, the collection consists of over three thousand file boxes transferred during the period of 1942 to 1951 to the National Archives from the Board of Economic Warfare, the Office of Lend-Lease Administration, the Foreign Economic Administration, the Department of Commerce, and the state department. The record group includes central and numerous files of officials of the OLLA, the FEA, the BEW, the Office of the Administrator of Export Control, the Economic Defense Board, and the Office of Foreign Relief and Rehabilitation Operations. The collection is enriched by the files of the lend-lease administrator, the BEW executive director, and the FEA administrator. It also contains the records of the FEA historian and the "History of Lend-Lease" completed by the state department in 1947. In 1951 the archives compiled a preliminary inventory, which serves as an indispensable guide for this huge collection.

The material on France and French North and West Africa is abundant though widely scattered. The records include interagency memoranda, voluminous correspondence from overseas missions, regional studies, financial and economic evaluations, understandings and agreements, analyses of the shipping situation, correspondence from private enterprises, presidential directives, and an assortment of miscellaneous material. Also included are the enormous requisition forms that arrived from West Africa, North Africa, and France. These contain descriptions of needed supplies ranging from nuts and bolts to tractors and locomotives. The nature and scope of the area programs create a lasting impression of the magnitude of the civilian supply operation. There is also valuable but unfortunately not voluminous correspondence from French leaders, in particular Jean Monnet. However, numerous summations of meetings and correspondence with French officials are available. Consequently on the major issues the position of the French is clear.

Like most record groups the FEA collection has basic weaknesses. The descriptive inventory in many cases is somewhat misleading. Too often boxes contain preliminary reports on crucial matters without including the information relating to the outcome or final decision. Generally the "history" is somewhat disappointing. A few of the sections on the French program are well done and documented, but much of it lacks citation.

The massive and comprehensive Stettinius Papers (University of Virginia, Charlottesville, Virginia) are indispensable. From 1941 through

1945 Stettinius was deeply involved with lend-lease affairs. His files for the period when he was lend-lease administrator include correspondence and reports on matters relative to his role in policy development and administration. Of special interest is the organized research material for his book, *Lend-Lease: Weapon for Victory.* The papers upon which he based the chapter on the North African operation offer considerably more detail than his account. The files covering his career as undersecretary of state and secretary of state contain reports on the progress of negotiations with the French as well as surveys of public reaction to the French Master Agreement. His diary and calendar notes are also useful in gaining an appreciation of the numerous issues involved in lend-lease. Evidently Stettinius instructed his staff to collect all the important newspaper and periodical commentaries on lend-lease. Thus the collection includes over twenty boxes of contemporary articles and newspaper clippings. These, along with a similar collection in the FEA records, expedite research on the subject.

The manuscripts at the Franklin D. Roosevelt Library in Hyde Park, New York, are extremely informative. President Roosevelt's Official File and the president's Secretary File contain information on final decisions on French lend-lease policy. The material deals almost exclusively with policy matters rather than the day-to-day operations of lend-lease. The Map Room collection includes correspondence from French leaders, which is very helpful. The papers of Harry Hopkins are interesting, for a number of officials, especially Stettinius, approached Roosevelt through Hopkins on lend-lease matters. The papers of Oscar Cox, the influential OLLA Legal Counsel, are useful, but except for a few items most of the material is also in the FEA files.

The most valuable material on French lend-lease at the Roosevelt Library is the information contained in the Henry Morgenthau Diaries. The term diary is misleading. The collection consists of over nine hundred volumes of correspondence, records of telephone conversations, and detailed accounts of important meetings. Morgenthau's records reveal the influential role that he played in French lend-lease matters and also shed light on his power within the Roosevelt administration. The diaries provide detail on Morgenthau's position on the French payments issue and clarify his opposition to a French agreement that did not include specific payment arrangements. Most importantly the Morgenthau manuscripts proved to be, at least thus far, the only source of information that thoroughly explained the position of the Roosevelt administration on French lend-lease policy in late 1944.

The war department's role in lend-lease matters is clarified in the Henry L. Stimson Diary (Sterling Memorial Library, Yale University, New Haven,

Connecticut). The Stimson Diary is an account of daily events, meetings, and reflections on important questions and is most informative. Here the secretary of war presents an impressive case for transferring the responsibility for civilian affairs in liberated areas to the military and is critical of the "loose" administration of Roosevelt, especially in North Africa. Furthermore, Stimson, experienced at testifying before Congress on lend-lease affairs, carefully explains his opposition to any employment of lend-lease as a postwar measure and accurately predicts the congressional reaction to the French Master Agreement.

The papers of Admiral William D. Leahy (Library of Congress, Washington, D.C.) consist of the manuscript source material for his published memoirs, *I Was There*. The manuscripts are more detailed than the published version and include a valuable collection of personal correspondence with Undersecretary of State Sumner Welles.

The letters and papers of Secretary of State Cordell Hull (Library of Congress, Washington, D. C.) contain very little useful material. The correspondence rarely mentions the French lend-lease program. Information on France refers mainly to the administration's Vichy policy and to relations with de Gaulle. This information offers no new insights. Of limited assistance is a manuscript by Stuart Graham, "The North African Economic and Political Program from Its Inception to the Invasion" (Department of State unpublished manuscript, 1944), which succinctly summarizes the role of the state department from 1940 through 1942 in North Africa.

The unpublished state department documents effectively supplemented the manuscript collections and published documents. They furnished important detail, especially on the negotiations leading to the *Modus Vivendi* and the French Master Agreement. For the period from 1940 to 1942 the unpublished material included nothing to significantly alter the information published in the Foreign Relations series. In fact the voluminous published material covering American relations with Vichy and North Africa prior to the invasion appears to indicate a strong desire on the part of the state department to make as much of this information available as possible. This would also reflect Hull's wishes, since the secretary considered the successful invasion of North Africa a vindication of the administration's controversial Vichy policy. The publication of Langer's manuscript in 1947 was the earliest example of the state department's eagerness to tell its side of the story. In contrast there is a minimal amount of published material on the less successful American-Free French relations.

Two interviews were extremely informative. Lloyd Cutler spent more than an hour recounting his experiences in arranging and supervising the distribution of supplies to the Arabs. He provided details on the early problems with civilian supply, the significance of these difficulties, and the attempts to remedy them. He also discussed the futile efforts to curb the Black Market and added a personal touch by describing his relations with Arab leaders. Cutler's lasting impressions relate to the Arab independence movement, and he emphasized that native officials felt that in some way the presence of Americans in North Africa would assist their cause.

Robert Murphy also found time to explain his thoughts on the North African experience. The former diplomat appeared to be exceptionally acute, and he was extremely persuasive. Murphy concentrated on the post-invasion period, and his interpretations of the French civilian lend-lease program were stimulating and provocative. He cited the major issues that arose and presented his views on their cause. He defended American policy on the payments issue and approached it in the same manner as Morgenthau. Murphy considered private trade an area in which the French could have offered concessions in return for civilian aid. The French refusal, he emphasized, was another example of French ingratitude and further evidence of their interpretation of the civilian program as something to which they were entitled. On the other hand Murphy believed that the extent of American assistance went far beyond the responsibility of the United States. His description of the French as "continually having their hands in American pockets" aptly summarized his views. As expected Murphy vigorously defended dealing with Darlan and still maintains that British and BEW opposition to aid for France and North Africa was unwise, short-sighted, and needless. The conversation with Murphy represented the highlight and most pleasant aspect of this research.

SELECTED WORKS

UNPUBLISHED MANUSCRIPTS

Cox, Oscar. "American and British Lend-Lease Reciprocal Aid Negotiations with the French Committee of National Liberation." 1943. Cox Papers, Franklin D. Roosevelt Library, Hyde Park, New York.

Culbertson, William S. "Report of the Special Economic Mission to North Africa, September 11, 1944." Boxes 970, 975, Record Group 169, National Archives Washington Records Center, Suitland, Maryland.

Cutler, Lloyd. "Manual of Operations for the Importation and Distribution of Civilian Supplies in Liberated Areas." July 19, 1943. Box 173,

Record Group 169, National Archives Washington Records Center, Suitland, Maryland.

Fennemore, George M. "The Role of the Department of State in Connection with the Lend-Lease Program." 1943. Historical Office, Department of State, Washington, D. C.

Graham, Stuart. "The North African Economic and Political Program from Its Inception to the Invasion." 1944. Historical Office, Department of State, Washington, D. C.

Herring, George C. "An Experiment in Foreign Aid: Lend-Lease, 1941-1945." Ph.D. dissertation, University of Virginia, 1965.

Holmes, James H. "Admiral Leahy in Vichy France, 1940-1942." Ph.D. dissertation, George Washington University, 1974.

O'Boyle, John. "Summary Report of Lend-Lease in North Africa." February 19, 1943. Box 234, Record Group 169, National Archives Washington Records Center, Suitland, Maryland.

Office of the Lend-Lease Administration. History: "France and the French Empire"; "Ships and Shipping"; "Liberated Areas." Record Group 169, National Archives Washington Records Center, Suitland, Maryland.

Short, Livingston. "Report on North Africa to the OLLA Executive Staff Meeting." July 5, 1943. Stettinius Papers, University of Virginia, Charlottesville, Virginia.

Wieschoff, Henry A., ed. "French North Africa: Area Study for the Army Specialized Training Program." 2 vols. 1943. University of Pennsylvania Museum, Philadelphia, Pennsylvania.

UNITED STATES DOCUMENTS

U. S. Congress. *Congressional Record*. Vols. 89-91.

———. U. S. Congress, House of Representatives, Committee on Foreign Affairs. *Hearings on H. R. 1776, A Bill to Further Promote the Defense of the United States and for Other Purposes.* 77th Congress, 1st Session, 1941.

———. *Hearings on H. R. 1501, A Bill to Extend for One Year the Provisions of an Act to Promote the Defense of the United States.* 78th Congress, 1st Session, 1943.

———. *Hearings on H. R. 4254, A Bill to Extend for One Year the Provisions of an Act to Promote the Defense of the United States.* 78th Congress, 2nd Session, 1944.

———. *Hearings on H. R. 2013, A Bill to Extend for One Year the Provisions of an Act to Promote the Defense of the United States.* 79th Congress, 1st Session, 1945.

U. S. President. *Public Papers of the Presidents: Harry S Truman* [1945].
Washington, D. C., 1961.
——. *Reports to Congress on Lend-Lease Operations.* Nos. 1-22. Washington, D. C., 1941-1946.
U. S. Senate, Foreign Relations Committee. *Hearings on H. R. 2013, A Bill to Extend for One Year the Provisions of an Act to Promote the Defense of the United States.* 79th Congress, 1st Session, 1945.
U. S. State Department. *Foreign Relations of the United States, 1940, 1941, 1942, 1943, 1944, 1945, 1946.* Washington, D. C., 1957-1969.
——. *Foreign Relations of the United States: The Conference of Berlin* [Potsdam, 1945]. Washington, D. C., 1960.
——. *Foreign Relations of the United States: The Conference at Malta and Yalta, 1945.* Washington, D. C., 1955.
——. *Treaties and Other International Agreements of the United States of America, 1776-1949.* Edited by Charles I. Bevans. Vol. 7, *Denmark-France,* 1971. Washington, D. C., 1968-.
——. *United States Treaties and Other International Agreements.* Vol. 9, 1958. Washington, D. C., 1950-.

NEWSPAPERS

Barrons Weekly
Chicago Tribune
New York *Herald Tribune*
New York Times
The Times (London)
Wall Street Journal
Washington Post

BOOKS AND ARTICLES

Acheson, Dean. *Present at the Creation.* New York: Norton, 1969.
Adloff, Richard, and Thompson, Virginia McLean. *West Africa: The French Speaking Nations, Yesterday and Today.* New York: Holt, Rinehart and Winston, 1964.
al-Fasi, Allal. *The Independence Movements in North Africa.* trans. Hazem Zaki Nusiebeth. New York: Octagon Books, 1970.
Ashford, Douglas. *Political Change in Morocco.* Princeton, N.J.: Princeton University Press, 1961.
Barbour, Nevill, ed. *A Survey of North West Africa.* New York: Oxford University Press, 1962.

Berque, Jacques. *French North Africa: The Maghrib between Two World Wars*. trans. Jean Stewart. New York: Praeger, 1967.

Blair, Leon Borden. "Amateurs in Diplomacy: The American Vice Consuls in North Africa, 1941-1943," *Historian* 35 (August 1973), 607-20.

———. *Western Window in the Arab World*. Austin, Tex.: University of Texas Press, 1970.

Blum, John Morton. *From the Morgenthau Diaries: Years of War, 1941-1945*. Boston: Houghton Mifflin, 1967.

———. *Roosevelt and Morgenthau*. Boston: Houghton Mifflin, 1970.

Brace, Richard Munthe. *Morocco, Algeria, Tunisia*. Englewood Cliffs, N. J.: Prentice Hall, 1964.

Brett, Michael. "The Colonial Period in the Maghrib and Its Aftermath: The Present State of Historical Writing." *The Middle East Journal* 30 (Summer 1976), 273-90.

Brockway, Fenner. *The Colonial Revolution*. New York: St. Martin's Press, 1973.

Burns, James MacGregor. *Roosevelt: The Soldier of Freedom*. New York: Harcourt Brace Jovanovich, 1970.

Byrnes, James F. *All in One Lifetime*. New York: Harper and Brothers, 1958.

Cantril, Hadley, ed. *Public Opinion, 1935-1946*. Princeton, N. J.: Princeton University Press, 1951.

Chandler, Alfred D., Jr., et al., eds. *The Papers of Dwight David Eisenhower: The War Years*. 5 vols. Baltimore: Johns Hopkins Press, 1970.

Churchill, Winston S. *Memoirs of the Second World War*. 6 vols. Boston: Houghton Mifflin, 1948-1953.

Clark, Michael K. *Algeria in Turmoil: A History of the Rebellion*. New York: Praeger, 1959.

Coakley, Robert W., and Leighton, Richard M. *The United States Army in World War II: Global Logistics and Strategy, 1943-1945*. Washington, D. C.: U. S. Government Printing Office, 1968.

Coles, Harry L., and Weinberg, Albert K. *The United States Army in World War II. Civil Affairs: Soldiers Become Governors*. Washington, D. C.: U. S. Government Printing Office, 1964.

"Compromise at Algiers." *The Economist* 144 (June 26, 1943), 816.

Copp, Philip. "French Morocco: A Land of Promise." *Foreign Commerce Weekly* 10 (January 9, 1943), 4-9.

———. "French North Africa: Economy of New War Vortex." *Foreign Commerce Weekly* 9 (November 28, 1942), 3-7, 33-35.

———. "Tunisia: Economy of Vital Protectorate." *Foreign Commerce Weekly* 9 (December 5, 1942), 10-13, 42-43.

Culbertson, William S. "Principles of Economic Policy." *Department of State Bulletin* 12 (February 25, 1945), 299-301.

"Declaration by the Government of the United States of America and the Provisional Government of the French Republic on Commercial Policy and Related Matters." *Department of State Bulletin* 14 (May 28, 1946), 995-97.

De Gaulle, Charles. *The War Memoirs of Charles de Gaulle: The Call to Honour, 1940-1942*. trans. Jonathan Griffin. New York: Simon and Schuster, 1955.

———. *The War Memoirs of Charles de Gaulle: Unity, 1942-1944. Documents*. trans. Joyce Murchie and Hamish Erskine. New York: Simon and Schuster, 1959.

———. *The War Memoirs of Charles de Gaulle: Salvation, 1944-1946*. trans. Richard Howard. New York: Simon and Schuster, 1960.

De Novo, John A. "The Culbertson Economic Mission and Anglo-American Tensions in the Middle East, 1944-1945." *Journal of American History* 63 (No. 4, 1977), 913-36.

Fighting French. "The Delegation of the French National Committee." *Fighting French Yearbook* (1943), 81.

"Friends of France?" *The Economist* 141 (July 19, 1941), 76.

Funk, Arthur Layton. *Charles de Gaulle: The Crucial Years, 1943-1944*. Norman, Okla.: University of Oklahoma Press, 1959.

Gardner, Lloyd C. *Economic Aspects of New Deal Diplomacy*. Madison, Wis.: University of Wisconsin Press, 1964.

Gilpatric, Donald S. "Resumption of Private Trade in Liberated Areas: A Progress Report on the Work of the Special Economic Mission." *Department of State Bulletin* 11 (December 10, 1944), 720-22.

Gordon, David. *The Passing of French Algeria*. New York: Oxford University Press, 1966.

Greenfield, Kent Roberts. *American Strategy in World War II: A Reconsideration*. Baltimore: Johns Hopkins Press, 1963.

Hahn, Lorna. *North Africa: Nationalism to Nationhood*. Washington, D. C.: Washington Public Affairs Press, 1960.

Haight, John McVickar, Jr. *American Aid to France, 1939-1940*. New York: Atheneum, 1970.

Hall, H. Duncan. *North American Supply*. London: H. M. Stationery Office, 1955.

———, and Wrigley, C. C. *Studies of Overseas Supply*. London: H. M. Stationery Office, 1956.

Hall, Luella J. *The U. S. and Morocco, 1776-1956*. Metuchen, N. J.: Scarecrow Press, 1971.

Halstead, John P. *Rebirth of a Nation: The Origins and Rise of Moroccan Nationalism, 1912-1944.* Cambridge, Mass.: Harvard University Press, 1967.

Heggoỳ, Alf. A. *Insurgency and Counterinsurgency in Algeria.* Bloomington, Ind.: Indiana University Press, 1972.

———. "The Origins of Algerian Nationalism in the Colony and in France." *The Muslim World* 58 (April 1968), 128-40.

Herring, George C. *Aid to Russia, 1941-1946.* New York: Columbia University Press, 1973.

———. "Lend Lease to Russia and the Origin of the Cold War, 1944-1945." *Journal of American History* 56 (June 1969), 93-114.

Howe, George F. *The United States Army in World War II: Northwest Africa, Seizing the Initiative in the West.* Washington, D. C.: U. S. Government Printing Office, 1957.

Hull, Cordell. *The Memoirs of Cordell Hull.* 2 vols. New York: Macmillan, 1948.

Jessup, Philip C. *The Birth of Nations.* New York: Columbia University Press, 1974.

Kanet, Roger, "The Soviet Union, the French Communist Party and Africa, 1945-1950." *Survey* 22 (Winter 1976), 74-92.

Kimball, Warren. *The Most Unsordid Act: Lend-Lease, 1939-1941.* Baltimore: Johns Hopkins Press, 1969.

Langer, William L. *Our Vichy Gamble.* New York: Knopf, 1947.

Leahy, William D. *I Was There.* New York: Whitlesey House, 1950.

Ling, Dwight. *Tunisia: From Protectorate to Republic.* Bloomington, Ind.: Indiana University Press, 1967.

McVey, Camden. "An American's View of France." *Department of State Bulletin* 13 (October 7, 1945), 523-27.

Matloff, Maurice. *The United States Army in World War II: Strategic Planning for Coalition Warfare, 1943-1944.* Washington, D. C.: U. S. Government Printing Office, 1959.

Morgenthau, Henry. "The Morgenthau Diaries: Part III, The Story Behind Lend-Lease." *Colliers* 120 (October 18, 1947), 16-17, 71-75.

Murphy, Robert. *Diplomat among Warriors.* New York: Doubleday, 1964.

Nurse, Ronald. "Critic of Colonialism: JFK and Algerian Independence." *Historian* 39 (February 1977), 307-26.

Ottaway, David and Marina. *Algeria: The Politics of a Socialist Revolution.* Berkeley, Calif.: Univeristy of California Press, 1970.

Paxton, Robert O. *Vichy France. Old Guard and New Order, 1940-1944.* New York: Norton, 1975.

Pendar, Kenneth. *Adventure in Diplomacy.* New York: Dodd, Mead and Company, 1945.

Penrose, Ernest Francis. *Economic Planning for the Peace*. Princeton, N. J.: Princeton University Press, 1953.

Quandt, William B. *Revolution and Political Leadership: Algeria, 1954-1968*. Cambridge, Mass.: M.I.T. Press, 1969.

"Restoration to Private Channels of Certain United States Exports to France." *Department of State Bulletin* 13 (September 9, 1945), 358.

"Resumption of Private Export Trade to French North and French West Africa." *Department of State Bulletin* 12 (April 29, 1945), 832-33.

"Reunion in Algiers." *The Economist* 144 (June 12, 1943), 747-48.

Roosevelt, Elliot, ed. *FDR: His Personal Letters, 1928-1945*. 2 vols. New York: Duell Sloan and Pearce, 1950.

Rosenman, Samuel I., comp. *The Public Papers and Addresses of Franklin D. Roosevelt*. Vols. 9-12. New York: Random House, 1938-1950.

Sherwood, Robert E. *Roosevelt and Hopkins: An Intimate History*. New York: Harper and Brothers, 1948.

Stettinius, Edward R., Jr. *Lend-Lease: Weapon for Victory*. New York: MacMillan, 1944.

———. "Lend-Lease Works Both Ways." *The Saturday Evening Post* 215 (September 15, 1942), 11, 117-18.

Stillwell, James A. "Civilian Supply Problems in Europe." *Department of State Bulletin* 13 (May 20, 1945), 917-23, 927.

Tompkins, Peter. *The Murder of Admiral Darlan*. New York: Simon and Schuster, 1965.

Truman, Harry S. *Memoirs*. Vol. 1, *Year of Decisions*. Garden City, N. Y.: Doubleday, 1955.

Vandenburg, Arthur H., Jr., ed. *The Private Papers of Senator Vandenburg*. Boston: Houghton Mifflin, 1952.

Vigneras, Marcel. *The United States Army in World War II: Rearming the French*. Washington, D. C.: U. S. Government Printing Office, 1957.

Walker, Richard L. *The American Secretaries of State and Their Diplomacy* Vol. 14, *Edward Reilly Stettinius*, ed. Robert H. Ferrell. New York: Cooper Square Press, 1965.

Wertenbaker, Charles. "White-Haired Boy: Stettinius." *The Saturday Evening Post* 214 (July 21, 1941), 9-11, 94, 96.

Werth, Alexander. *France, 1940-1955*. Boston: Beacon Press, 1966.

White, Dorothy Shipley. *Seeds of Discord: De Gaulle, Free France and the Allies*. Syracuse, N. Y.: Syracuse University Press, 1964.

Zingg, Paul J. "The Cold War in North Africa: American Foreign Policy and Postwar Muslim Nationalism, 1945-1962." *Historian* 39 (November 1976), 40-61.

INDEX

ABOUT THE AUTHOR

JAMES J. DOUGHERTY is a humanist administrator in the division of public programs at the National Endowment for Humanities, an editor-bibliographer of RECENTLY PUBLISHED ARTICLES of the American Historical Association, and lecturer at University College of the University of Maryland. His previous publications include an article on lend-lease for "Cahiers d'Etudes Africaines" and several book-length bibliographies and compilations on American history.